# Ships of the Chester River

Richard Martin

*Ships of the Chester River*
First published in Wales in 2018
on behalf of the author
by
**BRIDGE BOOKS**
Pear Tree Cottage
Worthenbury
WREXHAM
LL13 0BF



A CIP entry for this book is available from the British Library

ISBN: 978-1-84494-116-2

Cover illustrations:
*The Old Port of Chester.* [Courtesy of the Grosvenor Museum, Chester]
PS *Victory*, built by John Wilson & Son of Liverpool 1832.
[By kind permission of Merseyside Maritime Museum, Maritime Archives
*Jane Porter.* [Courtesy of Flintshire Records Office]

Printed and bound
by
Gutenburg Press Ltd
Malta

CONTENTS

## PLATES

# Preface

I began the research for this book back in1969, in the darkness of the pre-computer age. I realised then that so little had been written about the shipbuilding, or the commerce of the river Dee, particularly the period since the coming of the Industrial Revolution. Over the next forty years I gathered the odd relevant article and made a few interesting contacts in the course of my working life, but only in 2012 did I finally have the opportunity to seriously sit down and put the information in order and fill the gaps. I have used the term 'Chester river' rather than river Dee for two reasons. Firstly, more vessels were built at Chester than anywhere else on the river, and secondly the coastal schooner operators of the Victorian era always referred to the Dee as the 'Chester river.'

When I came to listing as many of the vessels as possible that had been built on the estuary, I was surprised to find that I was in fact trying to write about over 600 commercial and naval vessels built in the Dee yards established between 1800 and 1914 (excluding Saltney) which were considered to be worthy of a registration document! Whilst this is only a relatively small number compared with other shipbuilding areas of the U.K., particularly the neighbouring river Mersey, it was far more than I, or anyone else, had realised.

Many readers will expect this book to be all about small coastal vessels built to serve the ports of the Dee, and perhaps providing links with Ireland. So it is astonishing to find that many of the larger vessels, especially those built at Chester itself, served the deep-water trade of the British Empire for many years. Every imaginable cargo was carried, as well as passengers, emigrants, convicts and troops. Once launched, those deep sea vessels were destined never to return to the river Dee.

It is well known that the trade of the Chester river suffered as the channel silted up, whilst vessels grew in size and draught and, at the same time, Liverpool expanded. It is perhaps forgotten, however, that the shipbuilding industry required less depth of water in a port than did commercial cargo carrying because the vessels when completed, or were ready for fitting out elsewhere, could sail 'light ship' from the port, never to return. This is one reason why shipbuilding kept going longer on the Dee than foreign commercial trading in the ports of the estuary. Launches needed high spring tides in many instances, but once the vessel was launched its relatively shallow draught meant it could sail away on high water, or even move to Liverpool to be rigged or have its engines fitted.

I have tried to concentrate on the shipbuilding which occurred in those places on the river which have had the least written about them. I have therefore excluded J. Crichton & Co of Saltney and Connah's Quay, because there is already an excellent book on the subject written in 2002 by John Dixon and Geoff Pickard, which covers a further 180 vessels built on the river.[1] I have also excluded the pleasure yachts that were built at Chester in the late Victorian period as well as those vessels built in a number of locations within the Chester canal system.

It has only been possible to include the career details of a relatively few vessels built on the river, and no doubt some vessels are missing from the appendices. One has to stop writing somewhere, and hopefully, as additional entries and the inevitable textual errors come to light (for which I apologise), these can be added in a second edition. Please do let me know if you have anything to add.

I have tried to write the book for those readers who have a general interest in ships and maritime history, as well as those who want to know more about the local history of Chester and north-east Wales. Today, there is little surviving physical evidence of the former shipbuilding and maritime industry of the river. In Chester itself, nothing is visible apart from a few warehouse buildings at Crane Wharf where the main port activity was conducted. Walking along the river bank all the way from Chester to the Point of Ayr, it is so quiet and peaceful as most of the evidence of slipways and buildings has gone.

Apart from a few articles in magazines, very little has been previously written on this subject, particularly with regard to Chester itself. Many books have been written on the history of the city, but despite the fact that more than 250 vessels were built there since 1800, none has covered the shipbuilding industry of the period. As well as a dearth of books, there are also very few paintings surviving of vessels built on the river Dee before the age of photography. In several instances I have therefore utilised images of vessels that I believe to be similar in appearance to those built on the Chester river.

I trust this book will assist those who already know the area to realise what a hive of shipbuilding activity existed on the river bank 150 years ago, and inspire those learning about the Dee estuary and its history for the first time to go there, walk the bank, and imagine how it used to be in the days of sail and early steamships.

Richard Martin
2018


## Acknowledgements

It has only been possible to write this book with a lot of help from many very patient people. Thank you to all of them, but particularly my wife, Joyce, who is still waiting for all sorts of things to be done in the house and garden.

As I started the research more than forty years ago, many of my contacts and interviewees have sadly passed on. In particular, I think of those whom I met who had actually worked in the shipyards on Deeside, and individuals, such as Denis Branigan (the former Board of Trade Inspector in Liverpool, who with his articles in the local press in Chester in the 1970s, sparked my interest in the deep-sea iron vessels built at Chester).

I must also thank the inspirational Mike Stammers, formerly of Merseyside Maritime Museum, who I originally met through work, but who encouraged me to write about the shipyards and who was so knowledgeable about everything to do with sailing vessels. I cannot forget too the help and information about Queensferry vessels from Brian Hillsdon, retired Secretary of the Steamboat Association of Great Britain.

For much of the information on shipbuilding in Flint I am greatly indebted to the late Edward Hogan who did so much research and whose unpublished works 'The Streets and Lanes of Flint' and 'Notes on Shipbuilding at Flint', ably edited by the late Peter Bellis of the Flint Local History Society, have both been deposited at Flintshire Records Office.

In more recent times, since I retired, I must thank those individuals who have helped by listening to me rattle on about the challenges encountered in gathering information, and also with the many IT issues encountered by a dinosaur during preparation — Rosemary Waring, Chris Stork, Bill Bowley, David Cummings, Dave Davies, Pat Talbot, Nicholas Martin, Penny Senior and Philip Sutcliffe.

Fellow maritime authors and specialists have also been very helpful too: Tom Pritchard, Malcolm McRonald, Tony Barratt, Cath Turpin, Terry Kavanagh, Geoff Pickard ,Ray Buss, Mark Myers, Jeff & Cindy Grice, Paolo Piccione and members of the Liverpool Nautical Research Society. They all assisted me when I found there were so many unanswered questions being generated by my research.

Staff at the various archives visited were so helpful, especially at Merseyside Maritime Museum Maritime Archives and Library, the Cheshire Record Office, the Flintshire Record Office, the Liverpool Record Office, Lloyd's Register Library, the National Waterways Museum Archives in Ellesmere Port, the Grosvenor Museum in Chester, the National Archives in Kew, the Manx Museum, the National Maritime Museum in Greenwich, the Lincolnshire Museum of Rural Life and the North Devon Maritime Museum. Invaluable help also came from overseas, most notably from the Maritime Museum of Barcelona, theDevonport Naval Museum in Auckland and the Maritime Museum of Tasmania.

Finally, a special thank you to the staff of *Sea Breezes* magazine. This magazine has been part of my life since childhood when my father took took out a subscription. As a result of this, I started reading it from a very early age and today have a complete post-war set. Anybody out there who is interested in matters maritime but does not read it regularly should subscribe as soon as possible!

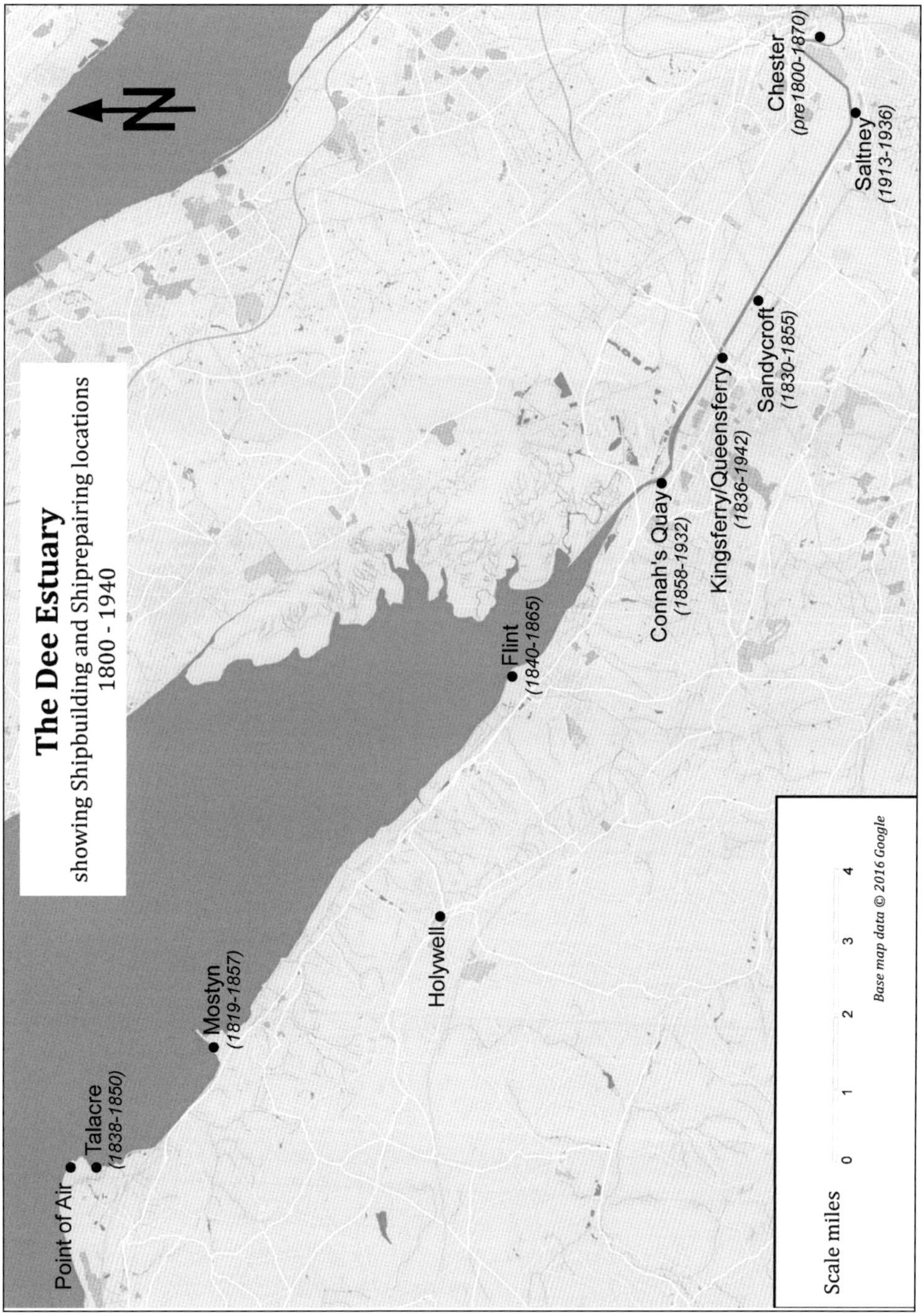
The Dee Estuary
showing Shipbuilding and Shiprepairing locations
1800 - 1940
Point of Air
Talacre
(1838-1850)
Mostyn
(1819-1857)
Holywell
Flint
(1840-1865)
Connah's Quay
(1858-1932)
Kingsferry/Queensferry
(1836-1942)
Sandycroft
(1830-1855)
Saltney
(1913-1936)
Chester
(pre1800-1870)
Scale miles
0 1 2 3 4
Base map data © 2016 Google

# 1

## Chester 1800–21: the nineteenth century before steam

By 1800, the port of Chester, including its outport at Parkgate, unlike other places on the river Dee, was already an important centre of wooden shipbuilding. There had been vessels built in the city of Chester since medieval times and by 1800 at least two shipbuilding firms were already well established — Joseph and John Troughton, and Peter Jackson. It seems that many of the vessels were built speculatively and were often initially owned, or part owned, by the builders. The Troughtons often built in this way and it is strange to record that between 1793 and 1803 they built five vessels called *Active* and it seems likely that they may also have built some of the other vessels of that name launched at Chester between 1787 and 1803.[1] Similarly, there are a number of press adverts for vessels for sale built at the Cortney yard. One such advert from 1812 recorded, '... a new vessel on the stocks in the building yard of Wm Cortney, Chester, 122 tons register — apply Mr John Carson, or Thos Bagot broker'.[2] Again, in 1815, '... a fine new ship, she has been 2½ years on the stocks, her frame is of timber felled in 1812.'[3]

Unlike the later periods of shipbuilding at Chester, and indeed elsewhere on the river, with reference to the first twenty years of the nineteenth century, there is relatively little information about the vessels that were built or which builder was actually responsible for their construction. This is a unfortunate, because it was by far the busiest period of building at Chester with 145 vessels identified as being launched between 1800 and 1821. I should, however, add that in this period there could be a small number of vessels (listed in Appendix 1) which may have been registered at Chester, but not actually built there. To further complicate matters the Chester Ship Registers for the period before 1836 are missing and it is hard to determine which builder was responsible for building which vessels.

In 1800, the shipyards, dry-docks and inlets used by the builders were located at Crane Wharf, where they were to continue in operation for the next 70 years.

The Roodeye (or Roodee) had reached its greatest extent in the early seven-

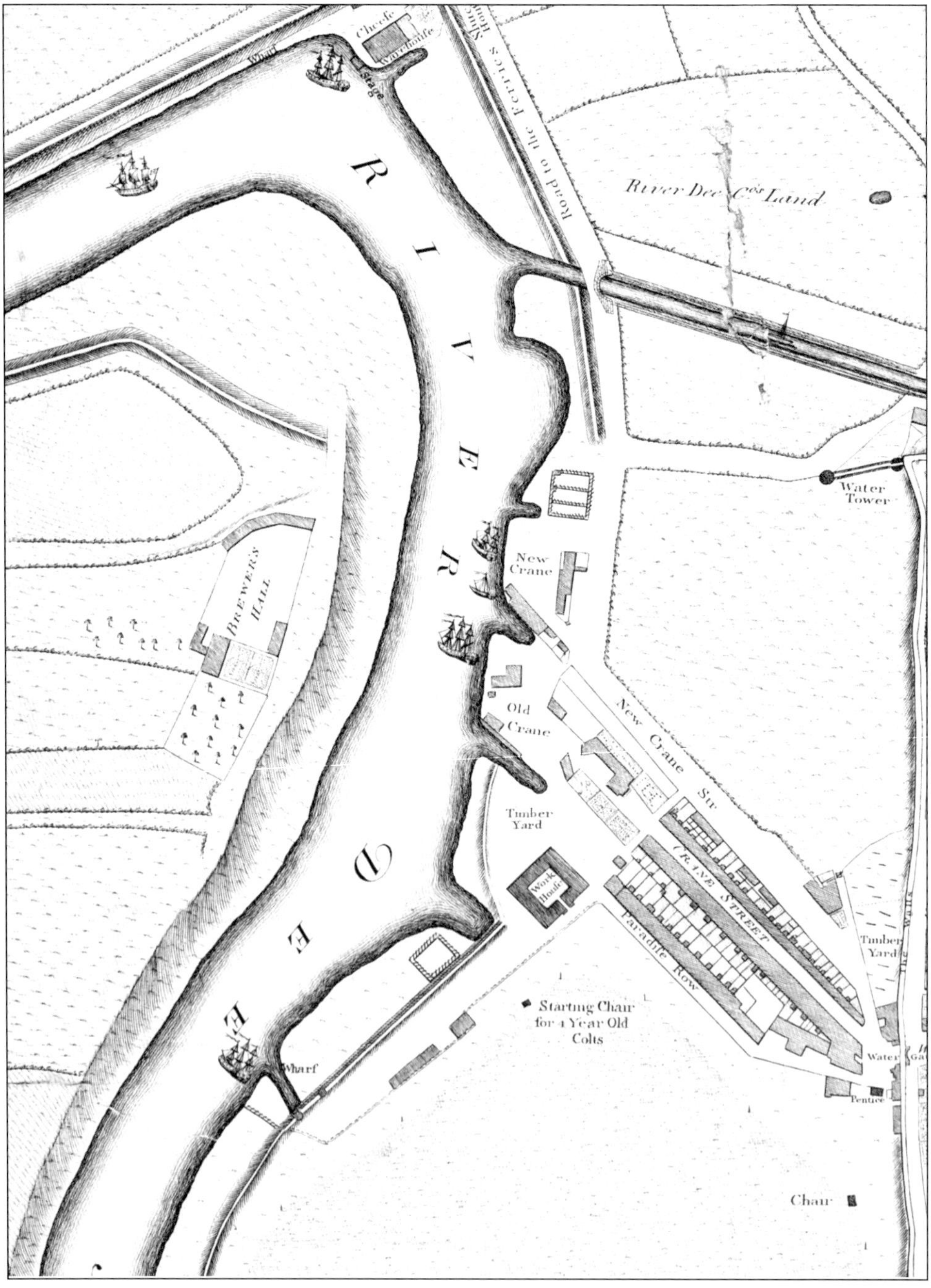


Plate 2: Hunter's map of Chester, 1789.

teenth century and thereafter it gradually began to shrink as various parts were leased for building purposes. The House of Industry was built there in 1757, a dock and quay were first constructed in the 1760s and an iron foundry and a mill in 1772.[4] Further major division of the Roodee was not to take place until the opening of the Grosvenor Bridge in 1832, and then the completion of the first railway viaduct and bridge over the Dee in November 1846 which was immediately adjacent to the main shipyard site, occupied by Cortney in 1802 and his successors.

The vessels built between 1775 and 1800 were of 150–300 tons burthen, and by the early years of the nineteenth century, this had increased to 400–500 tons; the largest being the *Lord Forbes*[1] of 556 tons, built by Cortney for Liverpool owners in 1803. The company of John Bruce and John Gunson also built vessels in the port before 1800, whilst Thomas Makin also built vessels at Parkgate.

Joseph Troughton had been building ships in Chester since at least 1787, but he died in 1800 and left his money to his son John and son-in-law John Hughes (who was married to his daughter Susannah). In 1782, John Troughton, shipbuilder, was elected a freeman, and in1785 John Troughton 'shipwright' was elected to the Common Council of the City of Chester. In 1790 he was appointed Sheriff of Chester for three years.[5]

After 1800 only John Troughton of these early builders continued in business, but was to be soon joined at Crane Wharf by William Cortney who set up in 1802 to start building at the Crane, a business which was to continue for the next twenty years.

It seems likely that William Cortney was a shipwright, born originally in Skerton, now part of Lancaster. He had married Elizabeth Hall in Lancaster on 24th September 1793 and they had children there, as well as three further daughters whilst living in Chester. After Lancaster, William went into partnership with a John Sause of Liverpool to build ships at Pwllheli, but this partnership was terminated on 3rd March 1800.[6] By March 1802 he had been appointed a freeman of the City of Chester and was negotiating to lease land from Chester City Council at Crane Wharf. In April of that year the Chester City Land Committee recommended that a lease for ten years should be granted to Mr William Cortney, shipbuilder, 'extending 70 yds in length of the foreland of the Roodee by the limekiln to extend from the river to the foot of the cops for a timber yard. He and his workmen must only use the footpath from the end of the old poor house to Paradise Row. He must also make an 8 ft fence round the said piece of land and to extend to the present building in his own yard He paying a rent of 10 guineas a year for ten years.' In May 1804, he extended his timber yard for another 70 yds and paid another 10 guineas per annum.[7]

From about 1803 William was in a partnership trading as 'Carson, Forbes, Cortney & Co', and this partnership was to last until 30th September 1810. The earliest known vessel built by this partnership was the *Lord Forbes* in 1803 for Forbes and Carson. William Forbes and John Carson were shipowners/merchants from Liverpool. The *Isabella* of 1803, and the *George* of 1805, also built at Chester, were both part owned by John Carson whilst William Forbes was part owner of the ship *Mary Ann* of 1806, and also the owner of a vessel of 340 tons launched at the Cortney yard in January 1810.[8]

The most well-known and best documented vessels built by the Cortney yard were the six vessels built for the Royal Navy.

In 1804 he completed the first two Royal Navy vessels, both gun-brigs of 178 tons, the *Contest* and the *Defender*. Only 80 ft in length and 23 ft beam they were the subject of some interesting correspondence with the Navy Board regarding the cost of building ships at Chester[8] 'The sole objection to Mr Cortney of Chester building another gun-brig for the Navy, is the cost of either sending the rigging to Chester to rig the ship there or of towing the ship from Chester to a naval yard to have it fitted there.'[6] The two brigs were part of a series of 58 Archer-class vessels ordered by the Royal Navy.

Today we would not think that towing a brig to a naval dockyard would be a problem, but in 1804 the tug had not been invented and neither had the marine steam engine! How was this operation undertaken? By 1800 the Dee had been straightened and effectively narrowed so sending another sailing vessel from a Naval Dockyard to tow the hull of a new brig must have been fraught with difficulty. The first tug was not to appear on the Chester River until the end of 1826.

A few days later William Cortney pressed his case for continuing to build. 'Mr Cortney is not interested in building just one gun brig for the Navy because he quoted his price on the understanding that two would be built.' He apparently got his way. 'We are sending a copy letter from Peter Kinnion, asking for Mr Cortney of Chester to build a second gun brig for the Navy.'[8] In retrospect, it is easy to understand the Navy Board's reluctance to use the Chester yards. All six of the Naval vessels built by Cortney were towed to Plymouth for fitting out.

Neither of these gun brigs was to have a long Naval career, as both were lost in December 1809. HMS *Contest* is presumed to have foundered in the Atlantic in December on passage from America, whilst her yard sister HMS *Defender* was also wrecked on 14th December 1809 off Folkestone, when her anchor cables parted; in this case all hands being rescued.[6]

Until 1813, Mr Cortney's yard then concentrated on commercial shipbuilding, but the missing Chester Ship records before 1836 mean that we are not sure which of the Chester builders were responsible for many of the Chester built vessels of this period. Some of the vessels built at Chester in these years were the deep –sea vessels of their time (see Appendix 1). Twenty -seven of the merchant vessels built in Chester in the 1800–21 period exceed 290 tons burthen and traded to and from West Africa, the West Indies, East Indies, North America and Australia.

It should also be mentioned that in this period more than 14 brigs and snows were completed in the Chester yards. A brig is a two masted, square –rigged vessel with a mizzen on the after mast and carrying three jibs. A snow was a variant of the brig when it was found that operating the main course and the spanker (mizzen) on the same mast proved difficult sometimes. The difference between the two types was simple-the snow had the spanker on a separate spar called the 'snow mast.' The larger brigs and snows such as the *Alice* of 1818 traded world wide, including voyages to Batavia and Singapore in 1828, Valparaiso in 1830 and Sydney , Australia in 1835. I am constantly amazed that these small wooden vessels, like the *Alice* had careers of more than twenty years hard voyaging. The *Ellen* of 1815 spent over 20 years trading to Brazil, Demerara and on the English Channel before her demise in 1838.

Some of the larger early wooden 'ships' ('ships' being defined as those sailing vessels square rigged on all three masts) built at Chester had interesting careers. The *Lord Forbes* of 1803 was built by Carson, Forbes & Cortney and at 556 tons and 121' x 32'.6" beam she was the largest ship built at Chester up to that time. She was to have a career of over fifty years, not being deleted from Lloyd's Register until 1855. The ship *Bostock* followed in 1805 and 1808 saw the completion of the *Nevis Planter* (see Plate 6 for picture of similar 'ships', the *Charlotte* and *John Campbell*) a West Indiaman for two Liverpool merchants. In December 1809 she arrived in Liverpool from St Croix with a cargo of muscovado sugar, castor oil, liquorice, sweetmeats, coconut shells and tamarinds. However she had only a brief trading life as according to the press in March 1810,[9] the *Nevis Planter* '... from Liverpool for St Croix was captured on 21st January by the *Astrea*, a French frigate, off Fayal (Azores) and burnt, but the crew reached Terceira (Azores). In April that year the vessel *Margaret* arrived at Liverpool and reported that she had seen an English frigate with a French frigate as a prize, in company, supposedly the same one that had captured and burned the *Nevis Planter*.

In 1809, Carson Forbes Cortney completed the brigantine *Lady Warburton*. Built also for Liverpool merchants she too was used in the West Indies/South America trade. In January 1810,[10] she was advertised as sailing for Rio de Janeiro, as a copper sheathed and fastened vessel carrying 18 guns with twelve and eighteen pounders and '... very superior accommodation for passengers, apply Clarke & Tods, Liverpool.' In January 1811, she arrived at Liverpool from Buenos Aires and on 15th March 1811 sailed back to Demerara. Due to the continuing war with France it was arranged that she should sail in convoy from Cork to Jamaica in 1813. It appears, however, that she went missing from a return convoy from Jamaica as in October 1815 the press reported '... the *Lady Warburton* is one of four vessels still missing from the 'Warrior' convoy from Jamaica.'[11] She does, however, reappear in Lloyds until 1820, but her ultimate fate is unknown.

In 1810 Carson, Forbes& Cortney launched the *Charles Mills*, with a slightly larger tonnage than the earlier *Lord Forbes* which was to prove to be Chester's sole connection with vessels of the East India Company [EIC]. Named after one of their directors (Charles Mills, 1755–1826, MP for Warwick), she traded successfully until 1822. In May of that year she was struck by a hurricane in the Bay of Bengal –Lat 15 N, Long 85-30E, 4–500 miles from land. She took with her the chief officer and 65 persons. Only the captain and six others survived in a lifeboat for six days, escaping just as she suddenly sank with 66 unfortunate beings standing on the poop.[12] It is said that the survivors lived on pumpkins. They reached a surf beach, but it was too dangerous to land and they were eventually picked up by a French trading brig and taken to Kedgeree on the east coast of India.[13]

The *Vere* of 1811 (see also Plate 6 below showing a similar vessel) and the *Clarendon* of 1813 were both ships built at the Cortney yard for Liverpool merchants France, Fletcher Yates & Co. These two vessels in their early years ran a 'liner' type of service to Jamaican ports from the Queen's dock in Liverpool. Up to 1828, the

*Vere* seems to have continued in the Jamaica trade to Liverpool typically carrying cargoes of rum, coffee, sugar, wine (possibly from Madeira), logwood, hides and cotton. In 1828 she is advertised as loading for West Africa for T. Tobin from Liverpool. By 1839 she had passed to G. Castle of London who sold her in that year to Selby & Son in Poole, Dorset, trading from south-west ports to Quebec. In 1843 she was on a voyage to New Brunswick and she was wrecked in a heavy snowstorm on 29th March on Campobello Island in the Bay of Fundy, but all her crew were saved.[14] The *Clarendon* had a similar length career trading to Jamaica until at least 1829. By 1835 she is owned by Young & Co of Leith and in 1840 is running from there to New South Wales. She is still in that trade in 1845, but by 1846, still owned by Young, she is on a voyage from London to Bombay. By 1848, however, she has disappeared from Lloyds List.

The *John Shand* (see Plate 5 for picture of a similar vessel) was a ship of 470 tons also launched by Cortney in 1813 for the West Indies trade, owned in Liverpool by Sir John Gladstone. The Gladstone family were already important merchants in Liverpool by this time and owned a number of plantations in the West Indies and throughout the nineteenth century they were to continue to have an involvement with shipbuilding on the Chester river in a variety of ways. Between 1814 and 1830 there are regular reports of the voyages of the *John Shand* to and from Jamaica. Early on in her career she had the misfortune to damage a naval brig, the *Araxis*, in Falmouth Harbour when she was sheltering from a storm and fell upon her.[15] She was named after John Shand , a victualler in Liverpool who also owned the Belmont estate in Jamaica. She disappears from Lloyds List in 1831.

In 1813, Cortney returned to naval shipbuilding with the construction of HMS *Cyrus* and HMS *Levant* in that year followed by HMS *Mersey* and HMS *Eden* in 1814. These vessels were 'sloops of war' classed as '6th rate' and part of the Conway class of vessels.

Plate 3: HMS *Eden* ½ model.

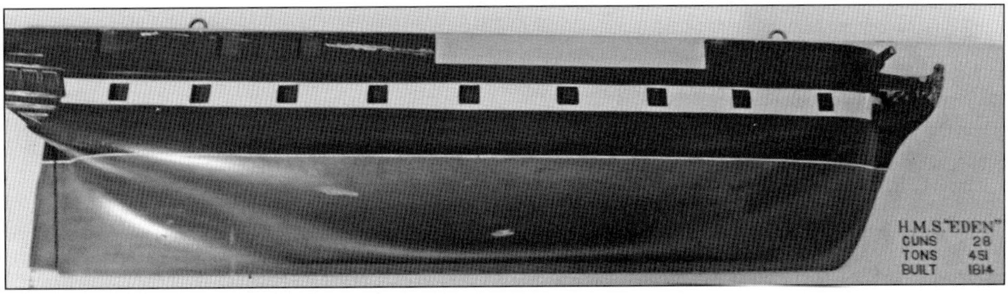

Plate 4: *Cyane* and *Levant* being taken by the *Constitution* in 1815.

The *Cyrus*, and *Levant* carried the same armament, two long 6-pounder guns, and 18 x 32-pounder carronades, with a full complement of 135. There were 16 Conway class vessels built for the Navy. During the Napoleonic Wars, the recently independent America supported the French side for a time and on 20th February 1815 the *Levant* was in company with another 6th rate of the Conway class, the *Cyane*, when they were taken by the American frigate USS *Constitution*, sixty leagues west south west of Madeira. On 11th March 1815, the *Constitution* was proceeding off Porto Praya, Cape Verde Islands with her two prizes, when she was sighted by a British squadron and chased, but due to the weather managed to escape, while fire from HMS *Leander* led to the crew of the *Levant* running her ashore from where she was subsequently recovered by the *Acasta*, a Royal Navy 5th Rate.

On 28th June 1815, a court martial was held on board HMS *Akbar* in Halifax, Nova Scotia, of the officers and men of the *Cyane* and the *Levant*. The *Levant* was returned to Plymouth on 3rd November 1815 where, with probably too much damage to repair, she was broken up in 1820, . Her Chester-built sister vessel *Cyrus* had a slightly longer career and took a couple of prizes, but in 1823 she was put up for sale and sold to Bennet & Son.[17]

In 1814, William Cortney applied to lease more land from Chester City Council '... a lot near the Workhouse now enclosed and in part converted to a graving dock and on which he has also erected warehouses and other buildings for the term of 50 years ... to leave all buildings on site and in good repair and pay the yearly rent of 5 guineas.'[16] On 5th January 1815, when the lease was signed, it was described as a ... piece of land in the Parish of the Holy and Undivided Trinity, bounded by the River Dee on the west, by the lands belonging to Chester City Council, now in the holding of John Troughton, shipbuilder ... and by the Harrison Iron Foundry to the east.' We know therefore that the yards of Troughton and Cortney were adjacent to each other at Crane Wharf and that John Troughton was still building vessels in 1815.

William Cortney also played a full part in the civic life of the City of Chester. In 1815 he was elected mayor. He had built two further 6th Rate Conway-class vessels, the *Eden* and the *Mersey* in 1814. Part of a series of sixteen vessels of the Conway class, they were built to an 1812 design by Sir William Rule. They had an armament of 26 guns –18 x 32 pounder carronades, 8 x 12 pounder carronades and 2 x 6 pounders. *Mersey* saw service on the South America station and in the West Indies. She was put on harbour service in 1832 and in1848 she was receiving ship at Portsmouth and was finally broken up in 1852.[17]

*Eden* (Plate3) had an unusual, but busy, naval career of only nineteen years. Soon after completion it is interesting to find that on 5th November 1816 she was in dock at Portsmouth, preparing for sinking at the bottom of the harbour, to test the effects of sea water on dry rot! On 17th February 1818 it was recorded that she had been raised from the Hamoaze and taken into dock, but '... the treatment of submersion has not been found to work, she remains rotten in every part and must undergo a thorough repair.'[17] It must be assumed that she was used in this way because the Napoleonic wars had ended in 1815 and she was surplus to requirements. It also raises doubts about the quality of the timber used in her construction and possibly could explain why no further naval vessels were built at Chester and Cortney's yard did not survive beyond his death in 1821.

Incredibly, however, the *Eden* was repaired and between December 1818 and January 1819 HM ships *Eden* and *Conway*, assisted by two East India Company cruisers carried out widespread operations against the Qawasim.[18] By the 18th August 1819 she was in Trincomalee, Sri Lanka and in November Major General Sir William Grant Kier was instructed to completely destroy all piratical vessels, together with stores to be found at Ras-al-Kaimah. To achieve this end he had under his command HM Ships *Liverpool, Curlew* and *Eden*, plus nine of the East India Company's cruisers and eighteen transports. There was also one company of artillery and two infantry regiments. Between the 24th November and February 1820, Arab power had been broken sufficiently for the bulk of the force to return to India. A garrison of 800 sepoys was left at Ras al Kaimah. In 1820 *Eden* was at Madras and by 1823 she was on the West Indies station, where she was to stay until 1825. She spent the years 1827 to 1829 on the West Africa station, detaining slave vessels running to Brazil.[19] On 10th June 1829 she reported at Fernando Po that she had buried 47 officers and men, including her doctor and two assistants. The ship was fumigated and the sick transferred to hospital ashore. On 18th July 1829 she sailed for St Helena to improve the health of the crew, '... having now lost 90 officers and men, leaving 40 in hospital.' She further reported from St Helena on 4th September 1829 that of the 173 officers and men who sailed for the west coast of Africa, only 6 officers and 11 men were left –'... now recruiting with a view to retuning to the Coast.' Recruiting for a disease –ridden vessel on St Helena must have been a real challenge, but somehow she did return to Sierra Leone for refitting. By 1831, she was on the South American station but she was broken up in 1833 –a remarkable career for a vessel which had survived serious dry rot and terrible disease.[17]

In April of 1814 Cortney '... shall have a lease of the Timber Yard adjoining the Roodeye called the 'Foreland' for seven years at the yearly rent of £21.' There is no doubt that William Cortney had an expanding business to accommodate at this time.

Writing in 1816, J. H. Hanshall, second editor of the *Chester Chronicle*, said '... the principal shipwright in Chester is Mr Cortney, but Mr Troughton's is the oldest establishment. There were lately 250 hands employed in the business, two thirds of whom were in Mr Cortney's yard, but the trade is at present flat.' Hanshall also indicated in1816 that '... for a number of years Chester has carried on a considerable business in shipbuilding. Within the last ten years the business has wonderfully increased, and even now it is not unusual to see ten or a dozen vessels on the stocks at a time. In fact, there are nearly as many ships built in Chester as in Liverpool, and the former have always a decided preference from the merchants. Indeed Chester lies particularly convenient for the trade, as by the approximation of the Dee, timber is every season floated down from the almost exhaustless woods of Wales, at a trifling expense and without the least risk.'[20] One can only assume that the floating of timber down the river was real, but it must have been an interesting activity to observe –were the logs rafted together? Were they hauled by watermen? Did they float down with an accompanying vessel? Not just allowed to go downstream on their own?

The next large wooden merchant sailing ship which Cortney built was the *Calcutta*, (see Plate 5 for picture of a similar vessel) also for the Gladstone family in Liverpool. Following the loss of the American colonies, which had meant great losses for many Liverpool merchants, came an event which was to expand the trade of the port considerably. The monopoly of commerce with Indian ports held by the East India Company (EIC) was finally ended, partly as a result of 45 years of campaigning by the Liverpool merchants. The first Indian bound vessel from the Mersey was the *Kingsmill* in 1814, a year after the end of the EIC monopoly, again owned by Sir John Gladstone.[21] She returned to Liverpool in 1816, and the appropriately named *Calcutta* joined the Gladstone fleet in 1817, from Mr Cortney's yard. However, the local press had noted in January 1817 that the 'fine ship which has been so long building in Mr Cortney's yard is purchased by Mr J. Robert Gladstone.'[22] She had

Plate 5: The *Princess Charlotte*, completed by Brocklebanks in 1815 at Whitehaven for the India/Far East Trade. She was similar to the *John Shand* (1813) and the *Calcutta* (1817) built by William Cortney.

been building for nearly 2½ years by the time she was purchased and put into service. Until 1834, she continued in Gladstone ownership in the Calcutta trade. In that year she was sold to Williamson. By 1840 she has been sold to J. Rogers of London and was trading to Quebec and Africa from London. In 1845, and again the following year, she made voyages from London to Quebec. Ten years later she was still in service with J. Rogers, making a voyage to Boston from London in 1854 and from Plymouth to Sierra Leone the following year. By 1858 she was no longer Lloyd's registered –a deep sea career of almost 40 years!

The demand for ships must have declined rapidly from the position in 1815. The war with France had ended with Napoleon's surrender on board HMS *Bellerophon* in July that year, after some twelve years of European conflict, the whole period of the Cortney yard's existence. In 1814 there were three shipyards in operation at Chester – Cortney, Troughton and William Mulvey – and 1816 proved to be the best year for building at Chester with at least eleven known vessels coming off the stocks. In March 1816 a reporter at the launch of the brig *John Troughton* stated that '... if we may judge from the number of vessels now on the stocks in Chester, we may imagine the business is in a very prosperous state – there are nine fine vessels on the slips in Mr Cortney's yard and three in Mr Mulvey's.'[23] Maybe the real impact of the end of the war had not yet been fully realized.

In November 1816, however, William Cortney put an advert in the *Chester Chronicle,*[24] 'In consequence of the total stagnation of new building and from a desire to employ the men now continuing in service, he undertakes to repair old vessels on moderate terms.' Dockage and warehousing were offered gratis!

By January 1817,[25] regarding his lease of the graving dock taken up in1815, William Cortney '... humbly prayed that he might have the Privilege granted to him of selling, letting, assigning or exchanging the said premises. It is ordered that the same is granted.' By April that year Cortney had also petitioned the Council Assembly that '... owing to the very depressed state of his trade and the remote prospect of its revival, the petitioner applied to release him from this engagement' (the 1815 lease of the Foreland for seven years). Again the request was accepted with the proviso that 'William Cortney lays the land down with seed to the satisfaction of the Treasurers.'

Later in 1817 matters deteriorated further for the Cortney business when, on the morning of Tuesday, 3rd June, '... fire broke out in the shipyard of Mr Cortney,

Chester and spread with such rapidity as to occasion considerable loss before it could be subdued.' The *Chronicle* reported the fire, '... as one of the most dreadful fires ever recollected in this city.' It seems to have spread from the smithy, over the whole east side of the yard and saw pits, moulding room and tool room were all attacked. There were great concerns about the safety of a new brig on the stocks, pitch being melted on its bow which was only 20 yards from the smithy and saw rooms. However, the wind was favourable and the vessel was saved. Two of the city's fire engines attended.[26]

Despite the problems experienced by shipbuilders following the end of the Napoleonic wars, in 1817 two vessels, both flats, the *Lord Hill* and the *Margaret* were built at Chester by J. Goolden & Co.[27] It is not clear whether these vessels were built at Crane Bank, in the Dee Basin, or at the site on the Ellesmere and Chester Canal, later occupied by the boatyard of the Shropshire Union Co. It seems that both these vessels were built for the canal/river packet service that operated between Chester and Liverpool. John Goolden was not a recognised shipwright, but at the time of their building, he operated as the wharfinger at Maesbury, Shropshire for the Ellesmere and Chester Canal Co and also had a cartage company. So far I have not come across any other vessels that he may have built.

During this period press reports were regularly written as if accidents in shipyards and at launches were the norm. In September 1813, a reporter recollected that, '... no accident had taken place on such occasions...' at the launch of the ship *John Shand,* although he went on to say that, at the time of launching, there was nearly an accident when '... the pressure on an anchor to which a check cable was fastened, was so great as to separate its shaft midway, the piece to which the rope was attached pulled for 30 yds, but happily without persons receiving injury.'[28] In May 1814, a Mr Llewellyn of Bridge Sreet Row, Chester, died of a fractured skull after he went on board the new sloop of war *Eden* to view the vessel and unfortunately fell from the deck into the hold. A month later, there was an accident at the Mulvey yard at the launch of the *Limerick Trader,* when a shipwright was '... hurt in knocking away the boult between the bottom of the vessel when he received an accidental blow from a maul of a fellow workman, shattering his arm in a dreadful manner above the elbow.'[29]

Later in 1816, the *Chester Chronicle* reported that two vessels were launched on the same day in March of that year; the *John Troughton* (from the yard of the same

Plate 6: 'Port of Liverpool' by Joseph Heard. *Martha*, brig, built at Chester in 1818, is the two-masted vessel in the background.

name) and the *Lord Nelson,* from Mr Cortney's yard. Again, the reporter made a point of saying '... no serious accidents occurred.'[30]

The reporter, however, did go on to say that, owing to the sudden swell of the water when the *John Troughton* went off, several people got a sound ducking on the wharf under the cheese warehouse! This incident also tells us that the Troughton yard was located more towards the northerly end of Crane Wharf, nearer to the Cheese Stage.

Throughout the period up to 1815, John Troughton continued to build a variety of types of wooden sailing vessels. The last we can identify being the brig *Belvedere* of 1818.

Also built at one of the Chester yards in 1818 was the brig *Martha*. Whether she was built as a 'cheese ship' to carry Cheshire cheese from the river Dee to London, is not certain, but she was working in that trade by 1822. She is the only merchant vessel from this era of Chester shipbuilding to have featured in a painting (see Plate 6).

She was originally owned by Stapp & Co, and was put into the Brazil trade. In 1829, she passed to the ownership of the Maxwells and William Rotherham, trading to West Africa. For the last ten years of her career she was owned by Isaac Bold who kept her running to West Africa. Both these owners had associations with other Chester-built vessels.

John Troughton died on 21st October 1819 and his business may have suffered after the end of the Napoleonic wars. Sadly, he had no direct heir to carry on the business and the proceeds of his will were divided among his three nieces.

The shipbuilders in Chester at this time must have worked together in an atmosphere of friendly rivalry, sharing labour and resources as required. Evidence for this is to be found in the order book of the Ellesmere & Chester Canal Co. [E&CCC] in 1820.[31] This company had a lot of problems with the contractors who leased the right to operate the packet boats, both across the Mersey and along the canal between Chester and Ellesmere Port, largely it would seem because the contractors could not make any money after they had paid the rent to the E&CCC. At a meeting held on 9th Sept 1820, the E&CCC Committee requested Mr Cortney, on behalf of the company, to meet Mr John Wilson, on the part of Mr Hickson (contractor), and Mr Mulvey on behalf of Mr Whittle (E&CCCo), to examine the state of the two canal packet boats –the *Telford* and the *Countess of Bridgewater*– as well as the luggage boat, and report back to a sub-committee on their state of repair.

Subsequently, the Mersey packets were found to be in good order but the 'canal packets, upon their bottoms being opened, appear very materially damaged by dry rot.'

William Cortney also gave up some more land in January 1821, just one month before his death on 9th February, aged 56, at about which time the partnership he had with a Samuel Newton also expired. How long this had been in existence is unknown, but there is a merchant named Samuel Newton, who was part owner of two vessels built at Chester –the three-masted ship *George* (built by the previous partnership of Carson Forbes & Cortney in 1805) and the ship *Mersey* (built in 1806). The last known vessel built by Cortney was the three-masted ship *Liverpool* completed in 1821 after his death.

The known children of William Cortney were all daughters, so there was no one to carry on the family business. In September 1821, the stock of the yard was advertised for sale at an auction to be held on 17th September. It comprised mainly timber and building materials, but also a '... new schooner of 88 tons with masts, spars and boat, complete.' It was reported in September 1821[32] that some Liverpool businessmen were taking the yard over and it must be assumed that this was John Wilson, the Liverpool shipbuilder, whose first recorded building at Chester is in 1822. Indeed, five years after the death of her father, Margaret Cortney, William's youngest daughter, married John Wilson who was to continue building vessels at the Crane from 1822–7.

Throughout the period that John Troughton and William Cortney were building vessels at the Crane, the involvement in shipbuilding at Chester of the family of Thomas Dixon should also be recognized. Thomas Dixon I (1755–1811) was a mariner based in Liverpool who owned vessels trading to the West Indies. He had three children, the eldest of whom Thomas II (1790–1878), founded a bank in Chester in 1813 which was his most significant achievement. A tablet in the church at Christleton, just outside Chester, records that Thomas II was Sheriff in 1813 and Mayor in 1835.[33] This bank more than likely financed some of the Chester shipbuilders and their shipowners. Thomas Dixon I's youngest son, James (1796–1866), is also recorded as having an involvement in the timber business.

Thomas Dixon I, had substantial shareholdings in sixteen Liverpool registered vessels between 1786 and 1788. He was described as '... a former Captain in the Navy, timber merchant and shipbuilder.'[34] Whether he had any direct involvement in shipbuilding at Chester or indeed Liverpool before 1800 is not really known.

In 1790 Thomas Dixon I was elected as a Common Councilman of the City of Chester (he had arrived in Littleton in 1779) and it is recorded that in 1802 the City Land Committee agreed that he should have '... the old dock between the House of Industry and Mr Harrison's foundry at 8 guineas a year for seven years from 10th October 1802 and that he should keep, the drain through the dock open at all times.'[35] By 1806, he must have been very prosperous as he had built Littleton Hall, designed by the architect Benjamin Gummow which still stands today, built on the site of his former house, Littleton Hill, and remaining in the Dixon family until 1980.[37]

In 1820, following the death of John Troughton in 1819, Thos Dixon II was asking for a committee of enquiry to be set up to look into a piece of land next to the House of Industry and in the same year he and the Guardians of the Poor took over '... a piece of land of the late Mr Troughton.'[36] It seems, therefore, that Thos Dixon II was also closely involved in the Crane Wharf site, where he took over the Troughton yard and expanded the timber yard and import facility. Taking account of its excellent location, this timber yard was probably a major supplier of timber to the Chester shipbuilders of wooden ships in the years to come. He was also involved in ship owning. The brig *Three Brothers*, built at Chester in 1812, was owned by Dixon in 1827 and then sold to a Mr Baile in 1831. Certainly, the Dixon brothers were importing timber according to newspaper advertisments in 1825 and 1826. In 1826 the press stated that '... now discharging from Miramichi, New Brunswick –pine lumber, planks poles and lathwood– apply Thos and James Dixon, St John St, Chester. We also have on sale Riga, Memel, Dantzic and Pitch pine timber, deals, boards, laths, slates tiles, Parkers Roman cement etc.'[38]

Summing up the role of the Dixon family in shipbuilding at Chester, there does not appear to be any evidence that they actually built any vessels at Chester after 1800 and it is more likely that they were major providers of timber and were involved in the finance through their banking interests in the city.

This snapshot of shipbuilding at Chester in this period would not be complete without reminding the reader that some of the larger vessels built there provided important links to the developing trade to the furthest reaches of the expanding British Empire, in particular taking settlers to Australia.

Two of the vessels built at Chester, the barque *John* (1810) and the ship

*Southworth* (1821) were successfully used for the transportation of convicts to Australia (a barque is a three-masted vessel, square rigged on two masts –the aft mast fore & aft rigged). Although it cannot be absolutely confirmed, it is likely that both these vessels were products of the Cortney yard.

The barque *John* made five voyages transporting convicts. In 1827 and again in 1829, she sailed to New South Wales. In 1831, she went to Van Diemen's Land (Tasmania), then again to New South Wales in 1832, and finally, in 1833, back to Van Diemen's Land.

On her first voyage, under Captain William John Moncrieff, she departed London on 22nd July 1827, carrying 188 male prisoners. She arrived in Port Jackson on 25th November 1827. The guard comprised a detachment of the 40th Regiment. On the outward voyage, one seaman died of typhus and the surgeon, James Mc Kerrow, in a fit of supposed lunacy, threw himself overboard.[39]

Two years later, she sailed with another 188 convicts bound for New South Wales, this time sailing from Sheerness. On this voyage, William Grant Broughton, who had been appointed as archdeacon of New South Wales, was aboard with his wife, two daughters and two servants. He kept a diary, and the entry for 26th May 1829[39] reads,

> ... the ship was commanded by Mr Robert Nosworthy, and as well as the convicts she had a crew of 32 men and boys and about 30 soldiers, under Capt Forbes of the 89th Reg't. The Archdeacon and his family were conveyed out to the vessel, anchored at the Little Nore, in a dockyard cutter, though the swell on the sea renders the operation somewhat formidable. Two steam packets going to Ostend found the weather too bad and turned back. After 15 minutes aboard the *John* all were affected with sea sickness. Sailed the following morning, but the crew were extremely unfamiliar with the vessel and many of them were ignorant of the orders that were issued, whilst the crowded state of the decks, the sight of the prisoners in chains and of the soldiers loitering about, neither able or willing to render assistance rendered our departure a scene of tumult and confusion. Our pilot did not spare his reproaches.'

Later on in the voyage, on 12th June, in a dead calm, the Reverend took advantage to describe the convict ship.

> On each side of the poop, as well as in front of the binnacle, we have coops containing fowls, ducks and guinea hens and abaft the cuddy skylight is a large pen filled with ducks and geese. The intermediate spaces are occupied by sailors refitting yards and sails and in the front are four privates and a corporal on guard with their loaded muskets lying near. Below, on the quarter deck, opposite to each other, are two unhappy wights, convicts afresh convicted of having towed their clothes alongside for the purposes of washing and suffered them to go adrift, which offence they are set in handcuffs and fetters and condemned to 24 hours bread and water. About the deck lie the soldiers off guard, some asleep, others employed in various occupations Two sentries with drawn bayonets parade the deck. From the barricade which goes athwart the ship, just after the main mast to the forecastle the prisoners are situated, some sitting idle on the spars and spare booms others cooking, washing, walking or sleeping as inclination leads.
>
> They appear neither discontented, dejected nor sullen and are in general far from noisy. In their behavior I find them universally respectful, though their characters are in general very unfavourable, most of them having been more than once, or even twice, convicted and sentenced. Add to this four or five women belonging to the soldiers and intermingled with them the crying of a child or two, the quacking of ducks, cackling of geese and fowls and the harsh grating cry of the guinea hens and you will have a fairly complete picture of all that is to be seen and heard on board of a convict ship.[40]

This voyage took 109 days.

In 1832, the *John* took 122 days to complete the same voyage, and she continued in the Australian trade for many years. During the last twenty years of her life she was in the hands of several different owners and served in a variety of trades, mainly across the Atlantic from Plymouth and Bristol. By 1848m she was owned by T. Evans and was registered in Bideford, running from Bristol to Quebec and the West Indies. After 1849, she passed to Rawle & Co of Plymouth who continued to operate her across the Atlantic to America and Canada, in the emigrant trade, running usually to New York. She was an astonishing 45-years old when she was wrecked on the Manacles in 1855, on an outward voyage from Plymouth to Quebec, on May 3rd 1855, with 282 persons on board. At 9.30pm she was within sight of St Anthony's Light at Falmouth, but failed to see the Lizard light. She was too close inshore and struck the Manacles travelling under full sail at nine knots. One boat got ashore with four of the crew who alerted the coastguard, but nothing was done until daylight.

In the meantime, the crew became intoxicated and neither they nor the captain made any attempt to save the unfortunate emigrants, although there were still three boats on board. At daybreak, boats from the shore approached into which the crew scrambled leaving the terrified emigrants to their own devices. All the crew of 19 were saved, but 196 men, women and children perished. The total survivors numbered 86.[41] An ignominious end for a fine, wooden barque which had certainly travelled the world.

Returning to the transportation of convicts. Immediately after the arrival of the *John* in New South Wales in 1832, the next convict vessel to arrive there was the *Southworth*, also built in Chester in 1821. Built for Liverpool owners, she sailed on her maiden voyage that year under Captain David Sampson, embarking 101 Irish convicts at Cork on 24th October and arriving in Port Jackson 111 days later on 9th March 1822. In April 1822, she left Port Jackson, and sailed north via the Torres Strait to Batavia (Dutch East Indies) where she arrived on 31st May 1822. In November 1823, she limped into Cowes with a cargo of tobacco from New Orleans having sustained so much damage that she had to be fully discharged before completing her voyage to Amsterdam. In 1825, she embarked part of the 99th Regiment at Portsmouth bound for Mauritius, and was expected to return with the 56th Regiment. In 1826, she took troops from Cork to Barbados and, in February 1827, arrived in Barbados with two companies of artillery, returning with invalids. In July she sailed from Quebec to Portsmouth in 27 days with a company of the Royal Artillery and invalids. In March 1830, having arrived off Deal from Valparaiso, she then made another convict voyage to Van Diemen's Land, returning via Manila. She made one further voyage to New South Wales in 1832, carrying 134 female prisoners from Cork, taking 129 days. The prisoners had an age range from 13–70.

Arriving at Port Jackson on 14th June 1832, the *Southworth* departed Sydney with the 39th Regiment bound for Madras in early August. In April 1833 she arrived at Portsmouth from Madras. In October 1833 she made a further voyage from Sheerness to Hobart with 190 male convicts.

In between her convict voyages, the *Southworth* was certainly fully occupied on routes world-wide, often as a troop transport but her end came in October 1834 when, returning from Batavia, she was lost off Holland, near the Oosterbank in a tremendous NNW gale. All on board were lost, including Captain Maltby and the two pilots she had taken on board off Goree on 19th October.[42]

From as early as 1814, the Troughton and Cortney yards were joined by a third shipbuilder, Mulvey and Evans, who continued their partnership until November 1820, when it was dissolved by mutual consent. Both parties are described as 'shipwrights of Liverpool.' The first vessel that can definitely be identified as theirs is the brig *Limerick Trader* (1814) built for the London trade. By 1820 she was running between Limerick and Liverpool. On 16th March 1816, a further brig was built, the flushed-deck *Hope*, a vessel that was probably also used in the coastal trade from Chester as a 'cheese ship.' By May of that year she was on the Thames, owned by Edward Savage and others, including William Bromfield of Greenwich, a pilot.

The brig *Velocity* (1819) has also been identified as a Mulvey-built vessel. In 1814 the shipbuilder William Mulvey was elected as a freeman of Chester. He was to have a long career as a councillor for the Holy Trinity Ward up to 1836. He had been born in Lancaster in1775, marrying Peggy (Margaret) Smith of Satterthwaite in 1795. It is likely that he was the son of John Mulvey and Elizabeth (née Wilkinson) who had been married at Melling in Lonsdale in 1765. The Mulveyfront website[43] also suggests that the Mulvey family built vessels in Frodsham and Liverpool at some time.

William and Peggy had at least three sons -John, Thomas Smith (born in Frodsham in 1809) and William Wilkinson (born in Chester in 1814). Both Thomas and William were destined to join the family business.

## Notes

1. *Transactions of the Lancashire & Cheshire Historical Society*, 'Shipping & Shipbuilding in Chester', by R. Craig, vol. 116, pp39–68. The *Lord Forbes* was the largest vessel built at Chester before 1808.
2. *Chester Courant,* 23rd June 1812.
3. *Liverpool Mercury*, 17th November 1815.
4. 'Chester – 1900 years of History', edited by Annette Kennet (1979, Chester). See section on the Roodeye by J. M. Grisenthwaite.
5. Chester City Council Records, 23/08/1785, Cheshire Archives, Ref. ZA/B/5/F.
6. www.hopkinsweb.org.uk.
7. Chester Council Land Committee Minutes, 02/04/1802 – Cheshire Archives, Ref. ZA/B/5/F88.
8. *Chester Courant,* 9th January 1810. Sadly neither the reporter on the *Courant*, or the *Chronicle* give the vessel a name. Both brief reports of the launch are written in flowery language, one in a classic Greek style.
9. See *Lancaster Gazette*, 10th March 1810, report of 8th March from Liverpool that vessel was burnt on 21st January 1810, BNA.
10. *Leeds Intelligencer*, 1st January 1810, BNA.

11. *Lancaster Gazette,* 30th September 1815, BNA.
12. Loss of the *Charles Mills*, see *Asiatic Journal & Monthly Register for British & Foreign India and China,* vol. 15 on google e-books.
13. *Caledonian Mercury,* 7th December 1822, BNA.
14. *Morning Post,* 17th May 1843, BNA.
15. *Morning Post,* 17th December 1814.
16. Chester City Council Assembly Book 1814, pp164–5, Cheshire Archives, Ref. ZA/B/5/F 12/08/1814.
17. www.pbenyon.plus.com – Naval database.
18. See *Sea Breezes* magazine July 1983, 'HMS *Liverpool* returns to the Gulf'.
19. The buying and selling of slaves was outlawed in Britain in 1807. The Royal Navy endeavoured to prevent other countries taking slaves from West Africa e.g. to Brazil.
20. J. H. Hanshall, *The Stranger in Chester* (1816).
21. *Portrait of Liverpool*, Howard Channon (1970, London).
22. *Chester Chronicle,* 3rd March1817.
23. *Chester Chronicle,* 8th March 1816.
24. *Chester Chronicle,* advert November 1816.
25. Assembly Book of the Chester City Council, 17th January 1817 and 10th April 1817, Cheshire Archives, Ref. ZA/B/5/f190 p379.
26. *Chester Chronicle,* 6th June 1817.
27. Chester Ship Register, 1827, BT107/290, The National Archives.
28. *Chester Chronicle*, 17th September 1813.
29. *Chester Chronicle,* 24th June 1814.
30. *Chester Chronicle,* 8th March 1816.
31. Order Book of the Ellesmere & Chester Canal Company, RAIL826/8, The National Archives.
32. *Liverpool Mercury,* 21st September 1821.
33. *Christleton, the History of a Cheshire Village,* Local History Group (1979).
34. *Christleton Local History Group Magazine,* vol. 1, issue 4, September 1998.
35. Minutes of the City Land Committee, Cheshire Archives, Ref. ZA/B/5/f 20/8/1802.
36. Chester City Council Assembly Book, April 1920, Cheshire Archives, Re.f ZA/B/5/f 3/4/1820.
37. Littleton Hill was divided into four units in 1969. Littleton Hall was built in 1806 and Hanshall described it about 1820 as 'the beautiful seat of Thomas Dixon.' This fine Georgian house looks just as splendid today.
38. Dixon's timber advert, *Chester Chronicle*, 1st September 1826.
39. See 'Voyage of the *John*, 1827' on the 'Free settler or Felon' website, www.jenwilletts.com.
40. 'Voyage of the *John* 1829', extracted from the diary of William Grant Broughton who had been appointed Archdeacon of New South Wales who sailed with his family on the *John* in May 1829. See 'Free Settler or Felon' website, 2015.
41. Charles Hocking, *Dictionary of Disasters at Sea in the Age of Steam 1824–1962*, Vol.1 (A-L) (1969, London).
42. *Morning Chronicle*, 4th November 1834 and 28th October 1834.
43. 'Mulveyfront' website, see www.bramhill.net, Mulvey family section.

# 2

## Chester 1822–35: the era of wood and steam

By 1820, Chester had passed its peak as a shipbuilding centre in the British Isles. It has already been noted in Chapter 1 that in 1816, immediately after the end of the Napoleonic wars, more vessels were being built in Chester than in Liverpool, and that it was not unusual to see 10 or 12 vessels on the stocks at the same time. Lloyd's Register of 1822 records the names of over 15,700 vessels, of which 109 had been built at Chester (0.69%). However, just looking solely at the 1,340 vessels listed beginning with the letter 'A', only 811 were actually built in the British Isles of which 13 (1.6%) were built at Chester. Not so important you may think until it is realized that those 811 vessels were built at no fewer than 117 different estuary, river and beach locations –an average of seven per site, so Chester was a relatively important shipbuilding city.

Following the deaths of John Troughton in 1819 and William Cortney in 1821, two of the three yards at Crane Wharf changed hands and also saw the building of the first steamships on the Dee, in addition to the traditional wooden sailing vessels, one of which was the largest built so far at Chester when launched in 1826. The Mulveys and the Wilsons became Chester's two principal shipbuilders.

John Wilson Junior was part of the Liverpool shipbuilding fraternity which had come to prominence in the early nineteenth century after John Wilson Senior took over a rival yard in Liverpool, formerly operated by Edward Grayson, another family with a long history of shipbuilding and repair on the Mersey. Grayson died in 1804, following a duel fought opposite the Chapel in Toxteth Park caused by a family dispute! An unusual reason for a business to be taken over, but Edward Grayson's will had stipulated that, although his son Charles was in the family business, it was to be sold on his death, and Charles was obliged to start up on his own.[2] A Charles Grayson applied in 1823 to become a Freeman of the City of Chester but was refused, '... until he took up residence in the City,'[1] no doubt with a view to taking on the Wilsons in a competing yard on the Dee.

John Wilson Senior was a shipwright in a small way of business and, although he never made anything of it, his son Thomas built it up to a very large concern. The site of the Liverpool shipyards at this time was broadly where the Albert Dock (opened 1846) can be seen today, so the shipbuilders there were limited in the size of vessels they could build and there was no space to expand. 'Thos Wilson was a very energetic sort of man and led the approach by the shipbuilders to the Dock Trustees to gain more space. Instead of getting more accommodation, he was given notice to quit, whereupon he sought land in Birkenhead and transferred his business to that town.'[3] The Liverpool builders were constantly unable to gain security of tenure from the Dock Trustees who would not grant leases of more than 12 months, which was far from ideal for the shipbuilding business and its 'feast or famine' type of operation and labour disputes. Although this appears to have been a harsh decision by the Dock Trustees, the shipbuilders of Liverpool in the nineteenth century were to find that they were always second-class citizens on the Liverpool side of the river as the Liverpool Dock Trustees (and from 1857, the Mersey Docks & Harbour Board) needed the land for the rapid expansion of the dock system to service ships and the rapidly growing trade with the Empire. The opening of the Harrington Dock (1839), Toxteth Dock (1841), and Canning Half Tide Dock (1844) and the Albert Dock (1846), saw the shipbuilders gradually forced out of Liverpool to sites in Garston, Birkenhead and Chester.

By 1840, Thomas Wilson (destined to become the largest shipbuilder of his time on the Mersey) was responsible for the construction of a number of well known early steamships; the *Royal William* of 403 tons (1837), the *Oriental* of 1,797 tons (1840), the *Hindostan* (1842) and the *Bentinck* (1843), the three larger vessels all for P&O and engined by Fawcett Preston.[4]

The Wilson family, perhaps under pressure for space and continuity of tenure, looked to Chester to create more building space and also embrace the new technology of steam power in ships. We know from the experience of Troughton and Cortney that Chester City Council were prepared to grant leases of riverside land for up to 50 years to shipbuilders, a very different situation from that existing in Liverpool.

'Thomas Wilson, shipbuilder' is recorded in the Assembly Book of Chester City Council in January 1825, proposing that John Axe, a Spirit Dealer, '... be admitted into the liberties and franchises of the City,' but it is John Wilson, or John Wilson Jnr, who is shown as the builder of vessels in Chester between 1822 and 1827. On 26th October 1826, John Wilson Jnr (aged 25) married Margaret Cortney (aged 23), daughter of the late William Cortney, at Holy Trinity Church in Chester. From this connection it can be assumed that, after William Cortney's death, Thomas Wilson /John Wilson Jnr had taken over the lease of the yard that Cortney had used at the foreland end of the Roodeye.

Wilson's yard in Chester was, however, relatively short-lived as there are vessels recorded as built there only in the period 1821–27. Of the twelve possible vessels identified, six were small, wooden, steam-paddle vessels, some for Irish Sea services and some for ferry services across the Mersey. It must also be borne in mind that between 1835 and 1839 'W. & T. Wilson' or 'T. Wilson' also built quite a few wooden paddle steamers in Liverpool/Birkenhead.

The other vessels Wilson built at Chester were wooden sailing craft of various types, ranging from brigs to the snow *Belem Castle* (built in 1824) and three-masted ships including the *Loretto* (1825) of 380 tons burthen, and the *St George*, 604 tons burthen, the largest vessel built on the Chester River up to that time.[5] Launched on 29th November 1826, by Mr Thomas Green, a local timber merchant, the *St George* was immediately towed to Liverpool by the tug *Ormrod* for fitting out, but sadly the company who had ordered her for the South American trade failed financially and she was not registered until March 1828 at Bristol. This explains the delay of 18 months between launching and her maiden voyage, and why her date of build varies in Lloyd's Register.

Not only was the *St George* the largest vessel built on the Dee until then, she was also one of the largest sailing merchant ships built in the United Kingdom, outside of the Thames. The only larger sailing ships registered with Lloyd's in 1829 were those built on the river Thames for the Honourable East India Company and other merchants in the Indian trade, or sailing vessels built abroad. Certainly by this time there were vessels of a larger tonnage built in India (using largely teak, and pine from Danzig) and the north-east seaboard of the United States.

Writing in *Sea Breezes* magazine in June 1947, John C. Hill gave an excellent account of the maiden voyage of the *St George* to Calcutta.

> ... built at Chester for Messr's Daniel & Acraman for the East India Trade, she was a frigate type ,built and equipped in a manner surpassing those ships operated by the East

> India Company, which were admitted to be the finest model of British merchant vessel, combining swiftness of sailing with large stowage of cargo.
>
> Under the command of Capt Swainson she left the Floating Light Liverpool at 6.00pm on Tuesday May 20th 1828 on her maiden voyage to India. She was spoken with at 11.00 o'clock on the morning of Wednesday, the following day, off St David's Head going at a rate of 9½–10 knots. On 29th idem she passed the ships *Herculean* (Brocklebank) and *John Taylor* bound for Calcutta. On the 31st she passed the *Scipio* for Singapore. Then on July 7th she came up with the Honourable Company's enormous ships *Prince Regent* and *Rose* well over 1,000 tons register each, and getting on for double her size; they had left England on May 13th. She kept company with these ships six days owing to variable winds, but on July 13th she left them astern. August 13th found her in the longitude of Madras, latitude 35° south, with the wind N.N.E to N.N.W until August 20th, when the wind changed for the better, and then for six successive days the ship ran from 9½ to 11½ knots. On September 9th she came in sight of Madras, the current running strong to the southward, a sure sign that no ship should visit Madras after September1st. She had made the voyage in three months, twenty-two days. On arrival, the passengers unanimously addressed Capt Swainson for his kind treatment during the voyage, and accompanied it with a substantial present of plate.
>
> The good folk of Madras were not a little astonished that the *St George* had beaten the Company's ships on her outward voyage. On September 20th she sailed for Calcutta. The *St George* commenced her homeward voyage leaving Calcutta on December 13th, arriving at St Helena island, February 15th and sailing again on February 23rd, eventually docking at Liverpool on the completion of her round voyage on April 7th 1829.

She was to spend the next fourteen years in the Indian trade, making voyages of around four months duration to Calcutta and Madras under Acraman ownership, but following the bankruptcy of the Acraman enterprises in Bristol in 1842 (which continued until 1847) she was sold. The financial failure of the Acraman group was claimed by the local press to be '... the collapse of one of the most extensive private commercial establishments in the Kingdom.'[6] The *St George* was sold to G. Marshall of London who put her into the Australian emigrant trade, sailing to Sydney in 1850 and again in 1851. In 1853, she went out to Port Philip again. Supposedly she was finally converted to a barge (in Australia?) and was out of Lloyd's Register by 1854.

One of the first wooden paddle steamers built by John Wilson, the *Lord Melville*, was launched on 9th March 1822 by a Mr Everden (who also built steamers at Deptford for the General Steam Navigation Co.). She was also one of the largest at 112ft in length and 137 tons burthen. On her maiden voyage it took her 11 hours to sail from Chester to Holyhead at 9mph. Fitted with a two-cylinder engine by Butterley & Co. in 1822, she is initially recorded as being owned by W. J. Joliffe & E. Banks of London. They were instrumental in the founding of the famous General Steam Navigation Co. and by 1825 *Lord Melville* had passed into their ownership where she remained until her register was closed in 1849 when she was broken up.

On arrival in the Thames in May 1822, she was advertised as the '... superb new and commodious steam packet under the command of Peter Black, R.N.. From her moorings off the Tower to Calais upon every Wednesday and Saturday mornings at half past six o'clock precisely, returning from Calais on Mondays and Thursdays.'[7] Each passenger was allowed one hundredweight of goods and she also took carriages (£4) and chaises (£2) each (one assumes the accompanying horses too)! How the horses and carriages were manouvered aboard/disembarked off the Tower on a tidal river stretches one's imagination. Perhaps this was a forerunner of today's RO-RO ferry services across the English Channel? Passenger fares were chief cabin – 32s, fore cabin and foredeck – 22s. The voyage was advertised as taking 12 hours.

On such a demanding mail packet service it is to be expected that the ship experienced bad weather problems and accidents. In 1824, her engineer, Mr George Beedmore, seriously crushed his leg when examining part of the machinery when entering Calais Harbour, and in November 1826 she had to return to Calais four hours into her crossing with boiler trouble. On returning, she missed the harbour entrance in the dark and at the second attempt put herself aground with her 'head down the bank' with the crew bailing water. She survived this incident, but the press reported that the Earl of Rockinghamshire and Lady Stewart were delayed as their carriages and horses could not be transhipped to the other packet the *Fury*.'[8] On several occasions during her career, the press reported that she had put into Ramsgate due to bad weather (1833) and hurricane force winds (1837).

By 15th May 1830,[8] the *Lord Melville* had undergone considerable alterations and improvements and the *Morning Post* was advertising 'London to Calais in 9 hours at reduced fares.' The chief cabin fare was then only 21s and the fore cabin 14s. Later that month, on 21st May, it was reported that the *Lord Melville* was the strongest and fastest sea-going vessel on the river, and on 12th May she made the passage from London to Calais in 9 hours 38 minutes –the quickest ever known– but not quite the 9 hours in the advert!

She had an impressive 27-year career as a wooden mail steamer from 1822–49 on the Calais route, occasionally also serving Rotterdam. Despite her long service on this route, there do not seem to be any surviving paintings of this vessel. However, when the author was by chance looking at the pictures in the house at Polesden Lacy in Surrey, he came across an atmospheric painting of the Pool of London by George Bough, painted in 1863, showing the Pool before the building of Tower Bridge in 1886. There, berthed on the north bank of the Thames, is a steamer which looked very much as I imagine the *Lord Melville* to have looked.

John Wilson Junior, after his initial foray into steam, seems to have built two or three traditional sailing vessels in Chester, before returning to paddle steamer construction in 1825 with the *Lee*, an even larger vessel at 131' loa and 205 tons burthen. At the same time, John Wilson Senior built a twin sister to the *Lee* in Liverpool. Called *Severn*, she was built for the Cork & Bristol Steam Navigation Co. of Dublin, and was also engined by Fawcett Preston, with a 130 h.p. engine. She had a similar career, lasting until 1849 when she was scrapped.

The first owners of the *Lee* were William Fawcett of Liverpool, John Watson the younger and John Robinson of Dublin, in the name of the Cork & Liverpool Steam Navigation Co.. She was also fitted with schooner rig and carried three masts. Fawcett Preston built the120 hp engine, and she initially ran from Liverpool to Cork. In 1826/7 she was running Bristol–Cork, and in 1829 was running Liverpool–Dublin. From 1832/3 she ran Bristol–Dublin. Interestingly, after 1833, she is registered at 142' 5", so had been lengthened by 10'. In 1833, she was employed on a Liverpool/Cork /London service, but in 1834 the company opened a base at Hull and both the *Lee* and her sister vessel the *Severn* moved round to the east coast. From 1834–9 they were both largely involved in running Hull–Hamburg and to Dundee and Rotterdam, together with another vessel, the *William IV*. From 1840–2 the *Lee* was employed on Cork–London service. In 1835, ownership had passed to the Saint George Steam Packet Co. of Dublin, and in 1843 both vessels were taken over by the newly formed Cork Steamship Company, headed by Ebenezer Pike who was to go on and build a number of steamships himself in Cork for the Irish Sea and European services from 1848. From 1845 the *Lee* was in the hands of various

Plate 7: P.S. *Victory*, built by John Wilson Senior in Liverpool in 1832.

London owners, until she was broken up in 1851.[9]

Although there are no known paintings of the *Lee* or her Liverpool-built sister *Severn* there is a painting of 1838 by Samuel Walters of the similar three-masted steam paddler *Victory* (see Plate 7), built by John Wilson Senior in Liverpool in 1832. She too was built for Irish sea service and was 20 feet longer than the *Lee* before she was lengthened in1833.

The first vessel out of the Wilson yard in the year 1826 was the *Kingstown*, which was also a 'paddle steamer with schooner rig.' Clearly, in the early days of steam, sails were carried as an insurance policy in the event of a technical failure and to speed up the passage when appropriate weather conditions allowed. At 91' 2" in length and of 71 tons, she was fitted with a 60 hp single expansion steam engine and was the first passenger vessel to run between Wexford and Liverpool. Built for the St George Steam Packet Co. of Dublin, the *Kingstown* initially ran from Dublin–Wexford and Dublin–Bangor (Caernarfonshire), but in 1827 was on a Liverpool–Isle of Man service. In 1828, she was again running Dublin–Wexford and by 1830 was on a Limerick–Lower Shannon service. In 1833, she was running Dublin/ Wexford/Cork, but was back on the Shannon the following year. The register was closed in 1845 when she was broken up.

These small, wooden paddle steamers, with a schooner rig, are frighteningly

Plate 8: *Kingswear Castle* on the river Dart. She is longer and beamier than most of the wooden paddlers built at Chester 1822–6 for English Channel and Irish Sea service.

small for the waters they operated in –the Irish Sea and the English Channel. Today, operating in the summer on the river Dart is the steel-hulled paddle steamer *Kingswear Castle*, built in 1924 and now restored by the Paddle Steamer Preservation Society and operated by the Dart Valley Railway. With an overall length of 113.77 feet and a beam of 27.97 feet she is longer and beamier than both the *Lord Melville* and the *Kingstown*, yet is restricted to river estuary service only. Admittedly, her moulded depth is only 4.49 feet compared with the 12' 11"of the *Lord Melville* or the 10' 4" of the *Kingstown*, but these Irish Sea and Channel packets were also much narrower in the beam than the river Dart paddle steamers built 100 years later.

*Maria II* was built for the Eastham–Liverpool ferry service, while the *Ormrod* of 77 tons was another 'schooner rigged paddle steamer.' She was used as a tug on the Mersey by a variety of owners, but also spent time as a tug at Goole where she was briefly registered in 1834, before returning to the Mersey where she came under the ownership of the Liverpool Steam Tug Co. from the end of 1838–1856, when she was broken up.

*Cymro* was built in 1826 at Wilson's Chester yard, primarily for towing the Union Companys' cheese vessels up and down the river Dee and to carry passengers and parcels etc between Bagillt, Flint and Chester, and was destined to have a long career as a tug. She was the first tug based on the Dee. By 1845, she was owned by J. Williams of Chester, who sold her in 1847 to owners in Dundalk. In 1848 she was back under Chester ownership with Thomas Evans, wharfinger of Chester. From 1848 she was owned by the Shrewsbury & Chester Railway and, in 1860, passed to the ownership of the Great Western Railway Co. for whom she continued to provide towage services on the river Dee up to their wharf at Saltney until 1880 when she was broken up. For an early wooden tug, this was a lengthy career of 54 years –a hard life for a wooden-hulled vessel originally with only a 33 h.p. engine.

The reason for John Wilson Junior not continuing to build ships in Chester after 1827 is a most unusual one. By 1828, he and his first wife were living at Minerva House in Newton Bushel, part of Newton Abbot in Devon. This was the former residence of Dr Green, maker of the then famous Royal Antiscorbutic Drops. In 1834 a piece in the *Dorset County Chronicle*[10] records that '... the above valuable article was invented and for many years prepared by Dr Green and since his decease by his "nephew", John Wilson Green, who as it will appear by the following certificate has disposed of all interest therein to Messrs Barclay & Sons Farringdon St, London in August 1830.' As recorded in the references, the 'drops' were a cure for all manner of illnesses, the only one with a strong relationship to shipping, being scurvy. How exactly John Wilson was Dr Green's nephew we do not know, but he certainly acquired considerable property and wealth as the heir to the good doctor.

In 1828, whilst living at Newton Bushel, John Wilson's first wife, Margaret (née Cortney) died at the age of only 24. Several of his children, however, were born in Devon between 1829 and 1840, and two of them were christened in Dartmouth in 1832 and 1834, where he seems to have operated briefly as a shipbuilder. This venture ended in bankruptcy at the beginning of 1840,[11] and by June 1841 he is back living in Liverpool, aged 40, with Eliza Green, aged 35, and four children, all of whom were born in Devon after 1829. By this time he was known as John Wilson Green, a name which he retained until his death in 1882.

The Wilson family continued to build vessels in Birkenhead and Liverpool until 1851. John Wilson senior died in 1829, but his sons Thomas and William, continued in the family shipbuilding business on both banks of the Mersey, whilst John Wilson Green remained in Devon until 1841.

William, who had been at his father's yard in Tranmere, Birkenhead (Lomax & Wilson) as draughtsman and foreman for many years joined John Lomax as his partner in 1829 after John Wilson senior's death. John Lomax died in 1832 and sadly William died at the age of only 39 in 1842.

Elder brother John had returned from Dartmouth to Liverpool in 1841 and was described as a shipbuilder in the census that year. Ten years later, in the 1851 census, he was recorded as being a 'Shipbuilder's Master employing 56 men and 12 apprentices' so he must have returned to the family business for those ten years. In 1844' he also re-married, to a Mary Parry, from Wrexham. Three further children were born but by 1861 Mary is living at a school in Sefton Road, Bootle, with her three children , all recorded as 'scholars', but there is no mention of her husband. Similarly, there is still no mention of John Wilson Green in 1871, by which time she has become the 'Proprietor of a Boy's School' and was living in Litherland, Liverpool.

One of the reasons for the Wilson family concentrating on the Mersey, rather than the Dee, could have been the fact that Fawcett Preston & Company, operating at York Street in Liverpool, were early builders of steam engines for which they developed a world-wide reputation, indeed the P&O history says that the engines they provided for the *Oriental* were 'regarded as the finest set ever built.'

Shortly after 1851 the Wilson yard at Birkenhead was taken over by Lairds[12] and Thomas Wilson retired. He died in 1885 aged 79. Meanwhile, John Wilson Green had been appointed Shipwright Surveyor of Steam Vessels to the Board of Trade in 1850, writing to the press in this capacity regarding the loss of the steamship *Royal Adelaide* in the Irish Sea in that year. He became President of the Master Shipbuilders Association of Liverpool in 1853 in which year he was much involved in industrial disputes amongst the shipwrights who had accused the employers of employing 'strangers' to get vessels completed in a reasonable time.

By 1856, John Wilson Green was being described as the 'Surveyor to the Board of Trade,' when giving evidence in a case involving the vessel *Hotspur*. In 1863 he was called as an expert witness in the case of the *Alexandra* which was seized by the British government under the Foreign Enlistment Act, the first time it had been acted upon since being passed 45 years previously, on the premise that she was built in Liverpool as a gunboat for the Confederate States of America. John spoke as a witness to confirm that the *Alexandra* was suitable for the purpose she was built for, and he had found when he looked at her that 'her bulwarks are differently formed from any merchant vessel or any vessel but a vessel of war.'[13]

After 1863, John Wilson Green seems to disappear from public life in Liverpool, but his death in the city is recorded in 1882 at the age of 80. His career in shipbuilding was a most interesting one, building early steamers and one of the largest sailing ships outside of the Thames at Chester before he reached the age of 25. It is most likely that his father, John Wilson Senior, set up the yard in Chester in 1819 and that it had continued in operation until he became unwell and died in 1829 at the age of 53.

During this early phase of steamship building in Chester the Wilson yard also had a rival operator at Crane Wharf in the shape of William Mulvey, who had ended his partnership with Peter Evans in 1820.

The first steam paddle vessel, of at least eight built by William Mulvey, was the *Sir Joseph Yorke*. Almost 85' loa and of 48 tons burthen, she was built in 1822 for W. J. Joliffe & E. Banks of London and fitted with a 30 hp engine from the Butterley Co.. She remained with these owners for many years, and her main employment seems to have been carrying passengers between Southend and Sheerness. She was named after Admiral Sir Joseph Yorke who had been M.P. for Sandwich from 1812–18. In

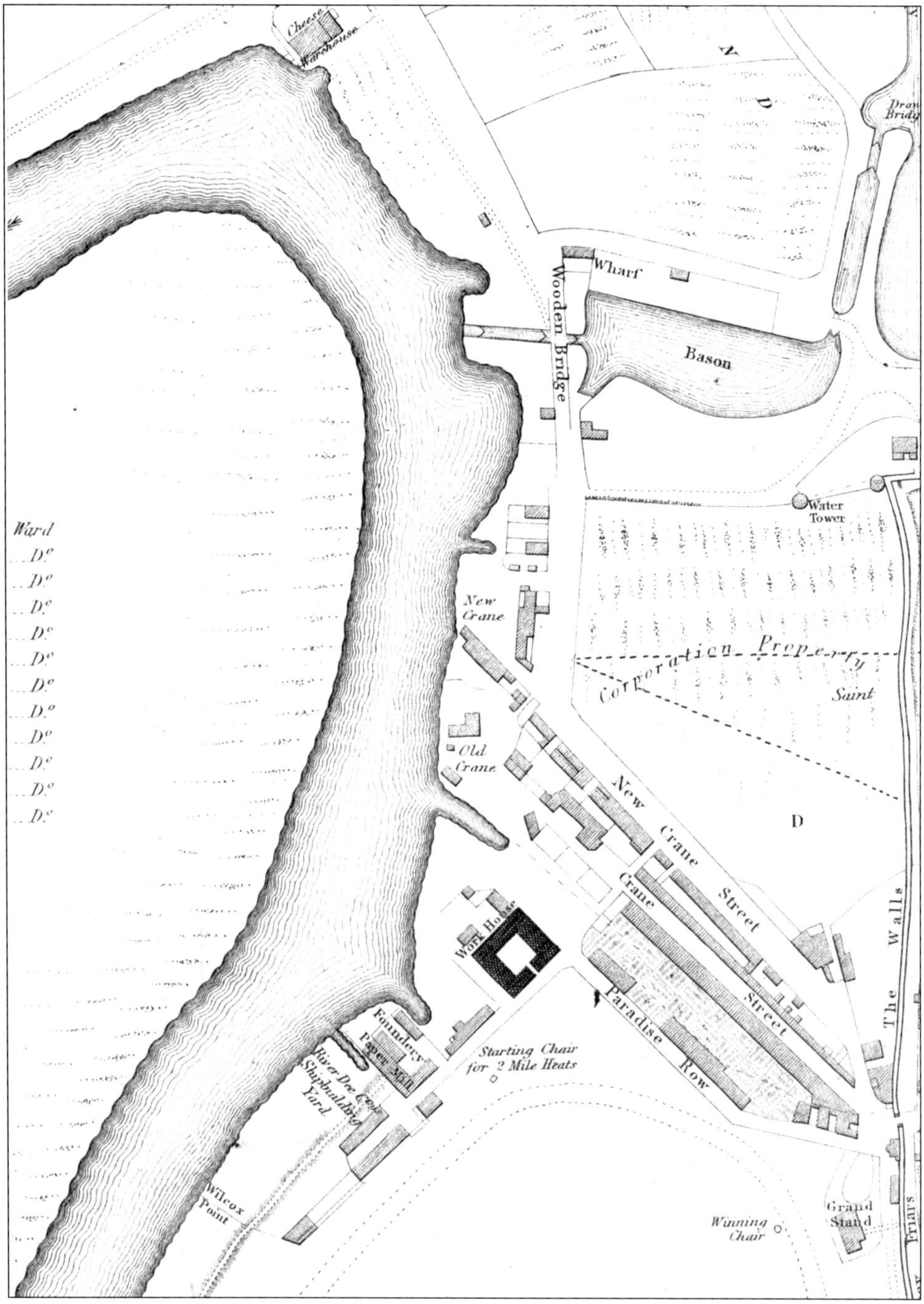


Plate 9: An extract, from John Wood's detailed map of Chester of 1833, covering the Crane Wharf area. The River Dee Company's Shipbuilding Yard is shown together with the adjacent iron foundry and House of Correction.

September 1823,[14] on the occasion of the opening of the new docks at Sheerness,

> During the whole of Thursday steam vessels and sailing boats of various descriptions were seen landing their passengers at the stairs. Among others who thus landed was Sir Joseph Yorke and about 60 fashionable friends, male and female who had come down the Thames in the steamer bearing the worthy baronet's name. The band struck up on the *Sir Joseph* Yorke' as the Royal Barge and his Royal Highness the Duke of Clarence passed.

John Wilson had also built the *Lord Melville* at Chester for the same owners, also in 1822.

By 1832, the *Sir Joseph Yorke* was operating in the Plymouth area, owned by a Mr Johnson. In February that year,[15] she was requested by the King's Harbour Master to attend the *Sir David Scott,* an East Indiaman, after the latter had got on shore at the east end of the breakwater. 'By indefatigable exertion she was got off and towed into the Cattewater.' Again, in 1833, the paddler was involved in the rescue of two females from a boat in stormy weather conditions in the same area. She was broken up in 1840.

The second venture into paddle steamer construction was the sloop-rigged *St David,* built in 1822 for the Chester Steam Packet Company. She was sold in 1828 to Hugh Williams, the innkeeper at Woodside in Birkenhead, who leased the rights of the ferry service to Liverpool from Francis Richard Price. Fitted with a 20 h.p. engine by John Rigby of Hawarden (see Chapter 11), she should not be confused with an Irish Sea paddle steamer of the same name built in 1824 on the Mersey by Humble & Hurry. She only lasted until 1832 when she was broken up at Liverpool.

*Dairy Maid*, built in 1827, was the next paddler. She was a sloop-rigged paddle tug for London owners where she remained until bought by Charles Davison of Shotton for towing on the Dee in February 1842. By 1850 she had passed to Neil Brodie –the 'Prestatyn chemist' (as I like to call him), but later in 1850 was owned by G. S. Sanderson in Liverpool where she remained until January 1853 when the register was closed with the note 'vessel lost.'

Also launched in March 1827 was the paddle steamer *Herald*, which appears not to have entered service with the Liverpool Steam Navigation Company until August 1828. At 174 tons burthen and almost 132' loa, she was the largest paddler built by

Mulvey family. Equipped with a 130 h.p. engine, she commenced operations running between Liverpool and Bristol, before transferring to Liverpool–Cork. In 1833, she ran briefly from Liverpool–London, calling at Cork and Plymouth. Her tonnage was increased to 218 tons and length to almost 146' loa in 1835, when she joined the St George Steam Packet Co. of Dublin. In 1837 she was running between Dublin and Glasgow. In 1838 she was running Dublin–Bristol, when she met the dismasted barque *Alexander Robertson* of London which was en route to Alexandria, and successfully towed her to safety. In May 1838 she transferred to the Liverpool–Newry service where she remained until March 1839. She only survived until 6th March 1839 when she was wrecked on Blockhouse Point, Carlingford on a voyage from Liverpool.[9] Some of her machinery was salvaged and arrived back at Liverpool on board the *Zephyr* on 18th March 1839.

No further steamers were built until 1832 when the *Zephyr* was built for the 'Company of the Proprietors of the Zephyr' of Liverpool (really the Saint George Steam Packet Company), with whom she was registered in 1833. She was fitted with a pair of engines by Fawcett & Co, providing 80 h.p. collectively. In 1832 the company took delivery of four new vessels and the *Zephyr* was placed in service between London and Exeter, calling at Cowes. By 1835, she was, however, formally registered as owned by the Saint George Steam Packet Company of Dublin who retained ownership and used her on many routes until 1844. In September 1837, when described as the 'Company's new steam yacht,' she was put on the North Wales service and was providing a back-up service to the Isle of Man when she took 25 hours for the crossing from Liverpool to the island in January 1839. She was the last ship owned by the company to be regularly operated between Liverpool and North Wales. When the Company split in 1843, she was retained by the English shareholders, but sold by them twelve months later. In 1849 she was advertised for sale and was described as 'having lately been running from Liverpool to Barrow.' She was described as suitable for towing and capable of carrying 110 tons. Until 1854 she had a chequered existence and a variety of owners. She was sold in 1858 to a Birkenhead shipbuilder and was probably broken up shortly afterwards.

The paddle steamer *John Watson* was launched from Mulvey's in July 1832. At 170 tons burthen she carried the same name as one of the individuals who registered early vessels for the Saint George Steam Packet Company, but little else is known about her, other than she was named after a well known Dublin merchant of the time who, among his many interests, was a retailer of ladies fashion wear.

Finally, in 1834, Mulvey launched the *George*, a sloop-rigged paddle steamer for Philip Laurence, innkeeper of Tranmere. At the same time he ordered the *Martha*, another wooden paddler, but this vessel came from the yard of Wilson & Lomax, based at Tranmere. Wilson & Lomax built several vessels of this type and are part of the same Wilson family shipbuilding business mentioned earlier in this chapter. Both vessels were laid up in 1845 and were broken up sometime before 1856.

It is interesting that it has been possible to identify some fourteen early wooden paddle steamers built by the Wilson and Mulvey yards at Chester in the period 1821–34. After 1834, the only paddle steamers built at Chester were the *Clive*, the *Earl Powis* and the *Victoria*, built in 1838 (see Chapter 3).

In between building paddle steamers, both John Wilson and William Mulvey built a variety of pure sailing vessels. Mulvey's largest vessels built in this period were the three-masted ship *John Welch* of 1825, at 259 tons burthen, and the *Laidmans*, a 360 ton, three-masted barque, built in 1832.

*Laidmans* was the largest vessel Mulvey had built up to 1832. She was ordered by William Laidman, a Liverpool merchant, primarily for the West Indies trade. On one of her early voyages she went aground at Fort Augusta when beating up to Kingston in Jamaica, where she did eventually arrive on 14th February 1834. She continued in the West Indies trade through to 1838 and then seems to have shared her time between the West Indies and Indian sub-continent trades. Late in 1847 she arrived at Liverpool from Calcutta having brought sugar from Mauritius to Bristol at the beginning of the year. In 1848 she was back sailing to St Thomas, and by 1850 she is owned by Moore & Co., the Laidman family having experienced financial difficulties in 1844.

In 1852, when bound from Calcutta to London, the *Laidmans* had to put into Mauritius for repairs after a severe hurricane in Lat 13S, Long 83E. She continued in the Indian trade until 1858 when it was reported in July[16] that, when bound from Rangoon for Cochin, she had foundered off Trincomalee sometime in June.

In 1833 two further barques were built. Firstly the *Jane Prowse*, which spent a large part of her life in the trade between Liverpool and the west coast of South America, until 1850 when she was employed in the West Indies trade. In 1852 she was homeward bound to Liverpool from Mauritius. However, by 1853, she was back in the West Indies trade and it was reported in the press from Puerto Rico that she had gone ashore when loading molasses in Arecibo and had gone to pieces.[17] Sadly the master, his wife and two children all drowned, along with the mate and a ship's boy. A sad end to a 20 year incident free career. She was the first of a number of vessels the Mulvey family built for the 'Prowse, Barklay, Radcliffe consortium.' William Prowse was a Merseyside based merchant. His son Joshua had married Miss Ann Bridson in 1831, daughter of the late Captain Robert Bridson, whilst on the same day at the same church in Toxteth, Miss Elizabeth Prowse, his eldest daughter had married Captain William Ratcliffe of the barque *Rowena*. Clearly the merchant shipping families of Liverpool were closely involved in more ways than one, a fact reflected in the names of some of the larger vessels the Mulvey family was destined to build in the next few years.

The bark (barque) *Mary & Ann*, also built by Mulvey in 1833 for John Adams Bartlett and Philip Whiteway, two master mariners, had a career in many various trades. In 1840 she was running to Buenos Aires from Liverpool, but between 1843 and 1845 she was under the command of Captain Whiteway, running to Sydney, Australia. In 1846–7 she passed into the ownership of Magey & Co. of Belfast and was running to the West Indies from Cork under Capt Nolan and in1848–9 still running to the West Indies from the Clyde. In 1851 she was outward bound to Singapore under the same ownership and captain, but disappears from Lloyd's in 1853; another twenty-year career for a hard working wooden vessel.

From the 1820s William Mulvey built many smaller craft, as well as three-masted ships and barques, and wooden paddle steamers. For example, the brig *William Mulvey* of 1829, which had a short career of seven years in the Brazil trade, before being wrecked in Mexico in 1835. The flat *Chester*, which was to have the longest known life of all the vessels the Mulvey family built, was completed in 1828 and, of 41 tons burthen, survived well into the age of photography.

In 1840 she was owned by the Trustees of Liverpool Docks and was used to move stone in the building of the walls of the Liverpool dock system. In 1830 the Dock Trustees leased a granite quarry at Kirkmabreck on the Solway, to ensure a supply of good quality stone for their dock building schemes. One of several flats they owned for this work was the *Chester*. The photograph was taken in 1907 and she was still afloat until about 1930, still carrying stone for the Dock Board.[18] There is no greater testimony to the craftsmanship of the wooden flat builders than the longevity of their products. With so little freeboard when loaded, the flats which

Plate 10: The flat *Chester* (left foreground) discharging stone in Liverpool.

were built on the Dee from the 1820s seem quite unsuitable for the conditions experienced in the river Mersey and the Irish Sea in an age when weather forecasting was non-existent and many were lost along with their crews. Wooden flats that lasted 50 years were not uncommon, but the sturdy craft *Chester* lasted at least 103 years!

Notes

1. Assembly Book of Chester City Council, 1823, Cheshire Archives.
2. Colin Books, *Graysons of Liverpool* (Liverpool, 1956).
3. A. R Burstall, 'Shipbuilding in Liverpool', *Sea Breezes Magazine*, vol. XX, p.194.
4. Horace White, C.B.E., 'Fossets', *Sea Breezes Magazine,* vol. 26 (new series), September 1958.
5. *Chester Chronicle,* 1st December 1826.
6. *Berkshire Chronicle,* 23rd July 1842, BNA.
7. *Public Ledger & Display Advertiser*, May 1822 and 17th December 1833.
8. *Morning Post,* 13th October 1824, 18th May 1830, 20 November 1826, 2nd January 1837.
9. Malcolm McRonald, *The Irish Boats*, vol. 2, *Liverpool to Cork & Waterford* (Brimscombe, 2006).
10. *Dorset County Chronicle* 17th July 1834 and D. M Stirling, *A History of Newton Abbot and Newton Bushell* (1830). Also see advert *Royal Devonport Telegraph*, 7th April 1832 which states that Dr Green's Royal Antiscorbutic Drops cure Scurvy, Scrophula, Erysipelas, Ulcerated Sore legs or wounds in any part of the body, fistulas, piles, in short every impunity of the blood, weakness and debility ... the skin becomes more fair than normal in spring, summer and autumn by taking one small bottle.
11. *The Jurist,* vol. 3.
12. *Transactions of the Liverpool Nautical Research Society*, 1955–61.
13. *Leicester Chronicle,* 27th June 1863, BNA.
14. *Caledonian Mercury,* 11th September 1823, reporting on the grand naval spectacle at the opening of the new docks at Sheerness.
15. *Plymouth & Devonport Weekly News,* 16th February 1832, and *Exeter & Plymouth Gazette,* 7th September 1833, BNA.

16 'Loss of the Laidmans', *Liverpool Daily Post,* 26th July 1858.

17. *London Standard,* 16 December 1853, BNA.
18. Michael Stammers, *Sailing Barges of the British Isles.*

# 3

## Chester 1835–52: back to basics – wooden sailing vessels

After 1827. the Mulvey family were to be the sole shipbuilders at the Crane for the next 21 years. William Mulvey carried on the yard in his name until he died in March 1839 at the age of 67.

Between 1832 and 1839 he completed at least nine wooden, three-masted barques (a bark/barque being a three-masted sailing vessel, square-rigged on the foremast and the main mast only) for various Liverpool merchant owners following the first of this type built at Chester, the *Laidmans* of 1832, and finally the *Margaret* in 1837. We must not forget that whilst these nine vessels were being built, the yard was also building flats, schooners and a pilot vessel.

The bark *Bee* of 1834 was built for Hatfield & Co of Liverpool and traded to and from Liverpool to the west coast of South America for the next twelve years. In 1848, she was sold to Cornish & Co who switched her to the Mediterranean trade for a couple of years, but in 1851 she was sold to C. Duncan, not entered in Lloyd's in 1850, but finally reappearing from 1851–6, but with no voyages recorded.

The *Elizabeth Radcliffe* of 1834 was built for the Hadfield family for trade with South America and named after a wealthy widow who invested in some of these vessels. She spent the first ten years of her career running via Cape Horn to Chile and Peru, with Valparaiso being her principal port of call. By 1840, she was owned by W. Prowse, on the same trade, which she continued to serve until 1850. By 1855 she was owned by Imrie & Co, but was not at sea. Her hard life had not yet finished, however, as in 1858–9 she was owned by J. Philips of Sunderland and operated as a collier between the Tyne and the Wear to Hamburg and various French ports until 1861.[1] She was out of Lloyds by 1862.

*Matilda,* also built in 1834, was another barque belonging to the Liverpool merchant William Rotherham. The main item of interest for the press during her early career was her arrival in London with a black man on board.[2]

*In coarse and rugged attire, he stated his name to be Georgius and the Captain had given him free passage from Antwerp, having run from the* Tournett, *an American vessel from Virginia on board of which he was a slave, born in Virginia, the property of a Mr Vandyke who traded in them among the several states of the Union. At the Court hearing, Mr Evans, Principal Surveyor of the Thames police was directed to find a vessel for the poor fellow —he should not go to slavery in America'.*

In September 1838, she sailed from Liverpool to Calcutta, and continued in the Indian trade until 1841, but in later years became a 'palm oil vessel,' but in 1854, and again in 1855, she sailed to Australia, finally disappearing from Lloyds in1859. During the whole of her career she remained with William Rotherham as the owner.

In 1834 the Mulveys built the wooden paddle-steamer *George,* one of two sloop-rigged paddlers built that year for Philip Laurence of Tranmere (the other was the *Martha* built by Lomax & Wilson at Tranmere). *George* was the first steamer built on the Dee since the *Zephyr* of 1832.

The barque *Queen Mab* of 1836 was also built for William Rotherham, and spent most of her time in the China and Indian trades. In 1840 the press reported that she had made a remarkably quick passage from Macao, leaving on 21st February and arriving at Liverpool in 106 days from China '... this we believe is one of the shortest passages between China and England on record.'[3] In 1848, when on her way to Calcutta, she experienced a severe gale off the Cape of Good Hope and was struck by a sea which carried away the larboard stanchions and stoved in the long boat and the caboose. Her 27-year career came to an end unexpectedly. On 19th August 1863 she arrived from Liverpool at New York, where she anchored in the North River. She was discovered to be on fire a couple of days later.

Her ensign was placed 'Union down' and many of the harbour tugs observing black smoke issuing from her were soon in attendance, streams of water being poured into her. The barque was subsequently towed under Jersey City, scuttled and sunk, her masts showing about half-way above water at low tide. She was laden with general cargo.[4]

Also in 1836, William Mulvey completed the barque *Frances Barklay,* again for William Prowse of Liverpool, initially with William's son, also named William, as master. Until 1850, she served the trade between Liverpool and Chile/Peru and then spent five years in the China trade before being sold in 1856 to Irving & Co of London. After a special survey in 1855 she did a couple of voyages to the Mediterranean, but by 1860 she was running to eastern Canada and was to continue in the timber trade, especially to Maryport, until 1862 when her entry in Lloyd's was endorsed 'wrecked.'

Little is known about the final barque built by William Mulvey in this period, the *Margaret* of 1837, again for the Prowse, Barclay, Radcliffe partnership. Sadly the *Margaret* only lasted until February 1840 when she was wrecked on the Brazilian coast.

The year before William Mulvey Senior's death, the yard returned briefly to building paddle steamers. The paddle steam tug *Clive* was ordered by the Ellesmere & Chester Canal Co in 1838, for the purpose of towing flats and timber floats between Ellesmere Port and the docks in Liverpool and Birkenhead. Up to this time, the Ellesmere & Chester Company had contracted out towage on the Mersey.[5] In February 1837, they had agreed with the Steam Tugs of Liverpool for flats and timber floats to be towed across the river at the rate of £3 for three vessels. The company quickly realized they could save money by taking the towage 'in house.' The Canal Committee asked for tenders for a wooden paddle tug, and William Mulvey submitted the successful bid at 11 guineas per ton. At her launch in July 1838, the *Chronicle* reported — '... she is called the *Clive* and is of 117 tons burthen and intended to be fitted up with 2 engines of 20hp each from the manufactory of Messrs Fawcett & Preston. We understand that the vessel is a very neat specimen of naval architecture.'[6]

Plate 11: *Clive* and *Earl Powis* at Ellesmere Port 1843.

Even before the *Clive* went into service, the Canal Co ordered a further steam tug, called *Earl Powis*, which entered service in July 1839. I believe that she also came from the Mulvey yard as she was also fitted with two 20hp engines. Both vessels were present at the opening of the New Dock at Ellesmere Port in 1843 (see plate 11) and indeed *Earl Powis* was to have been the first vessel into the new basin, but to the disappointment of all present it was discovered that, in consequence of her paddle-wheel bulwarks having been enlarged whilst she had recently been on the stocks, she was several inches too large for admission into the gut and a local schooner, the *Bridget* was the first vessel into the dock instead. In 1870, the by then owners of the *Earl Powys*, the SUR&C Co, sued the Wallasey Local Board for damage and demurrage after a collision with the ferry *Gem* off Alfred River Entrance, Birkenhead on a stormy night. The SUR&C Co lost the action. Similarly, in February 1872, the owners of the flat *Oliver* brought an action against the steamer *Earl Powis,* and again the judgement went against the SUR &C Co.[7] In 1875, the tug *Lord Clive* was brought into service on the cross river traffic, so the *Clive* of 1838 must have ceased operating on the traffic by this time.

The last survivor of the tugs that hauled barges between Ellesmere Port and Liverpool, the coal-fired, twin screw *Daniel Adamson* (ex *Ralph Brocklebank*), built

Plate 12: *Daniel Adamson* of 1903, last of the barge towing tugs across the Mersey.

in 1903, has recently been restored and is now in full working order. She can usually be seen in the Albert Dock complex at Liverpool and is well worth a visit.

In 1838 the Mulvey yard also produced another wooden steamer, the *Victoria*; the *Chronicle* recorded '... very early in the morning a beautiful steamer was launched and christened in honour of the day.' (the anniversary of Queen Victoria's coronation),[8] but there is no more information about this steamer or her purpose in life. Then, quite suddenly, no more steamers were built on the Chester River until 1853, by which time iron had replaced wood for steamship construction, because of its greater strength.

William, by the time of his death in 1839, was a well-respected shipbuilder and businessman of the city of Chester. At his funeral the *Chronicle*[9] said 'To show the esteem in which this lamented individual was held we need only state that his funeral which took place at Trinity Church on Tuesday last was attended by a number of gentlemen and about 100 of Mr Mulvey's men, most respectably attired, followed in the funeral procession.'

William Mulvey's will, written in 1834, appointed his wife, Peggy, John Dawson (his son-in-law, a Liverpool 'shipwright' who had married his daughter Jane) and Robert Roberts of Chester, a banker's clerk, as his executors. The will provided for his wife and whichever sons had become shipwrights to carry on the business. One son, John, was specifically not to benefit from the business under the will, instead he was made an allowance of 10s 6d per week, a codecil to this effect was written on 4th March 1839, just five days before William's actual death. The family was to continue to build traditional wooden sailing vessels for the next nine years.

In May 1836, Thomas Smith Mulvey married Ann Temple Yeoward, at Christ Church in Liverpool. She was one of the Yeoward family who had been involved in Liverpool shipowning since the eighteenth century and were to continue in shipowning and operating and ship's agency in Liverpool until the 1990s and, in the shipping business in Southampton, continued until 2012. In 1839 his brother, William Wilkinson Mulvey, married Elizabeth Moss.

By 1839, Thomas was aged 30 and William was 25. Both had joined their father's business and been apprenticed as shipwrights, but interestingly most of the registration certificates of vessels built by the yard in 1840 and 1841, were signed by Peggy, the widow of William Mulvey Senior. At this time, her two sons only signed certificates for small vessels, such as the flats *Trap* (1840) and *Lead Works* (1841).

She was clearly very much part of the shipbuilding management and the sons were perhaps not deemed to be experienced enough in the financial side of the business. It was unusual for a woman to be heading up an industrial enterprise, in early Victorian England, particularly in shipbuilding and Peggy Mulvey is the only woman I have come across in what was at the time a totally male dominated industry, although in the 1870s, Elizabeth Ferguson continued her involvement in the family shipbuilding business at Connah's Quay for many years.

Peggy Mulvey (née Smith) was a country girl, born far from the sea, probably in Satterthwaite in about 1775. She played a remarkable role in the shipbuilding history of Chester and continued to live in the city until her death in 1855, at the age of 80. Under her guidance four three-masted ships were completed in 1839–40 — *Pickwick* (1839), *William Prowse* (1839) and *Amiga* and *Lycee* (1840), all for a variety of Liverpool based owners. On registry all their builders' certificates were signed by Peggy.

The *Pickwick*, 343 tons burthen, was no doubt named after the Charles Dicken's character who appeared in the author's first book written in 1836. She was built for South American trading and sailed mainly to the west coast ports of Chile and Peru, particularly Valparaiso, for the whole of her twelve-year career. A strange incident aboard the *Pickwick* was reported in April 1843.[10]

> On Saturday 19th February, Mr Cooke, Chief Mate and a passenger, a Mr Henry J. T. Bone, off to make his fortune, were both involved in some horseplay on deck and fell over. As a consequence both rolled overboard and were drowned. At the time the vessel was making 7 knots before the wind in Lat 3.10N, Long 20.40 W.

In 1848, on a voyage to Valparaiso, she picked up the crew of an abandoned Brazilian polacca that had been sailing from Rio to Montevideo, subsequently transferring them to another vessel that was bound for Montevideo.

*Pickwick* continued in this trade until 1852 when she was reported as believed sunk[11] after sailing from Liverpool for Valparaiso on Wednesday, 11th February as did an American full-rigged ship, the 690 ton *Chimera*. Both vessels had proceeded without difficulty until about 3 a.m. on Thursday morning when they were both about 30 miles NW of Holyhead, the *Pickwick* being on the starboard tack and the *Chimera* on the port tack. The wind was blowing hard from the NW and the *Chimera* struck the *Pickwick* amidships. All but two of the *Pickwick's* crew jumped aboard the *Chimera,* The *Pickwick* lost her fore-topmast, bowsprit, mizzen mast and main rigging, and the Chimera, also damaged, put back to Liverpool for repairs. Although witnesses believed the *Pickwick* would quickly founder, she did in fact survive and was subsequently picked up by the steam tug *President,* eight miles NNE of the Calf of Man, and was brought into Liverpool where the cargo was found not to be damaged.

In July 1852,[12] judgement in the Admiralty Court was given in favour of the owners of the *Pickwick* following the collision and she returned to service owned by Cornish & Co, continuing to serve the west coast of South America trade until 1859 after which she disappears from Lloyd's.

This incident reminds us of two important issues. Firstly Mulveys' ships were soundly built having survived a collision with a larger vessel, and secondly navigating sailing vessels in the 1850s in a busy stretch of water was a tricky business, particularly at night, in strong winds or poor visibility.

1839 was also the year when the full-rigged ship *William Prowse* was completed for the Prowse, Barclay, Radcliffe partnership. Her eleven-year trading career was divided between the west coast of South America and the Far East and India. In 1839 she sailed for Valparaiso from Liverpool under the command of William Prowse's son, but by 1844 she was trading to China from Liverpool under Captain Thompson, and in 1845 to Calcutta. In 1846 and 1847 she was in Hong Kong and Whampoa. She was, however, lost in December 1849[13] whilst entering Valparaiso Bay carrying a cargo of copper ore and flour. In March 1850,[14] it was reported that 'the wheat cargo is totally lost but the copper will probably be saved, to judge from the arduous and steady persistence of the persons that have the wreckage.'

In 1840, Peggy Mulvey signed off the certificate for her third full-rigger the 350 ton *Amiga* for William and Charles Hadfield of Liverpool. This ship also traded worldwide throughout her career. In 1843 she was advertised as sailing for Port Philip and Sydney in New South Wales. 'The splendid Chester built ship *Amiga*, Capt Dalrymple, 316 tons register, 500 tons burthen, A1 12yrs, now only two years old.' From 1845–7 she traded to Hong Kong, but in 1848 was sold to McCullum of Glasgow and she ran from the Clyde to Valparaiso for the rest of her career until 1852 when she disappeared from Lloyd's Register.

In 1840, the ship-rigged *Lycee* was completed. At 467 tons burthen she was the largest vessel in terms of tons and length (140' 8") which the Mulvey-operated yard ever completed. Her first owner was William Rotherham, a merchant of Liverpool, who had previously owned a number of Mulvey built vessels, particularly the three masted barques *Matilda* (built 1834), *Queen Mab* (1836) and the brig *Martha* (1818 – see Plate 6). The ship-rigged *Lycee* only had a fifteen-year career as she is supposed to have been lost on a voyage from Bombay to Liverpool. The Registrar General being informed of her loss by letter from William Rotherham dated 3rd October 1855.

In 1841, Thomas and William signed off themselves their first deep-sea vessel. The three-masted ship *Ann Bridson*, was another order from the Prowse, Barklay, Radcliffe partnership. Her early career did not bode well for a long life as in January 1842, after her homeward bound maiden voyage from Valparaiso, she was driven ashore in Liverpool Bay, ending up on Bootle Sands without her rudder. She was soon back in service, however, and in April 1843 arrived back at Gravesend from Valparaiso. On this voyage she again reported an incident.

> After a quick passage of 84 days from Valparaiso to London she was off the River Plate when the Captain and crew suffered the greatest inconvenience from the state of the atmosphere which for two days was so fetid and oppressive as to make it difficult for them to breathe; and we regret to say that the effects of their exposure to this unwholesome air did not cease when the atmosphere became pure again. Many of the crew remained ill until they reached Liverpool. No explanation could be given by the Captain or crew and the conclusion seemed to be 'that a discharge of mephitic gas under the waters of the ocean from volcanic activity at the point the vessel was traversing' was the cause.[15]

The way such events were described in Victorian newspapers is truly wonderful. Between 1843 and 1847 she traded from Liverpool to the Far East and India and from 1847–52 returned to the west coast of South America trade. However, the arrival of the gold rush in Australia meant that in August 1852 she sailed from London to Melbourne and again in 1853 for Hobart. By the end of December 1854 she was once again arriving in London from Calcutta when she reported that she had fallen in with the *Express* (from Cardiff bound for Singapore) which had been abandoned on 24th October in Lat 36 S, Long 23 E. Presumably as the hulk was a danger to shipping, the crew of the *Ann Bridson* set fire to her and left her to sink. Such were the ways of best practice in Victorian seafaring.

Between 1855 and 1859, when she was lost, the *Ann Bridson* sailed to Australia, India and the west coast of South America. Perhaps a portent of her end came in 1858 when she grounded at Mauritius on a voyage from Moulmein (Burma). It was reported in May 1858 that, on 19th March, she had been hauled onto the hard to patch her copper which had been 'strained and wrinkled' very much on the port side, and put herself out of shape from the fore to the main chains. She got on a ridge of rocks whilst the pilot was hauling her out into the main stream and remained a whole tide. In April 1859, she was reported 'leaky' at Calcutta while en route to Colombo, but she left Tuticorin in September 1859 bound for Cork. Then came the news at the end of December 1859 that Messrs Barry & Nephew had heard from their agent in George (Cape Province) notifying them that Captain James Murray and fourteen of the crew of the Liverpool bark *Ann Bridson* had landed at Christina Bay after their vessel had capsized when she was carrying 2,061 bales of Indian cotton, destined for Cork. She had sprung a leak in a heavy gale at the end of October, and had to be abandoned. The master and the crew had escaped in the gig and longboat. The *Ann Bridson* later drifted ashore near Cape Point.[16]

To date, no paintings have come to light of the barques and full riggers built by the Mulvey family but Plate13 below, showing the ship *John Bibby* (loa 120' x 26' 7"

Plate 13: *John Bibby* built in Maryport 1841.

x 20', built at Maryport in 1841 for Liverpool merchants John Taylor and William Potter) would have been of similar appearance and size to those vessels built in Chester at this time.

Two years later, the three-masted barque *Templeman* was launched, marking a return to this style of rig. Yet another deep-sea sailer for the Prowse, Barclay group of merchants in Liverpool, *Templeman* served the west coast South American trade to Valparaiso without incident until October 1846 when the press[16] reported at Kilmore, Ireland that —

> … the ship *Templeman* of 4–500 tons of and to Liverpool from Valparaiso, Prowse, master, laden with 430 tons of copper ore, specie (11000 dollars), coffee, Peruvian bark, 10 bls of tobacco and some cotton came on shore at 10.30am on the north side of Forlorn Point, the weather very thick and blowing very strong. Crew consisting of 18 men, one cabin passenger, seven steerage passengers, five of which were children, all saved owing to the coastguard having succeeded in throwing a line over the ship by means of Dennet's rockets by which a hawser was hauled on shore and a cot, a boat peculiar to this place, at low water was enabled to be hauled under the bows and from the bowsprit the whole of the passengers and crew were lowered into the boat and conveyed onshore. If the weather moderates it is expected that the whole of the cargo will be saved but the vessel will not be got off, she being on the rocks with such a dead cargo.

The despondent reporter from the *Dublin Evening Mail*[17] was, however, proved wrong and by May 1848 *Templeman* was back in service, sailing in company with the *Ann Bridson* from Liverpool for Valparaiso.[18]

The *Templeman* continued in the trade to Peru and Chile until 1854 when she was advertised as sailing from Liverpool to Hobart Town, still under Prowse ownership, as she was to be until the end of her career in 1860. She continued serving Tasmania until 1856, but in November that year[19] was reported as 'being at St Helena en route from Madras for London she has arrived here very leaky, has had two surveys held on her and is discharging'. However, in 1857, she was back in the South American trade, before her final voyage to China in 1860, from which she did not return. At the end of September that year it was reported in the press[20] that, on a voyage from Nagasaki and Shanghai, she had struck a rock near Papenburg (Germany). One report says her back was broken and that she was likely to be condemned, with the cargo supposed to be uninjured; another report stated that the cargo was supposed to be uninsured. However, in 1861 and again in 1862, reports continued to appear in the Liverpool press up to March[21] which show her sailing between Nagasaki and Shanghai, after which she disappears from records.

In 1845, it was recorded that the partnership between Thomas and William Mulvey had been dissolved, by mutual consent, on 10th December 1844.[22] Thomas then took over the business on his own and 'all debts due from the said firm will be paid and received by said Thomas S. Mulvey'.

After the re-structuring, Thomas only built one further three-masted ship, before the business finally closed. All the other vessels built by the yard were schooners or flats of less than100 tons burthen.

The sole three-master, built in the year 1844, was the barque *Earl of Chester*. Of 462 tons burthen, she was also built for William and Joseph Prowse and H. M. Barklay, merchants of Liverpool. She is believed to be the last 'big' wooden ship to be built at Chester and traded for the next 22 years until 1867.

Built for the Indian trade, in 1847 she arrived at Liverpool from Bombay having 'lost bulwarks, stanchions rails, cookhouse, had her boats, spars etc started, one of the fore chains broke and topgallant [mast/yard?] lost, forecastle filled with water during the hurricane' of 6th & 7th in Lat. 50° N, Long. 8° W.'[23] During the next few years she traded worldwide to China, Melbourne, Victoria, the west coast of South America and Hobart in Tasmania. In 1855 she returned to London from Madras, via Mauritius, returning to Adelaide in South Australia, before once again returning to the U.K. via Madras. By 1857, she was homeward bound from Moulmein in Burma. In June 1858 she arrived at Queenstown for orders, with a cargo of guano from Callao in Peru, and sailed from the Tyne to the Far East in 1859. Continuing in the China trade, she arrived at Greenock in 1864, again from Moulmein, with a cargo of teak. Shortly afterwards she was advertised for sale by public auction at Greenock with a reserve price of £2,300. However, when she was lost in 1867, her owners were still the Prowse family, so perhaps the reserve price was never met? In 1865 she was back sailing to Liverpool from Iquique, and in 1866 made a further voyage to and from Singapore and Batavia to Liverpool.

Leaving Liverpool at the end of October, with a general cargo for Madras and a crew of about eighteen, she was wrecked on the 25th, two miles from Tŷ Croes, Holyhead, shortly after leaving port — '... for half a mile along the beach chests containing sailors' clothes, boxes with merchandise such as candles, wine and manufactured clothing, were scattered about' reported *The Times*. All on board, including Captain W. B. Nancollis and his wife were lost. They are buried at Llanfaelog nearby. This wreckage reportedly attracted hundreds of the notorious Crigyll robbers.[24]

The *London Standard* reported that 'Twelve bales, about 1500 rods, rails, bundles, and sheet iron and 200 sheets of yellow metal were saved yesterday from the *Earl of Chester*.' Elsewhere it was reported that 115 bundles of hides had been saved. By 30th November, the sale of the wreck was reported, '... including sails, spars, ropes, chains, timber etc and the attendance was very large.'[25]

Looking at the shipbuilding orders completed in Chester during the first half of the nineteeth century, the same owners' names appear many times. The Prowse family were part owners of the barques *Jane Prowse* (1832), *Frances Barklay* (1836) and *Margaret* (a three–masted bark built in 1837 by Mulvey and lost in 1840), *William Prowse*, the three-masted ship built by Mulvey 1839, that was lost off Valparaiso in 1850 and the *Ann Bridson* (1841), abandoned off Mossel Bay in October 1859. The final large vessels, *Templeman* (1843) and *Earl of Chester* (1844), were both built for the Prowse Barklay merchant partnership —seven Mulvey-built vessels in all. Similarly, three of the 16 three-masted barques and ships built by the Mulveys between 1832 and 1844 were for the Hadfield Brothers of Liverpool, and three were for William Rotherham. Ten of the sixteen deep-sea vessels they built were to last more than fifteen years and only one had a career of less than ten. It is fair to say that such a record is quite an achievement for wooden sailing vessels trading in an age that was without sophisticated navigational aids and weather forecasting services.

In 1838, William Mulvey Senior completed the brig *Margaret* (not to be confused with the 3-masted barque *Margaret* built by Mulvey the previous year), nine years after their previous brig *William Mulvey*. By 1838, the schooner rig was much favoured over the brig, square rigged on two masts, because of the saving in crew numbers and wages and new brigs were not being built. The brig *Margaret* was also to have a deep-sea career. From 1842–4 she traded from Leith to Mauritius and then across the Atlantic to Trinidad and Quebec, until 1848 when she was owned in Ardrossan and sailed to Moulmein before returning to the Atlantic trade. By 1851 she was sailing from the Clyde to Havana and was declared missing in Lloyds' Register in 1852.

Plate 14: 'The old Port of Chester' – a mid nineteenth century view of the shipyard area.

Another notable career amongst the smaller vessels the Mulveys built was that of the two-masted schooner *Ann Mulvey* (1842). Her career continued until 1887 when she was lost. Originally built as a cheese ship, she was first owned by Thomas Mulvey and eleven others. By 1853, she was sold out of the Chester–London trade to the shipbuilder J. H. Treweek of Amlwch. In 1874 his son, James, succeeded to the shares and they continued to operate her in the Irish Sea trades. On 6th April 1887, when on a voyage from Irvine to Newport, she stranded on the Crow Rock in the Bristol Channel and foundered.[26] With her withdrawal from service, the name of Mulvey was to finally disappear from the maritime scene, 71 years after the family had started building vessels in Chester.

The end of this phase of wooden shipbuilding in Chester came in 1852 after the building of two vessels. *My Lady,* a two-masted schooner for the lead ore trade in 1850, and *Tower,* a flat, in 1852. Both were built by Sir Edward Walker. Walker Parker had established lead ore mining in Flintshire, a processing plant at Bagillt as well as a leadworks in Chester, at the end of the eighteenth century. As early as 1833, Walker Parker had ordered flats from the Mulvey Yard (*Smelter* and *Pelter*) and owned and built other coastal sailing vessels, some of which they built themselves. Certainly before 1855 they had a shed and land leased from the River Dee Company at the Crane where they 'built and repaired flats.' No doubt they used one of the nearby slipways (see Plate 14). It is also possible that they built flats at the leadworks site alongside the Ellesmere & Chester Canal near Boughton in Chester (other people did so) and certainly the *Fume* of 1846 is recorded in the Register as 'built at the leadworks'.

*My Lady*, built by Walker Parker at the Crane in 1850, traded regularly between Chester and the Continent, and in 1872 was still in the ownership of the Walker family. She had a lengthy career which lasted until 11th May 1910 when she was sunk in a collision with the *Balneil II* in the river Mersey. Her wreck was destroyed by blasting.[27] Apart from the flat *Chester* (see Chapter 2), she is the only Chester-built wooden vessel from this era to have survived into the twentieth century. At her launch she was described as being 'launched from the building dock, the property of Sir Edward Walker' which makes one wonder whether they used one of the inlets in the area as a drydock, but more likely she went off a slipway, like the other vessels in that era.

The premises leased by Walker Parker at the Crane were the subject of another fire in the area in September 1855 when the *Chronicle* of Saturday, the 15th recorded '... that the men had left the yard about 6 p.m. and at 8.30 p.m. a fire was discovered' that consumed a stove for preparing wood for shipbuilding purposes [a steam box one presumes?] and a wooden building was destroyed. The fire then caught the rigging of the schooner *Liberty* that was lying alongside the adjacent slate wharf and her '... sails and yards were much injured.' It was 9.15 p.m. before the engine arrived, the delay being caused because no police could be found to escort her!

Frequently, the Mulveys owned a share in the vessels they built, particularly in the early years of the vessel's life. In most instances, this would be a means of helping to finance the building, as with other shipbuilders on the Chester River, but it is a particular feature after 1840 when there is a suspicion that the yard was not financially as sound as in its earlier years. The flats *Shifty* and *Trap* (1840), *Kitty* (1842), the schooner *Ann Mulvey* (1842), the flat *Brewer's Hall* (1843), the sloop *Fanny Truss* (1848) , the schooner *Punch* (1847) and the smack *Sarah Jane* (1847) were some of the vessels in which, at some period, the Mulvey family, especially Thomas, had a shared ownership. It is also interesting to note in the later years that schooners such as the *Gwenddolen* and *Sarah* (1845) and the *Punch* (1847) were owned by John Williams, banker of Chester. In the later years there was also an involvement of the Yeoward family of Liverpool, who were particularly involved with trade to the Iberian peninsula and the Canaries. As early as 1824, Joseph Yeoward had taken a shareholding in the *Belem Castle,* a John Wilson vessel built at Chester. Then, in 1836, Thomas Mulvey married Ann Temple Yeoward and the Yeoward family also had a shareholding in the flats *Shifty* and *Trap* (1840) and the schooner *Ann Mulvey* (1842).

After 1842, the Yeoward involvement in owning Mulvey built vessels disappears, and of course the partnership between Thomas and William Junior ended in December 1844.

In February 1845, there was a newspaper report of a fire at the yard,[28] in a shed between the Roodeye Foundry and the Pattern Room. The interesting feature of this incident is the response by the fire brigades — 'In a very few minutes the City engines were on the spot. The Castle engines did not arrive as the men were at the time engaged in Divine worship at St Mary's church!' One shed was completely destroyed, and the flames had just started bursting into the Pattern Room before they were brought under control. It was further reported that £50–60 worth of damage had been caused and that the cause had most likely been a spark from the adjacent foundry. This fire does not seem to have been a contributory cause of the closure of the business.

In 1851, William Mulvey is still shown in the census as a shipbuilder. In 1846 a newspaper report[29] on the building by Hawarden Ironworks of the *Forth* at Sandycroft states that '... the ship's carpentry work is being done by Mr Mulvey,' but it is unclear which brother was actually involved.

In April 1848 notice was given that Thomas Smith Mulvey was bankrupt[30] and in July that year there was an auction in Linen Hall tavern Chester of all his property, including his house and contents, the house his mother Peggy lived in, and his shareholdings in eight vessels which he had built. Seven of these were flats, together with his 16/64 share of the schooner *Ann Mulvey*. A dividend of 3s 9½d was declared on his estate in Liverpool in December 1849. After 1847, no further Mulvey vessels seem to have been built at Chester.

What then happened to Thomas Smith Mulvey is still a mystery. His widow, Ann Temple Mulvey, died on the Isle of Man in 1890, where she had been living since at least 1881 (she had been recorded as a 'widow living in lodgings' in Liverpool in 1871). Whether Thomas Mulvey died before 1871 is unknown, but after his financial ruin he just disappears and he does not appear in the census or the birth, marriage and death records recorded after 1841. His mother, the redoubtable Peggy, lived on in Chester until her death in 1855 at the age of 79, described as an 'almswoman', whilst his brother, William Wilkinson, also remained in Chester until his death in 1869 at the age of 55.

## Notes

1. *Lloyd's Register,* 1857 and 1859.
2. *Morning Chronicle,* 21st August 1849.
3. *John O'Groats Journal,* 19th June 1840, BNA.
4. *Liverpool Daily Post,* 5th September 1863.
5. Terry Kavanagh, 'Sailing Flats on the Chester and Ellesmere Canals', *Waterways Journal*, vol. 18, spring 2006.
6. *Chester Chronicle,* 27th July 1838.
7. Minutes of the Shropshire Union Railway & Canal Company, No. 8610, 8th March 1872, National Waterways Archive, Ellesmere Port.
8. *Chester Chronicle,* 29th June 1838.
9. *Chester Chronicle,* 15th March 1839, BNA.
10. *Salisbury & Winchester Herald,* 22nd April 1843, BNA.
11. *Limerick & Clare Examiner,* 18th February 1852, BNA.

12. *Greenock Advertiser,* 6th July 1852, BNA.
13. *Sussex Advertiser,* 12th March 1850,BNA.
14. *Morning Post,* 5th March 1850.
15. *Kentish Gazette,* 4th April 1843, BNA.
16. *Saunders' Newsletter*, 27th December 1859, BNA.
17. *Dublin Evening Mail*, 14th October 1846, BNA.
18. *Manchester Courier*, 3rd May 1848.
19. *Morning Post,* 12th November 1856.
20. *Morning Post,* 12th January 1857, BNA.
21. *London Evening Standard*, 29 September 1860.
22. *London Gazette,* 10th Dcember 1844.
23. *Morning Post,* 14th December 1847.
24. *Manchester Courier,* 29th October 1867.
25. *London Evening Standard,* 11th November 1867 and *Cheshire Observer*, 30th November 1867.
26. *Sea Breezes Magazine*, September 1967, letter from Sir Diarmid Conroy.
27. W. Martin Benn, *Closing Down Sail* (2011).
28. Fire at Mulveys yard 1845., *Chester Chronicle,* 7 February 1845.
29. *Chester Chronicle,* 9th October 1846. The article also refers to vessel is built under the inspection of Mr Wilson, shipbuilder, formerly of this City, but now in eminent business in Liverpool.
30. *Sussex Advertiser,* 2nd May 1848, reporting the bankruptcy of Thomas S. Mulvey in the *London Gazette.*

# 4

# Iron shipbuilding in Chester, 1853–5

This period is probably the most interesting in the story of shipbuilding on the Chester River, mainly due to iron shipbuilding taking place there for the first time and also, by 1850, more written information is readily available to the researcher than was the case for the first fifty years of the nineteenth century.

The principal yard at Crane wharf built more than twenty iron vessels, while smaller concerns continued to build wooden schooners elsewhere on the Crane from 1855, after a gap of five years. Chester was relatively late to embrace iron as a shipbuilding material; iron vessels had been built on the Mersey in the 1830s, but the first new iron vessel to be built at Chester did not go down the slipway until 1853.

Chester's first iron shipbuilder was George Cram who took over the lease of the Roodee Yard in 1853. His first venture into iron shipbuilding was the steamer *Amelia* for a Bristol–Liverpool service. At 145' 6" loa x 21' 2" beam she went down the ways on 12th March,[1] launched by Miss Elsee, Cram's niece. Interestingly, when first registered the *Amelia* was partly owned by George Cram (14 shares) and members of the Cornish family. Amelia Cornish, a widow of Bristol, held four shares and gave her name to the vessel. The vessel ran successfully between Liverpool and Bristol until 1857, when on Sunday, 29th March, at 08.00 hrs, on a voyage from Bristol to Liverpool, she struck St Govan's Head in Pembrokeshire in a thick fog, becoming a total wreck, but no lives were lost. According to the *Pembrokeshire Herald,* at the time of her loss in twelve fathoms of water, she was carrying a crew of 17 and 16 passengers, together with a general cargo valued at £1,600 (including printed calicoes, spirits, ale, tin and yellow metal or zinc).[2] The article also recorded that whether she was insured was uncertain.

One of the other owners was Frederick Hillman Powell, a Bristol merchant, who as F. H. Powell went on to become a major part of the Coast Lines empire. According to *Mersey Rovers* by Roy Fenton,[3] they originated as Cram Powell & Co in 1830 and operated regular services between Liverpool and London, and Liverpool and Bristol. The *Amelia* was their first experiment with steam powered vessels and for almost four years she ran between Liverpool and Bristol, but not on the full route they had been operating under sail to London. Her successor on the Bristol route, the steamer *Athlete* was far more successful, making hundreds of voyages between Bristol and Liverpool entirely without accident. Her master, Captain Laver, commanded her for thirty years until 1875.

In October 1855, the Chester Banker John Williams, had sold under mortgage the shares owned by George Cram in *Amelia* to Frederick Powell.

The *Chester Chronicle*[1] gives a quite detailed account of the launch of *Amelia* which is well worth recounting here.

First Iron Ship Launch in Chester

On Saturday last, according to announcement, this long expected event came with great éclat at Mr Cram's shipyard on the Roodee. Despite several untoward matters which had occurred a day or two before and to which every employer of large bodies of men is subject, only one day's postponement of the launch was necessary and on Saturday instead of Friday it took place. Soon after 12 o'clock, numbers of persons began to arrive at the yard and to congregate on Brewer's Hall, on the opposite side of the river. Flags were flying gaily from every place of prominence in the neighbourhood. The Mayor, Magistrates, Clergy and nearly all the principal families of the City were assembled in the yard. About 1 o'clock a steamer arrived at that part of the river opposite the shipyard. The crowds on both sides increased and the water was animate with boats filled with sight seers or plying to and fro. At 25 minutes past one, the stays being all unloosed, Miss Elsee, niece of Mr Cram, who was standing on the platform under the bow, and named her the *Amelia*. She immediately glided down the incline gradually and majestically into the waters of the Dee, amidst the plaudits of the crowd, her temporary crew and the firing of cannon. At this moment a train passed over the railway bridge and along the viaduct which contributed to render the scene still more varied and pleasing. The impetus with which the *Amelia* moved off the stays carried her to a greater distance in the river than the rope from the shore would allow. The rope broke and immediately she made use for the first time of one of her nautical appliances – the anchor.

Another rope was shortly attached to her, the anchor was raised and she soon afterwards hove to on the quay. As we have several times previously mentioned she is of 350 tons burthen, will be rigged out in Chester, whence she will proceed to Liverpool where she will receive her engines and make ready for her first voyage. She is intended to ply between Liverpool and Bristol.

After the launch, a number of ladies and gentlemen repaired to an adjoining warehouse where an elegant repast had been laid out by Mr Cram's hospitality. The dejeuner was furnished from Mr Bolland's establishment and consisted of a variety of substantial and fancy dishes, choice wines etc, sufficient to please the most fastidious taste. The room was tastefully decorated with laurel and lighted with gas which had been supplied for the occasion from the Roodee Gas works, (the expansion of which was to be partly responsible for the end of shipbuilding at Chester in due course). The name of the vessel *Amelia* blazed in letters of light over the President's Chair. On the tables were two beautiful models of the *Amelia*, surmounted with cornucopias filled with confectionary and bonbons. Mr Cram presided and Mr Titherington was Vice- Chairman.

During the repast, the Mayor of Chester (Mr H. Brown) rose and congratulated Mr Cram on the gratifying success which must be most interesting to all and especially to the trading and working classes of the City; and which he sincerely hoped would bring to the worthy chairman a substantial and well meaning reward of his energy and enterprise (cheers). All must be desirous of that success; for the progress and prosperity of the town were closely bound up with works of this description which were of essential importance to the community, and they could not fail to regard with good wishes and lively interest this bold enterprise in commercial affairs. He would therefore propose 'the health of Mr Cram and success to the *Amelia'* (renewed cheers).

Mr Cram thanked the Mayor and the company for this mark of their good will and respect (etc, etc cheers). MrTitherington proposed, 'the health of Mrs Cram' (cheers) etc, etc. The Reverend F. Ford said 'Mr Cram had brought life and animation to the banks of the Dee, which for several years had ceased to re-sound with the workman's hammer or the din of busy well-remunerated toil. If Chester should regain her old position and again rank as an old-established port, there must be less talk in the Rows, less walking on the Walls, fewer flounces, furbelows and satins and instead of these they must possess mental energy, greater application, a sincere determination to deserve the term once applied in derision to England and ambition to be called 'a city of shopkeepers and merchants' (cheers).

Following the address from the moral high ground taken by the Rev Ford, there were

> more speakers, the most noteworthy of which was again Mr Titherington, who proposed 'success to the Liverpool &London African Association.' It was brought to the notice of this meeting that 8–10 large steamships would be required for its service and through the influence of Mr Cram those ships would be built at Chester. He (Mr Titherington) had signed a memorial v the establishment of Mr Cram's works on the Roodee, but he now publicly recanted his having done so and he regretted he had been betrayed into signing the petition.
>
> In the evening, upwards of 300 workmen employed in Mr Cram's yard sat down to an excellent supper, provided for them in one of the workrooms at that gentleman's expense The men enjoyed the repast and will doubtless long remember the happy occasion.

So, George Cram's shipyard was up and running and giving people great hope for the future, but who was he and what was his background before arriving in Chester?

George William Cram was born on 9th November 1798 in Newcastle upon Tyne, the son of master mariner Ralph Cram and his wife Margery (née Fothergill). George married Elizabeth Gibson in April 1828[4] in Newcastle, the daughter of shipowner Thomas Gibson. By 1829, George and Eliza were living in Liverpool and had a son, Thomas, and in the 1841 census George is described as a 'shipbroker'. By 1851, George and Elizabeth Cram are living in Watergate Square, Chester, he being described as a 'merchant'. His niece, Catherine Elsee (who launched the *Amelia*) is living with them, aged 25. She must have been the daughter of his wife's sister, Ellen Gibson, who had married Charles Elsee, a papermaker. They were living in Henley-upon-Thames in Oxfordshire in 1841, with seven children, but Charles died in 1855 and Ellen had disappeared from the records before 1851, so Catherine was living in Chester by 1851 with her uncle.

Why George decided to move into the relatively new world of iron shipbuilding at the age of 55 (he would have been considered an old man in 1853), is something of a mystery. The historical connections with shipping are clearly in place, through his father and his wife, and also via his second cousin, Henry and his father, David Cram. David was born in Newcastle upon Tyne in 1772 and his son, Henry, was also born there in 1809, but by 1841 was living in Bebington on the Wirral. David Cram, a merchant, had moved from Tyneside to Birkenhead and in 1841 was living with his wife Mary, three of his children and five servants at N° 1 Hamilton Square in Birkenhead, a fashionable address indeed. Henry was also described as a shipbroker at this time. In 1837, the partnership between Henry Cram and James Trevelyan Raynes, the North Wales quarry owner with shipping interests, was dissolved, but nevertheless this could explain his strong connections with North Wales throughout his life. In 1851, he was living in Dwygyfylchi, near Conwy, and was described as a shipbroker. This was probably his large family's second home (there were at least seven children) and in 1861 he was back on Merseyside living in Liscard, near Birkenhead, again described as a shipbroker.

The Cram family had their origins in Newcastle and Northumberland, and certainly there are earlier generations of Crams who owned and built ships in the late eighteenth century.[5] All three of the Cram family involved in shipping were very much a part of the local shipping community, as well as being very involved in public service.

Prior to 1854 George and Henry Cram were in partnership in Liverpool with Frederick Hillman Powell as Cram Powell & Co, shipping agents, who operated a regular weekly steamer service between Liverpool and Bristol. As far as George Cram was concerned, the partnership was dissolved in 1854.

In June 1846, David Cram was one of eight people who, although not members of the Council in Liverpool, were chosen to be the Commissioners appointed to implement the Acts of 51st Geo III and 6th Geo IV.

Earlier, in May 1838, George Cram had paid an annual subscription of £1 to the Southern & Toxteth Hospital, and in June 1845 was one of the gentlemen re-elected as a Commissioner for auditing the accounts of the Dock Estate in Liverpool for the ensuing year. In 1847, he was sworn in as a jury member of the Liverpool May Sessions, and in 1850 was a signatory to a Liverpool petition to Parliament protesting about the levels of duty on tea and timber imports, especially the timber employed in shipbuilding. After his move to Chester, he continued to play his part in public service and in April 1852 was present at the meeting of the River (Dee) Pilotage Trustees. Incidentally, also present were John Myers, Thomas Dixon and James Eyton, all of whom appear elsewhere in this story of the Chester River. In July 1852 he was sworn in as Foreman of the Grand Jury at Chester City Sessions and in 1854 he was the house visitor at Chester Infirmary. In January 1855 he was again sworn in as a member of the Grand Jury at the January Sessions. Maybe George found public service a form of therapy to cope with his depressing family life – he and his wife had three children who, sadly, all appear to have died in infancy or of childhood disease before the age of twelve.

In September 1846, George's cousin, Henry Cram, was sworn in on the jury at the Liverpool Quarter Sessions and in 1857 he was again sworn in on the Jury at the Liverpool Borough Quarter Sessions. In January 1860, he wrote a letter to the *Liverpool Daily Post* concerning the discussion then taking place about keeping open a 'track' for ferries across the river Mersey. He had personally been involved when the Mersey ferry *Sea King* collided with the Seacombe ferry *Thomas Wilson,* and had climbed on to the Woodside boat when the *Thomas Wilson* sank. He demanded a public meeting with the Mersey Docks & Harbour Board Marine Committee and the Pilotage Committee. A further letter followed in February of that year about the danger caused in fog by vessels anchoring in the ferry tracks, and gave notice that the MD&HB '... will be held accountable in case of any act of neglect of their duty and not enforcing the bye-laws inherited from the Town Council.'[6]

At some point in the operation of the Cram yard at Chester, it was managed by one William Quiggin.[7] who was born on the Isle of Man and had come to Liverpool as a single man before he was twenty, and was a ship's carpenter. By the time of the 1851 census he was recorded as being a 'draughtsman (iron shipbuilding yard),' living in Toxteth Park, Liverpool, with his wife and child. It has been suggested that he designed the auxiliary-screw iron ship *Royal Charter* which George Cram built at Sandycroft. In 1859, however, assuming he had left Cram sometime earlier, he joined up with Josiah Jones who was building vessels under his own name in Liverpool from 1856–9 and he became a partner with Jones and the firm became re-styled as Jones Quiggin & Co (located on the river front at Wallasey).

Shortly after the *Amelia* was launched at Crane Wharf, the iron schooner *Cobre* (built at Swansea in 1849 by T. Hessleton), was hauled up one of the slipways at the Cram yard to be lengthened by 15 feet. Her name (meaning copper in Spanish), hinted that she was no doubt originally built for the Swansea copper ore trade. Described as a clencher-built sloop when first registered, *Cobre* was re-launched by moonlight at 9.15 p.m. on 19th May 1853 after having been in the yard for six weeks. She was also fitted up with new machinery and new boilers and she was re-rigged as a three-masted schooner, and extra accommodation was added. Her conversion was undertaken while she was under the ownership of a Captain Walters of Saltney

Plate 15: *Cobre* after conversion at Chester.

(probably the same Captain Walters who had earlier been master of an Irish Sea paddle steamer). Having been converted to a steamer she was intended to ply up and down the rivers of Australia. In July 1853 she made a voyage, with invited guests, to Llandudno; it had been intended to go as far as the Menai Strait but the weather deteriorated. In early August, the *Cobre* went to Liverpool where she was inspected by a number of 'scientific gentlemen' and Captain Mathews of the *Great Britain*. At his behest, the owner of the *Cobre* had her fitted out with water tanks that could contain 40 tons of water for the purpose of supplying vessels in the colonies, the water to be discharged by a steam engine fitted for that purpose. 'She will sail from Chester under the efficient rig of a clipper-schooner.'

The *Chester Chronicle* of 13th August 1853 stated that the

> … fast iron steamer *Cobre,* A1 at Lloyd's, 150 tons burthen, Thomas Hall master, will leave Chester for Australia, on or about 23rd August. This clipper proceeds out under canvas and is expected to make a quick run. She has room for light freight-make application to the owner, W. Walters, or to Messrs Taylor & Jones, ships' agents and insurance brokers, Saltney near Chester.

The *Cobre* was lying at Green's Wharf, Chester, prior to sailing. Her boilers had been made by Napier of Glasgow, and her anchor chains by Messrs Wood Brothers of Saltney. There were nine men in her crew —Captain Hall, Mr Anthony (engineer) plus five sailors and two firemen. Her cargo consisted of slates, chimney pots and fire goods. Evidently it took her 130 days to reach her destination, as on 25th February 1854 she was spoken to off the Australian coast by a homeward bound vessel. Captain Hall duly reported the safe arrival of the vessel and stated that the voyage had been prolonged by ten days as he had lost his rudder and a foremast. He also lamented that the sails were not of a larger size, and that he was short of canvas on board.

On 9th March 1853 she arrived in Melbourne.[8] On 5th September of that year she was sold by William Walters to a Mr William Hamilton Hart of Melbourne, South Australia, merchant, with Bright Brothers, merchants of Liverpool acting on his behalf. She was re-registered at Melbourne on 22nd November 1854, by which time she was described as a single decked, two-masted schooner, rigged paddle steamer. Her dimensions were 98' 8" loa x 13' 6" beam x 8' 9" moulded depth, and of 44.8 tons burthen.

However, by March 1855, *Cobre* was working in Launceston, Tasmania, and advertised for charter as a pleasure vessel and tug.[9] The *Launceston Examiner* tells us that she,

> ... made a trial trip yesterday. She left the ship anchorage at half past seven a.m., was abreast of Windermere at a quarter to nine, opposite Swan Point twenty-five minutes past nine; passed through Whirlpool Reach at ten and arrived at George Town wharf at eleven, making the distance (40 miles) in three hours and a half. She returned to Launceston in the same time and it says that she could work up to 36 revolutions per minute, but on this occasion did not exceed 33, which was maintained nearly the whole way.

The article continues,

> ... as the vessel is for sale, we hope local enterprise will secure her services for this port, for which she seems well adapted. She has taken an 800 ton vessel out to sea from Melbourne through the heavy ripple of the heads and it is not likely there will be a greater demand upon her here.

By the middle of the nineteenth century there were enough separate settlements in Tasmania to support river transport and communications. Launceston had taken on a major port and town function at the head of the Tamar navigation, and river craft were able to provide a feeder service to it from Georgetown and Kelso.

According to the *Parson's List,*[10] *Cobre* was sold to Launceston owners in November 1855, but the early steamers were small and relied on an assortment of tugs, tenders and steam launches. No regular timetable of services on the Tamar existed until the 1880s and there were 20 or more small steamers brought to the river in the next few years. The *Launceston Examiner*[11] reported that the

> ... steam tug *Cobre* was dispatched last night to bring the clipper *Whirlwind* up to the Bar, where she will probably arrive in the course of the afternoon-many persons are expecting friends and relations by *Whirlwind.*

Not surprisingly perhaps, *Cobre* was sold on to Hobart tug owners in August

1856. In March 1869 she was sold to Sydney where she became an excursion vessel/Manly ferry/tug, still known as the *Cobra,* and then again to Newcastle in New South Wales in October 1873, where she operated as a full time tug for 43 years. According to Graeme Andrews in his excellent book *The Ferries of Sydney*[12] she survived until 1917 and had a capacity for 60 passengers.

George Cram's third Chester vessel was also on the stocks at the time *Cobre* was undergoing conversion. The iron steamer *Golden Queen* was launched on 24th May 1853. Described as a fine steamer of 570 tons, the launch was attended by '... a large concourse of people in the yard, on Brewer's Hill and the quays on the river as far as the Sluice House.' Shortly before the launch the schooner *Lord Mostyn* was towed upriver by the steam tug *Test*, whose deck was crowded with gazers.. The *Test* lay alongside the yard nearer the railway bridge until after the launch. At twenty minutes to one o'clock, Mr Cram gave the signal and the *Golden Queen*, christened by Mrs Pegler, glided majestically into her future element while cannons fired and people hurrahed. She was built for the Australian (or New South Wales) Coal and Inter-Colonial Steam Navigation Co. After the usual elegant lunch, often as in this case, provided by Mr Bolland of Eastgate Street, in the mould room, Mr John Leonard, a director of the owners proposed the toast 'success to Mr Cram whose public spirit and enterprise is commended by everyone.'[13]

Building the *Golden Queen* seems to hint at the beginning of George Cram's financial troubles. As early as 2nd November 1852,[14] he had taken out a mortgage for £1,825 with the Williams Bank in Chester, and the indenture refers to 'the steamship now building of 550 tons' and similarly, in April 1853, a further indenture for £5,000 was signed with the same bankers regarding the vessel of 556 tons. The bank had the right to take possession of the vessel if repayment of these mortgages was not made.

A third indenture drawn up on 29th May 1854, again with the Williams bankers in Chester, states,

> ... the said George Cram has built a certain steam ship or vessel called the *Golden Queen* for Van Hoey Smith of the City of London, merchant, and she is now in the Birkenhead Docks for the purpose of having her engines and other machinery filled up. George Cram is at present indebted to the said Thos Peers Williams and John Williams on the balance of his account current with them in a large amount and having applied to them to

> advance further moneys for his benefit they have consented to do so upon the terms only of having payment of the present balance and all other money which shall from time to time become due and owing from the said George Cram to the said T. P. and J. Williams or other persons or person for the time being occupying the business of the said banking house secured hereinafter provided for-this indenture witnesseth that in consideration of the premium and of the further sum of £ 677 17s 3d, this day advanced and lent by the said Thos Peers & John Williams for the accommodation of the said George Cram, and the assignment.

There was an interval of twelve months between her launch and the fitting of her engines in Birkenhead. Again, was this an indication of the financial difficulties of the builder? It is not known what finally became of the *Golden Queen*. It is assumed that Van Hoey Smith and the Australian Coal & Inter Colonial Steam Navigation Co were the same organization? In the 1850s it is believed that James Smith was a shipowner in Rotterdam. Van Hoey Smith later moved their operation to Rotterdam, and James Smith & Zonen were still operating vessels post the Second World War.

In 1856, during the Crimean War, there was a heavy demand for merchant vessels, especially steamers for use as transports and store carriers. In 1856 *Golden Queen* seems to have made a number of trips to Balaklava in the Crimea, and in August that year was expected at Portsmouth with troops. There is no further information available on her career after that date.

Raising working capital for the business in the period 1853–5 could have been brought about by rapid over-expansion of the Cram yard. There were three vessels built in 1853, six in 1854 and two in 1855, and it must be borne in mind that George Cram opened up a second yard at Sandycroft in 1854 where he was to build his two largest vessels.

In December 1853,[15] the iron screw steamer *Sardegna* was launched from Mr Cram's yard for the Sardinian Steam Navigation Company, to run the mail service between Genoa and Tunis. At the launch, Mr Cram referred to the pleasing fact that on that day they had seen the Spanish, Sardinian and the Dutch flags flying from vessels built at his establishment.

In all, six vessels were converted or built in 1854 at the Cram yard in Chester. The first was the iron sailing vessel *Rosario,* launched on 28th January 1854 for

Messrs Charles Smith & Co. of Liverpool and others (including Joseph Edward Robinson also of Liverpool). At 131' loa and 22' beam she was named by Miss Lord of Liverpool , and needless to say there was a 'sumptuous lunch by Mr Bolland' to follow. After trading to Asia and South America under sail, by February 1860 she is recorded as having been 'sold to foreigners' by Hugh Crawford Smith, but was then a 'a steam powered vessel, schooner—rigged with two masts.'[16] Mr Smith was also the Argentine consul in Liverpool, so perhaps she was sold to the Argentine Government or to private interests there? In 1863 she is recorded in Lloyds certificate expired register, but still showing her master as Captain Forteath, in port at Liverpool, and with her name amended to *Rosaria*. In 1864, there was another vessel registered as *Rosario* running to Buenos Aires. By 1866 *Rosaria* had ceased to appear in Lloyd's.

In April 1854, the press[17] reported that '... we have before us a spirited lithograph, coloured, of the Spanish steamer *Mino*, recently launched at the Roodee shipyard for the line of packets between Barcelona and Liverpool. It is exceedingly well done by Mr McGahey[18] of Bold Square, showing the beautiful proportions of this vessel while it attests to the skill of the craftsmen.'

Sadly, the *Mino* did not have a long career. She was 197' 6" loa, 348 tons burthen and fitted with three masts, a screw steamer built for the Tintore Bros of Barcelona. The Aldersey papers[14] say that the Mino was,

Plate 16: The *Mino*.

> … in the Sandon Dock at Liverpool for the purpose of having her engines and machinery fitted up therin, and there is now or will be on the final completion of the work become payable to the said George Cram in respect of the said last mentioned vessel on the contract for building fitting and completing the same, the Sum of One Thousand pounds.

Initially, George Cram was shown as the owner, before transferring ownership to shipbroker George William Bahr in June 1854. Bahr in turn transferred ownership to Pablo Maria Tintore on 9th August 1854 and, on 26th October 1856, the Registry Certificate was cancelled.

In late March 1856, when the *Mino* was en route from Barcelona, Valencia and Malaga to Cadiz and Liverpool, she collided off Tarifa at about 2 a.m., with the British sailing transport *Minden*, which had left Gibraltar the day before, in tow of the steam tug *Bustler*.

> Melancholy to relate, the steamer which was going at the rate of 10 knots sank 5 minutes after she struck and it is feared 88 persons met with a watery grave. Capt Marquillas is supposed to have gone down with the vessel. Only 21 people were saved, 17 of whom were crew members. [19]

Plate 17: The *Mino* in fatal collision with the *Minden.*

Plate 18: The *Sardegna.*

In May 1854,[20] the trial trip of the *Sardegna* was reported. She left the yard at 12 o'clock and proceeded down river as far as Sandycroft, returning at 1.30 p.m.

> When the engines were going at full speed, 50 revolutions were made with 14 lbs of steam and a vacuum of 26". Under these circumstances, the vessel went at an average of 10¾ knots per hour, a rate of speed considered very good for a vessel of her power compared with her tonnage. The cylinders are placed at right angles and the connecting rod vibrated in trunks. The shaft was driven by means of gearing, which, being cut very accurately by machinery, caused no noise to be made as was generally the case. During the excursion no stoppages were made from hot bearings or other matters connected with the machinery. The screw propeller is made after Sir Thomas Mitchell's system, called the Boomerang Propellor. The engines were made by the eminent firm of George Rennie & Co London.[21] She is 180' loa and her screw is propelled by engines of 80 h.p. She is constructed on the clipper principal and is remarkably fine fore and aft. Her cabins fore and aft are fitted with bird's-eye maple and polished birch and will accommodate 35 first-class and 40 second-class passengers. The trial was witnessed to the entire satisfaction of Mr Rennie, Mr Cram and her intended captain and crew.

When built she was actually just 146' in length, which would help to explain how she managed to turn-round on the canalised section of river at Sandycroft on her trial trip, perhaps assisted by the inlet at the west end of Mr Cram's Sandycroft yard? Later, in her Italian career, she was lengthened to 205' (62.5m) by Fratelli Orlando at Leghorn in 1872. The press also reported that she was to be the first of a series of vessels built for the same owners, and that another of 600 tons was already on the stocks with 120 h.p. engines. Clearly the series was never extended beyond the first two vessels.

The early iron steamers built at Chester by Cram either had very short lives, or, they lasted many years. An iron steam coaster, *Helena*, was built in 1854 for J. Meek of Hull and was probably an early iron collier as she was 137' loa and had four bulk holds. Like the *Rosario*, she was later owned by Hugh Crawford Smith, a Liverpool merchant. She was of 181 tons burthen and was fitted with a 30 h.p. steam engine. Little is known of her subsequent career.

The *Chester* was the first of two steam colliers launched at Chester for the General Iron Screw Collier Company of London, built to work on the east coast carrying coals for the pits of the north-east to the Thames. Launched on Wednesday, 14th June 1854 at 2 o'clock, she was 183' loa with a burthen 5–600 tons — '... she will be fitted up at Sandycroft with engines of 70 h.p.' It is assumed that she was fitted with machinery at the yard George Cram took over at Sandycroft sometime in 1854, because the first Cram vessel was launched from there in December of that year (see Chapter 11). The *Chester* was the first of five steam colliers designed by the naval architect and marine engineer John Grantham.

After 1850 there was much interest in increasing the volumes and improving the reliability of the shipment of coal to London, particularly from the north-east of England, because of the surge in demand from the Thames-side gasworks which were serving the capital.

The General Iron Screw Collier Company had been set up in April 1852 by C. M. Palmer (later Sir Charles Mark Palmer, as Managing Director), with a capital of £250,000. The directors included Mr William Prinstep of the London Gas Co and Thomas Miers of the Commercial Gas Company.[22] In 1851, Charles and his brother George had commenced their famous shipbuilding business at Jarrow and the *John Bowes* was the first vessel they built at the Jarrow yard. She is of course well known as the first steam collier, measuring 150' loa x 25' 7"x 15' 6" moulded depth, and of 465 tons register. It was stated that she could carry 30 keels of coal and make 30 trips a year between Newcastle and London. The steam-collier owning business was to prove a very successful one as the business of moving coal from Newcastle in small sailing vessels had always caused problems of reliability of supply. One assumes that because of the two colliers built by George Cram at Chester, the *Chronicle*[23] reported in August 1854 that,

> ... there are now 14 screw colliers employed conveying coal between the Tyne and London. In July they carried 23,587 tons – or 8% of the coal imports by sea to the Thames and most of these vessels make a voyage every week.

In a speech to the Institute of Civil Engineers the following year in 1855 it was reported that in a 2½ year period 36 steam colliers had already been completed.

Returning to the situation in August 1854 in Chester, as well as reporting the growing tonnage of coal carried by steam colliers, the *Chester Chronicle* reported the bad news of the 'Suspension of Business at the Roodee shipyard', going on to say that,

> ... on Wednesday afternoon, while the men at the Roodee Ship Yard were in full occupation, they were startled by the announcement that all business was suspended and that they must attend on Friday (yesterday) for the amount of wages due. The men immediately left and it is but justice to them to state that their own difficulty was almost lost sight of in sympathy for that of their employer. We understand that these difficulties have been considerably enhanced by the strikes that have taken place in this establishment. One which took place a fortnight ago entailed a loss of at least £200 on Mr Cram. The extensive works at Sandicroft are, of course, in the same predicament as those at the Roodee. Of the cause of this commercial catastrophe we are uninformed. All we know is that an assignment for the benefit of creditors has been executed and that Mr Roberts of the Old Bank, and Mr Septimus Edward of Liverpool are the Assignees. Indeed the Conveyance of Real Estate and Assignment of a Personal estate were dated three days earlier and were to benefit Septimus Edward of Liverpool, iron merchant and Robert Roberts a slate merchant of Chester. In early September these two gentlemen called a meeting of all the creditors of George Cram at the Clarendon Rooms in Liverpool and it was declared lawful for the Trustees to complete any vessel at the Chester or Sandycroft yards.[24]

The financial situation provoked another interesting incident as, on the previous Wednesday evening, a sensation was caused in the shipyard, by an attempt of a creditor, Iron Trade, to obtain possession of a recently delivered anchor. When the object of the party and his men were known, the police were sent for and it was frustrated by their resistance. This coup was very nearly successful in the attempt, but of course it could have no result as the property was vested in the assignees. It was a realization of the 'good old rule, the simple plan.' The party, which came in a boat, obtained hold of the anchor and dragged it from the wharf into the water. When the police appeared on the scene, those attempting to take the law into their own hands had to drop the anchor, which fell to the bottom of the river, and the 'raiders' had to escape as best they could, some in the boat and the others by swimming.[23]

> We earnestly hope that this suspension will only be temporary, as well for the sake of the respected and enterprising proprietor as for the sake of the many hundreds employed by him. We understand that upwards of 1100 persons are thrown out of work by this event. We understand that yesterday morning a deputation of the workmen resident in Chester, heretofore employed at the Roodeye Shipyard waited upon Mr Cram in their own name and that of their fellow hands, placing their services at his disposal gratuitously for a fortnight, for the completion of works on contract, the non-fulfilment of which might expose that gentleman to additional loss. We understand from the latest information that the yards and works will be opened this day (Saturday) and business resumed as usual.

Despite all the financial problems that arose during August 1854, the second collier, the 'Derwent' from the yard was launched on Saturday 13th.[23] At 185 feet in length, the near sisters were 35 feet longer than the pioneer *John Bowes*. (See illustration of the *Lambton* in 'The Steam Collier Fleets' by J. A. McCrae, which is thought to have been a near sister vessel —bibliography).

The two Chester-built colliers were the first of a planned series of five designed by the naval architect John Grantham and are probably the most significant vessels he designed. He specified that his tried and tested oscillating engines were to be installed in the vessels and included features that were very advanced for the time and that were to be later incorporated in colliers and bulk carriers. These included the positioning of the engines and boilers in the aft part of the hull to provide a clear cargo space of maximum size, the provision of water ballast in a false bottom and wide hatches.[25] Both features were practical responses to the one way trade in which these vessels were to be involved. It is assumed that the other three vessels were built at other U.K. yards, not necessarily because of the financial problems experienced by George Cram, but because so many iron steam colliers were needed at this time.

Both of these colliers continued in service with the GI Screw Collier Company until 1873–4 after which they cease to appear in Lloyd's.

Born in 1809, John Grantham's early work as a naval architect was designing and building steam boats for use on the Irish canal system between Dublin and Limerick. He returned to England and worked in Liverpool, becoming a partner in Mather, Dixon & Co. They closed in 1843, and he then practised on his own. It is recorded that he was aboard the experimental screw steamer he designed and built at Liverpool, the *Liverpool Screw,* when she came round from the Mersey to the Dee on 30th April 1843 —the first screw-driven steam vessel to enter the Chester River. It was stated at the time that '... she is the first (vessel) upon the Archimedian principle seen in Chester, the rapidity and ease with which she glides through the water is astonishing. A number of Chester citizens were treated to a trip on this vessel to Flint and back (there and back in 3hrs 10 minutes and a very strong tide).'[25] The *Liverpool Screw* was built as a tug for the Mersey and Irwell Navigation Co with a 20 h.p. engine, fitted up by the celebrated engineers, Mather, Dixon and Grantham of that city. In 1843 John Grantham had visited the *Great Britain* at Bristol during her construction and was convinced that screw propulsion was the way forward. His design philosophy was summed up in a discussion at the Institute of Naval Architects in 1861 — 'I am not fond of new plans and sudden innovations. I would rather go on with improvements.'[25] He designed a wide variety of sail and steam vessels, but in 1859, at the age of 50, he left Liverpool and returned to his birthplace in Croydon. No doubt George and Henry Cram had met him during during his time in Liverpool where they were all part of the maritime community.

After the launching of *Derwent* it seems that no further vessels were completed at Chester in the name of George Cram as builder, even though the Trustees did not file for bankruptcy until 16th May 1855, and the indenture relating to the demise of the Sandycroft yard was not finally signed until 7th January 1856.

The start of 1855 was not a good time to be in shipbuilding. The winter proved to be bitterly cold for a long period. The *Chronicle* reported in February that '… the Dee is frozen and thousands have been promenading on it and the ice will bear pedestrians as far as Holt!'[26] It was indeed so cold that Liverpool docks could not work and easterly winds prevented the arrival of vessels into the river Dee. A week later, the *Chronicle* was still reporting on the extreme weather, saying there were '… 5,000 people on the river last Sunday and people had skated up the river to Bangor-is-y-Coed!' In the sixty years the author has been living in Chester, he can only recall the Dee freezing once, when he was taken to see a Mini car being driven on the ice. 160 years ago, the impact of weather like that on industry generally must have been indescribable.

At the beginning of May 1855, however, it was reported that

> … on Tuesday last an elegantly modelled iron steamer was launched from Mr Cram's yard on the Roodee. She glided into the water beautifully and was the long awaited sister vessel to *Sardegna*. Doubtless because of the financial problems the yard was experiencing, her construction had been greatly delayed as she had already been on the stocks in December 1853. Her name was *Italia,* and of 600 tons burthen and she is already chartered by the French Government to carry horses and soldiers to the Crimea. At the close of the war she will ply between Genoa and the coast of Barbary. She was rigged before she left the stocks.'[27]

Both the *Italia* and her sister vessel were destined to have long and successful careers in the Mediterranean.

It would be interesting to know how the George Cram enterprise became involved with building vessels for Italian/Sardinian owners. Living in London at this time was Mr Charles Pietroni who, according to the *London Evening Standard* was a 'gentleman of great experience in steamship building, an experience extending over thirty years.'[28] He was originally connected with the Imperial and Royal Steam Navigation Co. of Vienna, and superintended a number of steam vessels on their account that had been constructed at Trieste and Britain, including the *Sardegna*, the *Italia* (both from Cram), the *Vittoria Emmanuele*, the *Conte di Cavour*, the *Torino* and and the *Genova* (all built by C. J. Mare of Blackwall). His company in 1857 was Draper Pietroni & Co, located at 81, London Wall and they were also agents for the

Plate 19: The *Italia.*

Transatlantic Steam Navigation Co. of Genoa who ran a service from London to Genoa, via Leghorn, Naples and Marseilles.[29] His company also appears to have experienced bankruptcy in June 1855 and again in April 1865,[30] but Pietroni seems to have had the right connections, visiting Garibaldi in London in 1864. It seems likely therefore that he was involved with the building of the two Cram vessels from the beginning, and was instrumental in choosing the Chester yard for their construction.

The early lives of these two vessels is complex. According to *The Ships List,*[31] Compagnia Transatlantica di Navigazione a Vapore, Genoa (CTG) bought *Italia* from Rubattino with the intention of using her on a feeder service for emigrants between Rio de Janeiro and Buenos Aires, where she replaced the *Sardegna* which CTG had also been using. But in 1857, she returned to Rubattino ownership and CTG closed their operation to South America. CTG were declared bankrupt in 1859. The existence of this feeder service helps to explain why there is a report of a sighting of a vessel named *Italia* off Pernambuco (Recife) in February 1857.[32]

*Sardegna* was registered to the Merchant Navy of the newly formed Kingdom of Italy on 17th March 1861. Her passenger capacity was 31 1st Class, 26 2nd Class and 100 3rd Class. Lengthened in 1872, and re-engined in 1876, she was transferred to NGI (Italia Line) in September 1881 and was then running from Genoa to

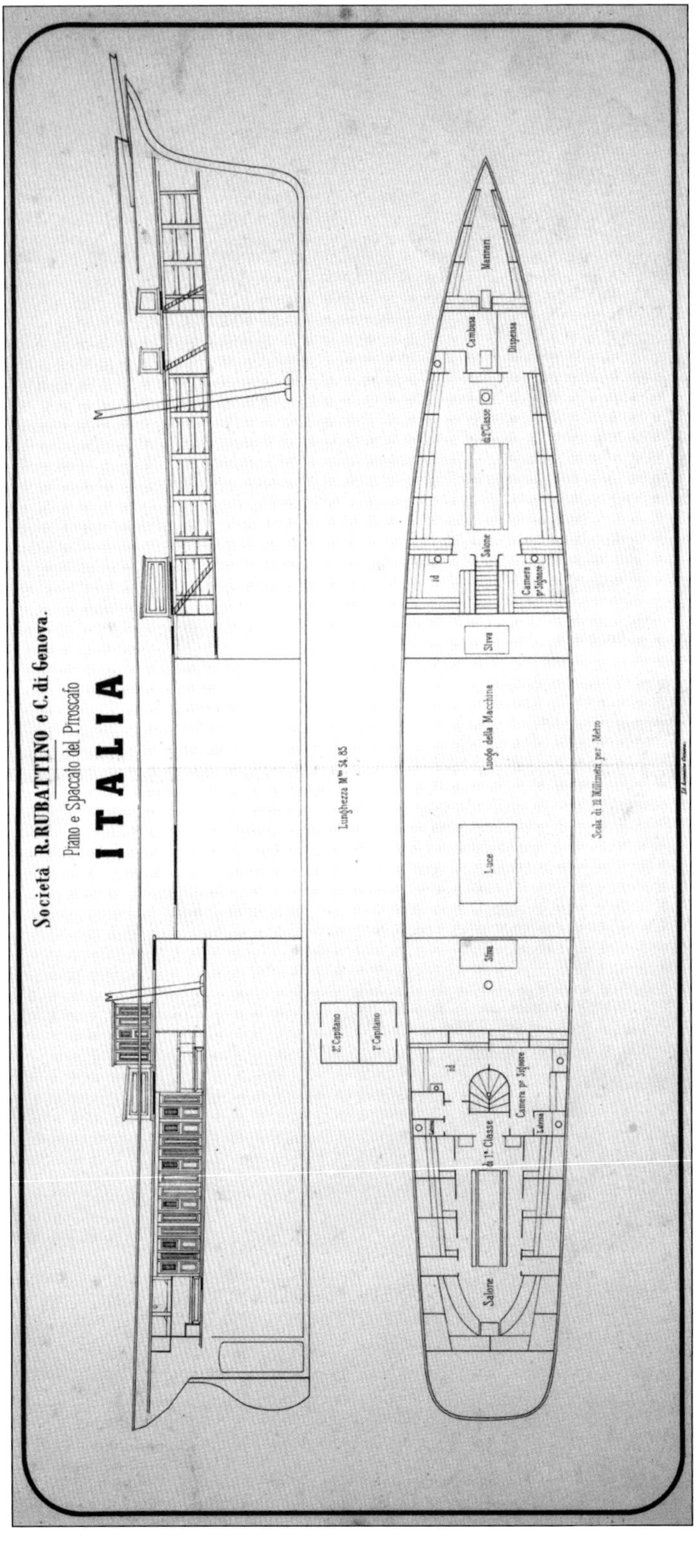


Plate 20: Plan of the *Italia*.

Leghorn, Cagliari and Tunis. In 1886 she was re-registered at Palermo, Sicily and in 1893 declared unsuitable for mail service by a government commission and subsequently sold for breaking at Genoa in June 1894.

*Italia* was actually launched for Rubattino and registered at Genoa in the Kingdom of Sardinia, sailing from Genoa to Corse and Sardinia. She carried 22 1st Class, 26 2nd Class and 61 3rd Class passengers. In 1856 she was sold to CTG and sailed to Brazil where she replaced the smaller *Sardegna* on their feeder service from Rio to Montevideo and Buenos Aires. After the bankruptcy of CTG, she was auctioned in 1859 and repurchased by Rubattino. Her claim to fame came in 1869 when she sailed from Genoa to Leghorn, Messina, Alexandria, Port Said and Suez, arriving in Ismailia on 17th November where she attended the opening ceremony of the Suez Canal and became the first Italian registered ship to sail the Canal. In 1877, like her 'sister', she was fitted with a new engine at the Ansaldo yard. In 1881 she was also transferred to NGI in Genoa, sailing from Genoa to Leghorn, Cagliari and Tunis. On 5th December 1891, she got heavily ashore at Terranova Pausania (in north-eastern Sardinia) but was later re-floated and towed to Genoa. After a twelve-month layup she was hulked in March 1893 in Genoa harbour.

Both vessels were operated for Raffaele Rubattino, the first Italian owner of steamships, until 1881. He had been born in Genoa in 1810 to a family of merchants. In 1838 he founded the first Italian shipping Company —De Luchi-Rubattino. After twelve months the line started operating between Genoa, Marseilles, Livorno and Naples. Rubattino also provide ships to Garibaldi in his 'Expedition of a Thousand' which brought about the unification of Italy in 1861. Indeed in 1860 there is a report of *Italia* being used to ferry troops for Garibaldi.[33] In 1851, Rubattino had obtained permission to operate a steam packet service connecting Genoa and Sardinia. In 1881, shortly before his death, his shipping line merged with the Florio Co. of Palermo to found the Italian Navigation Company (NGI). Both vessels then transferred to the newly created Italia Line for the remainder of their careers. In 1876 *Sardegna* was re-engined by Gio Ansaldo in Genoa and the *Italia* was re-engined the following year by the same yard.[34]

When they first appear in *Lloyds Register* in 1881/2 these two ships were listed as being built at Chester by 'Graham', but given the financial collapse of George Cram at this time, it is either a poor transcription of 'G. Cram', or possibly of (John) 'Grantham', the naval architect and marine engineer who already had connections with the yard and may have been employed by the trustees to oversee the completion of the two vessels? Grantham had also been involved with Palmers on the Tyne who were also building vessels for Italian shipowners at this time.

The Trustees filed for bankruptcy of the Cram undertakings at Chester and Sandycroft on 16th May 1855 and there was a further indenture drawn up in January 1856, relating specifically to the ending of the lease at Sandycroft. However, despite his bankruptcy, George Cram continued his association with the Roodeye Yard as the manager of the facility, with other directors and bankers providing the finance.

Remarkably, two further iron vessels were launched from the Roodee site in 1856. The *Chrystaline*, a three-masted iron barque, 112' loa, which was employed in the trade with West Africa in 1856, but by 1857 was running to South America. 24/64 shares in her were owned by F. H. Powell, (also a shareholder in George Cram's first iron vessel the *Amelia*) and 8/64 were owned by Henry Cram, George's cousin. Were they involved in trying to keep the business going? Did they buy the vessel at a cheap price on the stocks after it was built speculatively, or were they creditors who took shares in lieu of repayments that were not forthcoming? *Chrystaline* continues to appear in Lloyds until 1859, then disappears after which she re-appears in Lloyds of 1861, registered as *Crystaline*. Between 1855 and 1873 there was a serious falling out between the Liverpool underwriters and the committee of Lloyds of London regarding iron vessels, particularly those propelled by steam, and a separate register was created in Liverpool.[35] They were to finally resolve their differences in 1885. These registration issues may be connected to the disappearance and re-naming of the *Chrystaline.*

It is worthwhile spending a little time looking at the long career of the *Crystaline*, the latter part of which involved carrying bulk cargoes round the coast of the British Isles. F. H. Powell used her in deep-sea trading until the late 1860s. In 1857 she was reported having sailed from Matanzas (Venezuela)[36] and in 1860[37] was off the Isle of Wight bound for Mauritius. In December 1865,[38] she had sailed for Galveston from Glasgow.

In July 1870, the *Crystaline* was advertised for sale by Tonge & Co. of Water Street in Liverpool and subsequently passed into the ownership of W. McMaster of Liverpool and was put into the coastal trade where she was to be gainfully employed for the next 24 years.

Plate 21: McGahey view of Chester, 1853.

In 1881 she was reported bound from Liverpool for Devonport with coals, 'but put into Milford Haven on Tuesday afternoon with sails blown away, six chain plates broken and part of her bulwarks carried away.[39] Worse was to happen in November 1884[40] when she collided with the brigantine *Water Lily* of Fowey, four miles off the Longships. Initially locked together, the six crew of the *Crystaline* got aboard the *Water Lily* and were brought into Hayle. At the time the *Crystaline* was bound from Garston to Plymouth with coal, but she was subsequently picked up off the Scillies by a tug and brought into New Grimsby Harbour (Scillies).[41] The salvors accepted £250 for their services, arranged by the Receiver of Wrecks, Mr Henry Hicks. In this incident she received two holes in her stove in bow, lost her bowsprit and her fore compartments were filled with water.

Further problems occurred in February 1889[42] when information was received from Prawle Point and Torcross signal stations that she had been seen off Start Point flying distress signals and was drifting up channel on her beam ends.. The steam tugs *Hanley* and *St Patrick* found her, bound to Liverpool in ballast from Plymouth. She was taken into Dartmouth by the *Hanley*. The captain reported that he and the crew were exhausted and that the ballast had shifted in a gale. The gunwhale of the vessel heeled over almost to a level with the water and on arrival the captain was too ill to make a deposition at the Custom House.

She must have been a well-built vessel to survive these incidents and by 1890 she was back in the Plymouth coal trade, making the local news for being handled there by non-union labour when the coal porters went on strike.[43] In November 1892 she was offered for sale by public auction, but the highest bid of £400 fell below the reserve price[44] and she was withdrawn from sale.

Nevertheless, in 1893–4 she was all over the west coast of the UK — Connah's Quay, Glasson, Cardiff, Limerick, Fowey, Weston Point, Irvine, Stornoway, Plymouth and Holyhead. Sadly, in May1894,[45] she was reported ashore in Kylerhea, Sound of Skye, and no more is heard of her. Not a bad 38-year career for a vessel built in a struggling shipyard.

The second vessel built at the yard that year, *Deva*, is most probably the first launched by the Roodee Iron Shipbuilding Co., so will be covered in Chapter 5.

Regarding the interest of the other Cram family members at this time with George Cram's Deeside shipbuilding activities, David, described as a 'retired merchant' in the 1851 census, died at his Hamilton Square residence aged 85, on

23rd January 1856 and probably was very little involved.

We have seen that Henry was living in North Wales in 1851, but by 1861, after the bankruptcy of the shipyard, he had moved to Liscard on the Wirral and was described as a shipbroker, living with his wife and their seven children, one of whom, Henry, is described as a shipbroker's clerk. In November 1854, Cram Powell, agents in Liverpool, were advertising ships to Le Havre and Cram was advertising ships, as agent for both the East Indies and West Indies. In August 1856 there is an advert for Cram, Powell & Co. of 35, South John Street as agents for the 'direct steam communication between Liverpool and Bristol by one of the new screw steamships *Amelia* or *Athlete*. On 30th January 1868 the press noted that 'Henry Cram, Liverpool, Shipbroker, was declared bankrupt, composition of 2s in the pound in 14 days from registration of deed.'[46] Henry died in 1873 at the age of only 63, having gone back to live in Caernarfonshire.

## Notes

1. *Chester Chronicle*, 19th March 1853 – first iron ship launch at Chester.
2. *Pembrokeshire Herald*, 3rd April 1857 – BNA, loss of the *Amelia*.
3. *Mersey Rovers* by Roy Fenton – see Bibliography.
4. *Liverpool Mercury*, 25th April 1828.
5. Ancestry.co.uk.
6. Letter from Henry Cram to the *Liverpool Daily Post*, 19th January 1860 regarding the accident when the Mersey Ferry, *Thomas Wilson* sank in collision with the ferry.'
7. *Merchant Sailing Ships, 1850–1875* by D. Mc Gregor.
8. *Streets and Lanes of Flint* by Edward Hogan, unpublished MSS, FRO, Ref. NT1573.
9. *Launceston Examiner*, 13th May 1855.
10. See www.australian shipwrecks.info/easw-parsons, list a–i.
11. *Launceston Examiner*, 5th April 1855.
12. *The Ferries of Sydney* by Graeme Andrews, published by A. H. & A. W. Reed, Sydney, 1975.
13. *Morning Chronicle*, 26th May 1853.
14. See the Aldersey Papers – Deeds and Papers relating to the financial affairs of Geo. Cram, shipbuilder, debtor to Williams & Co. bankers 1854–56. Ref ZCR 69/33/10–20, Cheshire Archives.
15. *Chester Chronicle*, 24th December 1853 re launch 17th December 53.
16. *Cheshire Observer*, 4th February 1854 re launch 28th January 1854.
17. *Chester Chronicle*, 29th April 1854.
18. In 1851 John McGahey was described in the census as an artist and lithographer, aged 34, living in Liverpool with his wife, Jane, seven children and a governess. According to the Farle & Free Library he moved to Chester later in 1851 and was still there when he painted the *Cobre* in 1853. By 1871 he was again living in Liverpool with his wife Agnes, whom he had married in 1867. By 1891 he was living in

lodgings in Manchester with his second wife, still described as a lithographer/artist. He seems to be the only artist who painted more than one Chester-built vessel in this era and he also produced views of Chester and the port. Few of these exist today.

19. *Monmouthshire Merlin*, 12th April 1856, newspaper archive, National Library of Wales.
20. *Cheshire Observer*, 20th May 1854.
21. George Rennie (1791–1866) was a very versatile engineer who had a number of connections with Chester and Merseyside. Son of the famous Scottish canal engineer, in 1822 he was elected to the Royal Society and in 1826 completed a report on jetties and their interference with tidal flow on the Upper Mersey. He was engaged by the architect Thomas Harrison to build the Grosvenor Bridge in Chester, which was completed in 1832. He made engines for the Admiralty at his Holland Street works in London and he was very interested in the screw propeller and his firm built the engines for the *Archimedes*, the world's first propeller driven steamship (1839). Subsequently, in 1840, the firm built the *Dwarf* for the Admiralty, the first Royal Navy vessel to be driven by screw. (Wikipedia)
22. *The Steam Collier Fleets* by J. McRae & C. V. Waine, published in 1990 by Waine Research and paper by E. E. Allan to the Institute of Chartered Engineers (ICE), February 1855.
23. *Chester Chronicle*, 19th August 1854.
24. Trustees authorized to complete vessels Report of Creditors meeting 8th September 1854, Aldersey Papers see Note14 above.
25. Paper to British Association Festival, Liverpool, 6th September 2008, 'Pioneer Marine Engineer & Naval Architect' by Mike Stammers, Mersey Maritime Museum.
26. *Chester Chronicle*, 23rd December 1854 and 17th February 1855.
27. *Chester Chronicle*, 5th May 1855.
28. *London Evening Standard*, 11th December 1863.
29. *Public Ledger and Daily Advertiser*, 17th June 1857.
30. *Perry's Bankruptcy Gazette*, 9th June 1855 and April 1865.
31. www.the shipslist.com/.
32. *Morning Post*, 25th March 1857.
33. *Reynold's Newspaper*, 8th July 1860.
34. See 1891 entries in RINA register, showing re-engining by Ansaldo,1876 (*Sardegna*) and 1877 (*Italia*) respectively. RINA S.p.A is an operational company created by Registro Italiano Navale founded in Genoa in 1861.
35. See 'Underwriters Registry for Iron Vessels' by David Eccles, published in *Current Research in Maritime History*, published by Liverpool Nautical Research Society, 10th February 1996.
36. *Liverpool Mail*, 11th July 1857.
37. *Public Ledger*, 26th November 1860.
38. *Glasgow Morning Herald*, 9th December 1865.
39. *South West Daily News*, 13th April 1851.
40. *Edinburgh Evening News*, 17th November 1884.
41. *The Cornishman*, 27th November 1884.
42. *Western Times*, 16th February 1889.
43. *Exeter & Plymouth Gazette*, 6th November 1890.
44. *Glasgow Herald*, 5th November 1892.
45. *Hartlepool Northern Daily Mail*, 7th May 1894.
46. *Liverpool Daily Post*, 30th January 1868.

# 5

# Chester, the final fourteen years

## Part One — The Rise and Fall of Nathaniel Cox

The year 1856 was one of change in the shipbuilding industry on the Crane Wharf Roodeye site in Chester. The Roodee Iron Shipbuilding Co. had taken over the former George Cram yard in order to continue building in iron, whilst just downstream, on Crane Wharf, William Bishton of Wolverhampton had built his first wooden schooner in 1855.

The Roodee Co. had been set up by Nathaniel Cox and William Miller, both based in Liverpool. Cox had been born in Liverpool on 9th June 1820, the son of George Lissant Cox, an iron merchant and nail supplier, originally from Nottingham. George was a partner in the Liverpool firm of Cox & Yates, but Richard Yates died in November 1856 after which the business did not prosper and was destined to fail in 1860. In 1847, Nathaniel, then aged 26, had married Mary Griffiths in Ffestiniog, and by 1851 was living with his wife and mother-in-law at Ynysymaengwyn, a 160 acre farm just north of Aberdyfi on the west coast of Wales. Nathaniel was described as a 'commercial traveller in the iron trade'.

Quite how Cox and Miller got together is not known, but Nathaniel had grown up in Liverpool and there is a record of his eldest sister, Ann writing to her fiancée, William Holt in January 1830, one of the well-known Liverpool Holt family, saying that Nathaniel had gone skating with his brother Edward at Otterspool, so the family certainly had the right social connections with shipping as well as a probable business relationship.[1] Nathaniel wrote to William Holt in March 1830 saying '... as this is the first time I ever wrote a letter.' His actual partner in Chester, Thomas Lodwick Miller (born in 1835), was the son of William Cowley Miller from Plymouth who, in 1836 had moved to Liverpool to be a shipyard foreman in the firm of Miller & Mackay, who built vessels there for the famous Black Ball Line. In 1851, William

Cowley Miller was described as 'employing 104 men', and by 1855,[2] was building ships in his own name. By 1857, when his son Thomas built his first vessel in Chester, he was a mere 22 years old. His elder brother, William, was in the Liverpool business as a shipbuilder's clerk six years earlier, and Thomas may have felt stifled in his father's business. Alternatively, as we have already seen, Cox & Miller could have been set up as a vehicle for expansion by his father as space for shipbuilding was at a premium in Liverpool at this time.

The Roodee Iron Shipbuilding Co. built its first vessel, the *Deva,* in 1857, a 130' loa twin-engined screw steamer, of 79.3 tons burthen, first registered in June of that year by William and George Fosberry (16/64 each) and others, including one George Cram, holding 16/64 of the shares. It is therefore likely that the *Deva* was originally ordered from the George Cram controlled undertaking before it finally went into receivership. At her launch in May 1857[3] she was described as 'a fine new steamer from the shipyard of Mr Cram, 280 tons builder's measurement, and intended for the iron ore trade. Her engines which are being made in the yard will be 40hp'. She did not stay with them long, however, as she was transferred to Goole registry in September 1859 when she was owned by the Goole Steam Navigation Co. In 1861 it is recorded that she was running a regular service every Tuesday, Wednesday and Saturday between Goole and Antwerp/Ghent, along with *La Plata, Eagle* and *Cheviot.*[4] Sold out of their fleet in 1870, she was re–registered in 1877 at Glasgow as the *Doon* owned by Peter Barr. In 1883 she is recorded as having a 50 h.p. engine, built by David Rowan of Glasgow, and in 1889 she had been bought by them. In 1900 she was owned by David Rowan Jnr, and in her last year of registration, 1902, she was owned in Ayr, along with other coasters, by the Ayr Steamship Co., in which D. Rowan Jnr was a partner. She had lasted 45 years in the coasting trade.

Following *Deva*, the iron brig *Cymbeline* was built at the Chester yard. At 120' loa this single-deck vessel was jointly owned by Charles Tricks Bowring and Henry Price Bowring, the well-known Bowring Bros of Liverpool. In 1834 Benjamin Bowring had returned to Britain from Newfoundland and commenced trading between Liverpool and St John's. By 1856, the brothers had developed their trading routes and fleet and were regularly trading to Brazil as well as Canada. *Cymbeline* served in their Newfoundland trade until 1863 when she was sadly lost. It was probably decided to test an iron-hulled vessel in their trade because of the greater strength of iron hulls when trading on routes which were regularly affected by ice.

George Cram's involvement with the yard seems to have finally ended in the Autumn of 1857. On 8th August the press reported that 'Mr Ford attended at the Town Hall pursuant to the arrangement at the last hearing, to ascertain what arrangement had been come to by Mr Cram for the payment of wages due to his men. After waiting some time it transpired that Mr Cram had made no arrangements whatsoever and had not even the courtesy to appear according to the undertaking with the magistrates and upon Mr Walker being applied to ascertain what position matters were in, stated he had no instructions at all. After further discussion Mr Walker informed the magistrates that Mr Cram had been declared a bankrupt, but that the hostile creditor, at whose instigation the fiat was issued, regretted the course of action he had taken and that proceedings would be adopted at once to supersede the bankruptcy and that the men would be paid at a very early period.'[5] At the previous meeting, the Mayor had advanced £20 himself to pay the men's wages and indeed the following week the press reported that '… the Mayor had been kind enough to advance an additional sum of £30 to the workmen, but the £20 was repaid to Mr Eaton by the parties of the joint stock company who will in future work the business.' By the end of November, the house where George and his wife had lived in Watergate Square was available for let, including the greenhouse, coach house and stabling.

In the autumn of 1857 there was a fire at the yard, caused by a cinder from the adjacent railway viaduct. How much this affected the business and its finances, we do not know. It is interesting to note that in nearly all the Chester chapters of this book there is an instance of a fire at the main Roodeye shipyard site.

The next we hear of George Cram is in 1861 when he and Eliza were living in lodgings at Monk Coniston in the Lake District. He was described as a 'Merchant'. George died nine years later in Hexham, his wife living on until 1889. Latterly, she lived with her widowed niece, Catharine Vaughan, née Elsee, in Newcastle, who had lived with the Crams in Chester in 1853 and launched the *Amelia*.

Twenty-eight years later, in 1885, a letter appeared in the *Cheshire Observer* which shows how those who worked for George Cram were still lamenting the disappearance of shipbuilding and the inspirational Mr Cram from Chester. After all, he did have the vision to build the two largest vessels ever constructed on the Chester River, albeit both at Sandycroft. It reads as follows:

> The improvement of the River Dee, was much discussed at the Chester election of 1857. Mr George Cram had his shipbuilding yard near the Gasworks at this time and I happened to be engaged under him. He said to me one day 'Jack if these Chester people would get the river improved between the Yard and Connah's Quay, friends of mine would put a fine shipbuilding yard below Brewer's Hall and would give employment to more than 500 men.
>
> Of course the river was not improved, poor Mr Cram himself got into trouble and the old city lost a chance which has never been given to her since.

Realistically, as vessels were gradually increasing in size, the river Dee was never going to accommodate them without continuous dredging which would have been prohibitively expensive.

The joint stock company which took over the yard seems to have quickly evolved into a partnership between Thomas Miller and Nathaniel Cox but this was not destined to last long. It was announced on 11th February 1859 that '... the Partnership heretofore subsisting between us, the undersigned Nathaniel Cox and Thomas Miller as iron shipbuilders at the city of Chester under the firm of Cox and Miller has this day been dissolved by mutual consent — dated this 22nd day of July 1858.[6]

After 1858, Nathaniel Cox carried on, completing the first of the full-rigged iron sailing ships to be built at the yard. *Wayfarer* was built for the recently established firm of Messrs G. H. Fletcher of Liverpool, designed to operate in the Calcutta trade. She was launched by Mrs Hamilton Fletcher in July 1860 and was of 1,321 tons burthen and loa 212', and was fitted with iron masts, steel yards and wire rigging. The journalist reporting on the event clearly felt that his readers would be interested to know that the figurehead was a massive 7' 6" long figure of the Wayfarer, depicted leaning on his staff with his water bottle at his side, dressed in eastern costume! Interestingly, the reporter also took the opportunity to inform his readers that 'several of the vessels of the Sardinian Navy and which did good service in the late war with Austria were built in this yard.' After launching, *Wayfarer* was towed alongside the quay by the tug *Test* to be partly rigged before being taken to Liverpool. Nathaniel Cox, however, was ill at the time and therefore unable to attend the launch, but amongst those who were present was Mr G. W. Bahr of the Liverpool ship agents and owners (who were still trading as Bahr Behrend there until the

1990s) and Robert Gladstone of the Liverpool merchant family and elder brother of W. E. Gladstone, the future prime minister.

*Wayfarer* lasted until January 1871 when she had the misfortune to go ashore at Kilmore Quay in southern Ireland. Wedged upright on the rocks it was said that she could have been salvaged had a dispute had not broken out among the salvagers. By the time it had been resolved, wind and sea had damaged her beyond repair. In the 1970s bits of her rusting ironwork could still be seen among the rocks.

In 1861, *Eastham Fairy II* and *Swiftsure* were completed, both Mersey ferries of the same dimensions and registered to H. M. Lawrence & Henry Gough. Gough soon became the sole owner of both vessels and, following his death in 1871, his fleet of five steamers was advertised for sale and *Swiftsure* was bought by J. Lancaster for service in North Wales, whilst the others, including *Eastham Fairy II,* were sold to Thomas W. Thompson, who thereafter traded as Thompson & Gough.[7] *Swiftsure* lasted on the Mersey until about 1875 and *Eastham Fairy II* continued to work as a Mersey Ferry until the 1890s. Sometime after 1875, *Swiftsure* operated on the Liverpool–Mostyn service, operated by the Mostyn Coal & Iron Company and their Liverpool agents R. & D. Jones. She was regarded as 'neither swift nor particularly sure', as the timings of her 2/3 sailings each week depended more on tide tables than a time table.[8] R. & D. Jones survived into the late 1960s as agents in Liverpool. They were given an appropriated berth in Trafalgar Dock in the port in 1882 for the *Swiftsure* service, together with a service by sailing vessel to Greenfield on the Dee, and for steamers running regularly to other Welsh ports, Lancashire, and Cumberland. The *Swiftsure* service ended in 1893.

1861 was to witness probably the greatest achievement of all the shipbuilders at Chester when the iron full-rigged ship *Gitana* was launched, the largest vessel (in tonnage) ever to be built at the Roodeye or Crane Bank yards. At 210' in length, with a 36' beam and a 25' 2' moulded depth, she was, like her earlier almost twin sister, the *Wayfarer,* intended for the Indian trade. She was over 100 feet longer than most of the full-rigged vessels built at the same yard by the Mulvey family earlier in the century. Of 1,366 tons burthen and fitted with two bulk holds, she was initially owned by Moore & Co. of Liverpool, and was launched in February 1861 by Miss Laura Moore. She was sold to Edward Bates of Liverpool in 1870, who had opened a Liverpool office in 1848 and started running chartered sailing vessels to Calcutta and Bombay. By 1870 he had 44 vessels flying the white flag with red Maltese cross

Plate 22: The *Gitana.*

and was trading all over the world. In 1916 Bates' shipping interests were incorporated into T. & J. Brocklebank.[9] In February 1881, G. R. Leyland (of Leyland Line fame) wrote to his sister Mary saying that he had just purchased the iron ship *Gitana* for £10,400. Although he acknowledged that she was already twenty years old, he felt '... that we think there is a good prospect of making money out of her'. He encouraged two friends to take one share each in her, saying you may reasonably reckon 20% per annum out of it.'[10]

In 1883 the *Gitana* was abandoned off the west coast of Denmark, but was presumably brought to port and repaired, because she had a career that lasted for 35 years. On 21st March 1893 she sailed from Liverpool but grounded and had to put into Dublin where there was a case of insubordination on board when 9 of the 18 crew members refused to sail. Her end finally came in 1896, when she was sighted in dismasted condition with only the fore lower mast standing, near Cape Horn, by the barque *Edinburghshire*. She had been on a voyage from Pisagua in northern Chile to Hamburg and was badly damaged and leaking. The captain wished to abandon ship as the boats had all gone and he and his crew were landed at Durban.[11]

At the time of the census in April 1861, 40-year old Nathaniel Cox, 'an iron merchant', and his wife, Mary, were living in Pennal, near Machynlleth, some 80 miles by road from Chester. The had five children and George F. Cox, Nathaniel's brother, aged 50, a retired iron merchant and his wife, were visiting, along with an Alistair Gaskell, described as a 42-year old 'railway proprietor.' Two things need to be borne in mind concerning the fact that Nathaniel was living many miles from Chester where he was building his ships. Firstly, the Cambrian Railway opened as far as Machynlleth on May Day 1862, so Cox and Yates may have been a supplier of railway materials until their demise sometime around 1860. Nathaniel's father died at Conwy in July 1860, but was buried in Toxteth, Liverpool, while the failure of the Cox & Yates business could also explain the presence of George F. Cox and his wife at Machynlleth in 1861.

By November 1861, the Liverpool press was announcing that the '... Roodee Co was proposing public investments when the surrender of the business by its former proprietors opens a fine opportunity for the formation of a substantial and remunerative Joint Stock Co.'.[12]

London shipowners were complaining at this time of the cost of shipbuilding on the Thames and saw an opportunity to build ships with lower labour costs in the north, but not in Liverpool where there was a history of troublesome strikes as well as a lack of space for shipbuilding. The new joint stock company published a table in its prospectus comparing the cost of labour and materials in London and Chester. Independent of the saving in rent, taxes and management, this shows an actual gain of 20% in favour of building iron ships at Chester —for every £400 spent in wages per week, which would represent a comparatively minimum scale of business, there would accrue a positive advantage to the shareholders of £72 3s, equivalent to £3,750 per annum The saving in the cost of materials would be even larger.

The detail is impressive and the prospectus continued by saying that the yard was '... currently active and capable of turning out £200,000 worth of work in a year, but that amount may be increased to £500,000.' The 'project is a brilliant one'!

In November 1861 *The Times* provided a record of the incorporation of the Roodee Iron Shipbuilding Company, (RISB —details shown in Appendix 7). Nathaniel Cox was still very much involved in the business, but of the seven directors, apart from Nathaniel Cox himself, all were businessmen based in London or Devon. The chairman of the company was Admiral Sir Henry John Leeke, KCB, MP, and there was a further naval connection in that the appointed marine engineer and draughtsman was Mr E. C. Wheeler, formerly of Devonport dockyard, who had been employed at the Roodee shipyard since 1858. The prospectus noted that '... the Directors have been enabled to secure the whole property at a valuation, the proprietor receiving the whole of the purchase money in shares. A minimum profit of 10% is calculated upon all estimates for work to be undertaken, the subscribers may confidently contemplate dividends of at least 20% per annum on the capital invested.'

In 1862 Nathaniel Cox took a ten-year lease on the Roodeye yard from the city of Chester at a rent of £15 per annum, the frontage on the river running westwards from the railway viaduct for 116 yards, and inland alongside the railway for 48 yards. The rent was to be paid in two half-year instalments and all machinery and erections on site were to be removed at termination.

In February 1862, the RISB put an advert in *The Times*[13] saying that they were prepared to enter into contracts for building iron steam and sailing vessels of all sizes and every description of wrought iron work. Enquiries could be made to either the Secretary at Gracechurch Street in London, or to Nathaniel Cox, the resident director at the yard in Chester. Clearly opportunities for the yard were not quite as 'brilliant' as anticipated a year earlier.

In September 1863 Edward Cole Wheeler left his job as manager of the shipyard and was presented with a silver tea service subscribed to by the workforce of 300. Mr Brocklebank, his successor as yard manager, gave the testimonial and said that they wished to convey the great esteem in which he had been held by them for upwards of five years. It was clear therefore that Mr Wheeler had been in the yard's employ since 1858, probably arriving after George Cram's departure. In his reply to the assembled company, Wheeler said that he had always found disputes could be settled amicably; many yards had endured strikes but this one avoided it. He left the yard to take up an appointment as a surveyor to Lloyd's British and Foreign Registry.

Edward Cole Wheeler had clearly played a very important part in keeping the yard operating for the previous five years, particularly as Nathaniel Cox spent a lot of time living in Aberdyfi, possibly for health reasons. Born in Torpoint in Cornwall, the son of Thomas Wheeler, a dockyard shipwright, and Emma Ann (née Cole), Edward may have had personal reasons for deciding to move north to Chester in 1858. In 1851, both he and his father were working at Devonport dockyard, but he also went to sea with the merchant service, gaining his First Mate's ticket at Torpoint in September 1854. After leaving the Roodee yard he worked as surveyor to Lloyd's Register of Shipping, based at Liverpool, for at least 28 years, until sometime after 1891. By 1871 he was living in Tranmere with his wife and six of his children. In 1881, his eldest son, also Edward C. Wheeler, then aged 16, was following in his footsteps and was an apprentice engine fitter, but by 1889 had gained his Master's Ticket and as Captain Ted Wheeler, became the Superintendent of Pilotage at Liverpool for many years. There were two pilot boats named *E. C. Wheeler* after him. There is no doubt that maritime matters were very much in the blood of the important people involved in shipbuilding on Deeside, in this case for at least three generations.

John Brocklebank who took over the yard as manager in 1863, had been born in Lancashire in about 1840, the son of a timber merchant. In 1861 he was only 21 and was a draughtsman at the shipyard in Chester, and was therefore only 23 when he took the job as manager.

Business seems to have been thriving at this time and the Roodee Iron Shipbuilding Co. patented two inventions related to dry docks. Firstly, in July 1862, the *London Gazette* recorded the granting of a patent '... to Daniel Lancaster Banks of the RISC Ltd of N$^{o.}$ 17 Gracechurch Street, London, for the invention of a new method of constructing a portable coffer dam or apparatus for facilitating operations under water, in the water, or out of the water and apparatus connected therewith.'[14] Banks, the son of a retired mariner, was living in Toxteth Park in Liverpool at the time of the patent. Aged 42, he was described in the census of 1861 as a 'millwright and engineer'. On 11th December 1863[15] a further patent was granted to him '... for the invention of a method of construction of a portable sectional drydock and apparatus connected therewith.'

1862 saw the launch of the *Robinson Crusoe* the first of two iron, full-rigged ships at the Roodee yard for the Liverpool owner, James Beazley. She was launched by Mrs Wheeler on 22nd November and had originally been ordered by Mr M. I. Wilson of Hargreaves Buildings Liverpool for the East Indies trade, but he had sold her on to Mr Beazley, a Liverpool merchant. She was described as having the three lower masts and bowsprit of iron, and the lower yards of steel. The iron masts also acted as ventilators for the hold of the ship, having an inlet for air at the head and a delivery for same at the heel. Among the guests on the launch platform that day,

Plate 23: The *Roodeye* and *Robinson Crusoe.*

were Nathaniel Cox, his father George and his brother Henry and his wife. This may well suggest that the other members of the Cox family were financially supporting the venture. Also present were a Mr Andrew Dunn, a director of RISB (together with his wife), Mr J. Ramsden and Mr J. Crowder from the firm of Rose & Crowder of London. The latter two had been invited to the launch because, in addition to having three iron sailing ships on hand, the RISB was building a 'large parallel lift', or floating dock, to a design with lifting arrangements patented by Rose & Crowder. The construction of this floating dock no doubt followed the granting of patents to Daniel Lancaster Banks, engineer of the Roodee Iron Shipbuilding Company. Quite how he fitted in with the day to day operation of the shipyard is not clear. He died in Liverpool in 1869 at the relatively young age of 53.

The floating dock constructed at Chester was to be erected in the London docks where dry dock accommodation was much in need at this time. The dock was 100' in length x 60' broad x 17' deep. The dock was a rectangular iron vessel, or pontoon, of proportionate dimensions, designed for lifting and carrying vessels of any size. The arrangements for lifting the dock after the vessel had floated on it were very simple; the dock was lowered or sunk by admitting water to the required depth for floating over it the ship that was to be lifted. Once the ship had been properly placed and shored over the blocks, water equal to the weight of the ship was pumped out of the pontoon thereby raising the ship. After the vessel had been repaired, water was again admitted to the pontoon which then sank and the vessel floated off. The rapid action of this system of dock could be completed in 15–30 minutes. A working model of the dock was exhibited in Class 12 of the International Exhibition was awarded honourable mention for the novelty and simplicity of its design.[17] It is unclear whether the floating dock ever reached London.

In February 1863 the *Robinson Crusoe* was registered with the Liverpool Underwriters Registry for iron vessels, then in January 1864 the *Roodee* was registered. They were similar ship-rigged vessels of around, 1,116 tons, bm, 200' loa x 34' beam x 23' depth of hold, fitted with two bulk holds.

At the launch of the *Roodee* at the end of September 1863, Mr Brocklebank, the manager of the works, gave the order 'Down daggers' and the christening was performed by Mrs Beazley. For the *Chronicle* reporter at this event the most important feature of the vessel was the figurehead which represented the successful jockey John Wells who had ridden Sir Joseph Hawley's horse Asteroid, the winner of the Chester Cup at the last spring meeting (at the famous Roodeye racecourse) —in colours of a cherry jacket and a black cap.[18] After the launch and the luncheon, toasts were proposed to the owners, James Beazley (the principal owner) and Nicholas Duckworth. In his response, Mr Brocklebank proposed the health of these two gentlemen and apologised for the absence of Nathaniel Cox, again due to ill health.

In a 1925 article , F. C. Beazley wrote,[19]

> Another of Mr Beazley's ships was the *Roodee*, 1036 tons, built of iron by the RISC and employed in the India trade. While she has no special place to her credit, she is notable as having been launched, probably sideways [unlikely], on the River Dee and also for what is probably one of the most extraordinary occurrences in the annals of British shipping. She was scuttled, on fire, at Manila in 1875 in 12 fathoms of water and sold for 70 dollars. Four years later, she was thrown up by an earthquake into 2 or 3 fathoms, when her cargo was found to be little damaged.'

The *Robinson Crusoe* did not have a lengthy career either, going missing when homeward bound to Liverpool in 1872. Identifiable wreckage was found off St David's Head.

In 1863 two ship-rigged iron, sailing vessels were completed for Couborough Boyd, merchants of Liverpool. The *West* was commenced in 1862, launched on 6th April 1863 by Mrs Couborough. The yard had been thrown open to the public at 11 a.m. and at one o'clock there was sufficient water to send her down the ways with the two steam tugs the *Test* and the *Cymro* in attendance. According to the reporter for the *Chester Record*, '... people gathered on both sides of the river and some were immersed by the swell and baptised by immersion.[20] At the time the reporter observed that there were five other vessels on the stocks besides an immense floating dock for use on the Thames and noted that the yard employed upwards of 700 people. A month later, in May, she was registered. The *Chester Record* carried another report, presumably by the same journalist, who had been invited to make the voyage aboard the *West* from the Dee to the Mersey.[21] By this time she was lying at the Cheese Stage, attended by the tugs *Tiger* and *Test*. The invited guests had great difficulty boarding the vessel up a ladder from a floating stage in the river. and were accompanied by Messrs Cox and Brocklebank (the temporary manager of the yard).

This report is particularly interesting because it recounts the *West* meeting a schooner under full sail off Saltney as she was making her way upriver, and then overtaking the tug *Cymro* which was towing two outward bound schooners. The *West* also met four further vessels, all under full sail and bound for Chester. In its canalised section the river Dee is extremely narrow and today it is hard to imagine how a sailing ship under tow could pass these other vessels without incident. It also demonstrates the great skill of the mariners of the time. During the voyage to the Mersey the guests toured the vessel-holds, coal ballast in the stem, upper masts lashed on deck for fitting at Liverpool and the crews quarters which were described by Captain Wylie as the most comfortable he had seen in any ship he had served. After passing Hilbre, the weather got rougher and the Liverpool pilot took over from the Dee pilot. Remarkably, when the Rock Light was in sight, a boat approached and a ladder was lashed to the ship's side and a Lloyd's inspector came aboard and she dropped anchor. All the passengers got off the same way onto the tug *Tiger* and were taken to Woodside from where they could make their way back to Chester by train.

*West* sailed for her owners for almost six years, but after leaving New York on 4th February 1869 she was sadly not heard of again.

Her almost identical sister, the *North-East* was 193' in length and 998 tons burthen, with two bulk holds, but she too did not have a long career. In December 1872, on a voyage from Manila to New York, she had been running by dead-reckoning for several days when the master altered course to the north, only to go aground on the Cape of Good Hope and become a total loss.

Financial matters finally came to a head in December 1863 when, in the Court of Chancery it was reported that,

> In the matter of the Roodee Iron Shipbuilding Company Ltd., and in the matter of the Companies Act 1862, by an order made by the Master of the Rolls in the above matter, dated 5th day of December 1863 on the petition of Nathaniel Cox of the Roodee Iron Works at Chester in the County of Chester, Ship Builder, it was ordered that the said RISB Co be wound up by this Court under the provision of the Companies Act of 1862. The application was made by Neal & Martin of Liverpool, solicitors for the Petitioner.[16]

Was this another case of a shipbuilder trying to expand too quickly without the necessary financial backing?

The end of shipbuilding at the Roodee yard did not come until the completion of three more vessels in the following year. In 1864, the full-rigger *Cheshire* was completed for Boult, English & Brandon of Liverpool, but she was sadly lost on her maiden voyage to Calcutta in 1865. Near Madeira she had been spoken to by another vessel, the *Inkerman*, and reported 'All well', but she was never seen again.[22]

Next was the barque *Delmira,* a vessel which was to have the longest career of any of the iron sailing vessels built at Chester. She was ordered in April 1863 by Thomas Henry Ismay, as managing owner (12/64ths), the principal shareholder being James Hainsworth, a Liverpool merchant with 40/64ths. Only 134' in length and 380 tons burthen, she had a varied career until 1896, a remarkable 32 years. In 1867 the she was one of five vessels bought by Thomas Henry Ismay when the rival White Star Line, owned by Wilson and Cunningham, was struggling financially. In the closing days of 1867, Henry Threlfall Wilson sold the goodwill, the name and the famous flag to T. H. Ismay for £1,000. Almost immediately, White Star was back in business with iron ships on the Liverpool–Australia run, much to the chagrin of James Baines and his reduced Black Ball Line. In 1870, the *Delmira* was running between Liverpool and South America. By 1872, however, Ismay sold off his sailing vessels as using steamers on long voyages became achievable, and she was sold to Sumner & Benn of Melbourne, Australia.

At the time of her loss in 1896, she had passed to the ownership of Messrs Grice, Somers & Co. of Melbourne and was under the command of Captain Frederick A. Hutchinson. Her loss has been extensively recorded. She had been bound from Bluff, New Zealand to Malden Island, in ballast to load guano for Dunedin. By this time in her career she had been re-rigged as a three-masted schooner. Until Monday night, 7th December 1896, she had experienced light winds and was off the Banks Peninsula. The wind then veered to the south and brought her off Cape Palliser. At 8 p.m. on the 8th the wind dropped when the vessel was close inshore. A heavy sea swell then sprang up gradually carring the *Delmira* into the land. The master tried to wear the ship round, but in the absence of wind failed and she continued to drift until 10 p.m. when she struck, bow first, on a reef off Te Kaukau, two miles from White Rock in the vicinity of Cape Palliser. The following morning, her bottom was ripped open and the ship became a total wreck. When she struck, the boats were got out and fully provisioned. The captain and chief officer remained on board while the crew in the boats stood by. The steamer *Kahu* passed the wreck early the next morning and took them all on board. The subsequent Court of Enquiry found that the master did not make sufficient allowance, when crossing the Cook Strait, for the inset of the current, but that he had subsequently done all he could to try to save the vessel, and probably would have done so if the wind had not failed. The Court returned his certificate and made no order as to costs.[23] This was a sad end to a fine sailing vessel which could not have occurred almost any further from her birthplace.

One further iron sailing vessel was to be completed at the Roodee Yard, again in 1864. The barque *Terpischore* was completed for David Attwool of Liverpool, William McCormick of Dublin and Richard Cottew of Egremont (and Kingstown). By 1868, the 32 shares owned by David Attwool had passed to Samuel Gale, her master. Most of her career seems to have been spent in the west coast of South America trade. At 528 tons burthen and 154' 6" in length, she was a smaller vessel than some of the earlier vessels. She came to grief in January 1870 when, after sailing from Buenos Aires to Valparaiso, she was wrecked at Cape Corrientes, about 100 miles south of Buenos Aires. The point where she struck was an area of quicksand but the crew managed to save themselves. The loss was not recorded in the Register until 1876.

By February 1864 legal action had commenced and the affairs of RISB were being wound up in the Court of Chancery. It was reported that the debts of Nathaniel Cox were £13,056 (£1.48m at today's prices), contracted as guarantee for goods supplied to the Company. Mr Justice Thring stated that 'The assets are doubtful and depend upon the validity or otherwise of a mortgage deed of the shipbuilding yard and machinery which was given by the bankrupt two months previous to his bankruptcy as security for the sum of £15,000 advanced to him by a relative.'[24] A further interesting legal case developed in early 1864 involving the famous Holt family of Liverpool and Thomas W. Ismay, managing owner of the *Delmira* which had been ordered from RISB in April 1863 at a contracted price of £6,400. (£729,600 in 2016). By October, Ismay contended that the vessel had not been fully plated as agreed, and therefore he was not liable for the stage payment of £500, particularly as he had already loaned RISB money to complete the vessel. Nathaniel Cox was declared bankrupt on 5th December 1863.

One assumes that the Holt family must also have provided a mortgage to Nathaniel Cox/RISB at some time in order to keep the yard going. As we have seen, the Cox family had originally hailed from Nottingham, whilst the Holt family originally came from Rochdale. It is likely that Nathaniel grew up in Liverpool with George Holt Jnr (born 1824) of Lamport & Holt, and Alfred Holt (Blue Funnel) who had been born 1829. In 1828, with both families living in Liverpool, there was a family connection as there is a record of Nathaniel's sister being engaged to William Holt, an elder brother of George and Alfred.

The Holt v Ismay case was heard in the Assize Court in Liverpool in April 1864 and the jury found that Ismay was not liable for the stage payment of £500. The case was referred to the Court of the Queen's Bench and was heard in June 1864; again the judgement was in favour of Ismay.[25]

Also in April 1864 the Court of Chancery called all creditors of the RISB to contact Edward Crosland, solicitor of Neal & Martin of 21 Harrington Place Liverpool, the official liquidator of the said company. Legal arguments concerning the failure of the RISB were ito continue until 1869.

On 7th November 1864 there was a hearing at the Liverpool Bankruptcy Court where Mr Rae, solicitor for T. H. Ismay made an application to be awarded damages for the costs that his client had incurred in paying for the vessel (the *Delmira*) to be completed. The judge directed that the damages should be assessed in the Court of the Queen's Bench in an action which Mr Ismay was the plaintiff and the assignees of the bankrupt were to be the defendants.[26]

As with all bankruptcies, there was legal action taking place on many fronts. In February 1864, in a further case at the Bankruptcy Court, the solicitors for the widow of Nathaniel Cox's father, George, who had died in 1860, sought to recover £10,000 from Nathaniel which his father had leant to the business partnership between George Lissant Cox (his father), George Frederick Cox (brother) and Nathaniel, which had been dissolved in1856. It was resolved that the bankruptcy of Nathaniel Cox did not mean that the money was still owed to his creditors.[27]

During his time as Managing Director of RISB it is likely that Nathaniel Cox wished to enjoy the life of a wealthy, propertied business man. As well as the estate at Ynysymaengwyn, he also leased Wepre Hall near Connah's Quay, only twelve miles from Chester, and in January 1864 there was an advertisement for the auction sale of the contents of Wepre Hall, whilst in March that year a further auction was held on the Ynysymaengwyn estate, '... including a waggonette, phaetons and a pair of handsome match grey ponies.'[28] Wepre Hall was not blessed with good fortune during its later existence. In August 1889 it was leased by Daniel Adamson, the famous engineer who was the man who championed the building of the Manchester Ship Canal. Sadly, he died aged 71 in January 1890. The Georgian Wepre Hall was abandoned after being used by the army during the Second World War and was demolished in the 1960s.

No vessels were built at the yard after 1864. D. P. Branigan[29] says that there was a slump in the U.K. shipbuilding industry at this time and in 1870 the land was sold by Chester City Council to extend the gasworks, an enterprise that was to remain on the site until the1980s.

In February 1865 the *Liverpool Mercury* reported that Nathaniel Cox '... has set himself up as a shipbroker for the sale and purchase of iron ships and steamers at 19 Brunswick St.' but there is no further information on this venture. By 1871, aged 53, he was living with the Pierce family in Machynlleth, described as an agent, while his wife, Mary, was living in Bangor as a 'powder merchant and wife' with the younger children. Nathaniel died in July 1897, aged 77, whie living at New Quay in Cardiganshire. His son, Llewellyn, a medical superintendent, was granted probate. Mary died in 1905, aged 87, having lived in the asylum at Denbigh for number of years.

### *Part Two: William Bishton and William Parkes*

This final chapter of shipbuilding at Chester would not be complete without reviewing the building of wooden vessels at Crane Wharf beween 1855 and 1870, principally by William Bishton and William Parkes. To date, little has been written about the wooden shipbuilders who operated on Crane Wharf in this period, but between them they built at least 22 schooners and smaller vessels as well as one larger vessel. The situation as to who built which vessels is confused by the building during this time of single vessels at Crane Wharf by Thomas Hughes and William Allsup, and several vessels by Edward Walker of leadworks fame.

In 1855, even before the final demise of George Cram, the first of at least seven two-masted schooners built by William Bishton was launched. The wooden schooner *British Oak* remained in Bishton ownership until 1866, but by 1872 she was owned by Charles and Sarah Davison of Connah's Quay.

Plate 24: Looking upstream towards Crane Bank at the turn of the nineteenth century. One of the Crane Bank building slipways can be seen on the left.

At the end of February 1857 a serious accident that occurred in Mr Bishton's shipyard was recorded in the *Chronicle*:

> On Wednesday last an accident of a very serious nature occurred by which several persons received severe, and some almost fatal injuries. Soon after returning from dinner, fifteen men and boys were engaged in carrying a piece of timber, weighing 6 cwt called a 'pall bit', up the gangway to a schooner now building in the yard and had got nearly on board when one of the men thought the gangway was cracking under him. He cried out and all hands swerved to the other side when the 'pall bit' fell off their shoulders and the sudden movement of the men shifted the gangway and they all tumbled to the ground in a heap. All of them got up, but two, Edward Price and Thomas Gibson, who were seriously injured, but most of the persons were injured more or less. Price and Gibson were taken to the Infirmary where the extent of their injuries has scarcely yet been discovered. Price fell with his head in contact with a lamp of iron and has a dangerous laceration of the skull and concussion of the brain and Gibson has received an internal hurt, the nature of which has not yet been ascertained. Several others are out-patients at the Infirmary suffering from sprains, cuts and bruises.[30]

The schooner under construction at the time of the accident was probably the *Hagar* which Bishton definitely built in 1857, and which was named after his eldest daughter. She was a 122 ton schooner, 87' 6" in length, initially owned by Bishton himself until 1863/4 when she was transferred to the New Quay registry and owned by Evan Jones of Newcastle, Cardiganshire and traded to Malaga. Hagar was and still is a most unusual girl's name. In the Old Testament, Hagar, or Agar, is an Egyptian slave girl who was the surrogate mother of Abraham's child, Ishmael, when his wife Sarah was thought to be barren. Certainly an unusual choice of name for your eldest daughter, born in Dudley in 1821.

The *Chester Chronicle*[31] reported the launch of the *Hagar* (or *Agar*) in May 1857, as follows:

> A few days ago a handsome schooner of 125tons register was launched from the yard of Mr Bishton in this city. Serious doubts were entertained as to the safety of launching, owing to the height of the ground above the river, but the skilful arrangement of Mr Henry Ball, foreman of the yard enabled the vessel to safely plunge into her proper element. She was christened the *Agar* by Mr William Bishton, the younger (he was only 6 years old at the time) and as she sits in the water she looks a remarkably trim and handy craft. Her real burthen is about 230 tons, length 36', beam 21' 8", drawing 7' aft and 5' 2" fwd. After the launch the hands of the establishment, with several friends, dined together at the White Lion Hotel and we trust that shipbuilding under such circumstances may long flourish in Chester.

Only one further schooner can definitely be attributed to Bishton in this period, the *City of Chester*, built in 1858. She survived until April 1898 when she was stranded near Carmel Head on a voyage from Swansea to Mostyn with a cargo of burnt ore.

In 1859, the name William H. Parkes first appears as a shipbuilder in Chester. He was the son of Joseph Parkes who, in 1841, aged 30, was a boatbuilder in Wolverhampton. By 1851, William Parkes, aged 18, together with his mother and father, were living at Canal Wharf in Chester. Joseph was then described as a 'Boat Inspector' and his eighteen year old son as a 'Boatbuilder.' Ten years later, the census described William as a 'journeyman boatbuilder', aged 27, living in Chester with his parents. The first vessel attributed to Parkes is the schooner *Eclipse* of 1859.

After that, there are a further five schooners which he built by 1863, after which his name does not appear as a shipbuilder at Chester. These five schooners included vessels for the Reney, Davison, Coppack and Bennett families, all Shotton and Connah's Quay-based owners at that time.

One of these five vessels was the two-masted schooner *Hannah Coppack* of 1861, built for J. Coppack who was also her master. She traded round the British coast for the next sixteen years. In 1869, and again in 1872, she is recorded making voyages with bricks and fire clay from Connah's Quay to Belfast. In March 1877, a John Morris Jnr was found guilty of unlawfully piloting the vessel into Rye. In August of that year, she was reported as being ashore near Scarborough on a voyage from Sunderland to Dartmouth with a cargo of coal and had started to fill with water.[32]

In April 1862, the *Chester Chronicle* announced the launching from the 'Dee Bank Shipbuilding Co.' (William Parkes) of the *Magnet*, a beautiful coppered vessel of 550 tons burthen.[33] She was the largest vessel to be built at the Dee Bank/Bishton/Parkes yard at Crane Bank. The christening ceremony was very nicely carried out by Miss Mary Ann Parkes and the launch itself was successful, but owing to the negligence of the pilot in not letting go the bow anchor that was prepared to bring the vessel up, she came in violent contact with the opposite bank, smashed the rudder, the replacement of which was estimated to cost £100. She was intended for the West Indies trade and classed A1 for 10 years, but was destined never to appear in Lloyd's Register under this name.

It may be a coincidence, but a vessel called the *Florie* was also listed in the *Liverpool Ship Registers* as having been built at Chester in April 1862, but no builder's certificate is recorded. She was a square-sterned barque of 273 tons under deck loa 117' x 24' beam, first owned by Samuel Wylde of Runcorn, a corn merchant and miller, who was only 32 at the time of her purchase. The Registration was dated 3rd September 1862. Assuming that the *Florie* and the *Magnet* are one and the same vessel, she did not have a very succesful start to her career. Following the rudder incident on launching, she sailed from the Mersey for Montevideo with a general cargo, and on 25th October the *Lancaster Gazette* reported that the *Mary*, a Fleetwood fishing smack, had fallen in with the barque *Florie* off Duddon Sands in a disabled state. The master of the fishing vessel could not get aboard the *Florie* because of the heavy sea raging, but returned and led the barque to a safe anchorage off Fleetwood. She was later towed into the port by a steam tug. One cannot help but think that she set off on her maiden voyage with an inexperienced crew. She stayed with Samuel Wylde until 1867 when she was advertised for sale, the advert stating that '... she sails remarkably fast and has delivered at this port 444 tons of nitrate from the West Coast (of South America) and is now discharging her general cargo at Queens Dock.'[34] Despite the suggestion of her being a fast sailer, in 1865 she had taken 125 days from Iquique to Liverpool laden with nitrate of soda. It also stated that she had been caulked and re-sheathed in yellow metal in 1866. She was later sold to T. Maxwell and continued in the South American trade until just before her loss when she was sold to T. King & Son.

In 1871 the *Florie* was again in the headlines when her master, Captain Hicks, rescued the three surviving crew from the Aberdeen barque, *Mary Davidson,* on 20th September. The latter had been wrecked on one of the Jason Islands in the Falklands, in Lat 50.59 S, Long 61.28 W on 24th August. The other crew had perished through exposure and want. Captain Hicks was presented in 1872 with a binocular by the Board of Trade for this humane act of seamanship.

The *Florie* met her end in December 1874 in Cape Colony. It was reported that she, with a part discharged general cargo, together with the *Compage* a British schooner, the *Western Star*, a British barque, the *Coquette*, a British barque, and the

Plate 25: The wooden barque *Kaskelot.*

*Verulam*, a British barque from Penang, were all wrecked at East London.[35]

In June 2016 when the author was checking some of *Florie's* details in the Maritime Museum archives in Liverpool, berthed in the Canning dock was the visiting wooden barque, the *Kaskelot,* built in 1948. Although little bit bigger, at 153' loa, rounding the Horn in such small vessels with such tall masts and no engine seems unthinkable! The *Florie* was the only three-masted wooden sailing vessel, to have been built at Chester after the *Earl of Chester* in 1844.

In February 1863, for reasons unknown, William Parkes set up on his own at nearby Ellesmere Port.[36] This move may have been brought about by the launch disaster with the *Magnet* which was a much larger vessel than the others he had tried to build at the Bishton yard, or perhaps William Bishton had sacked him?

> A shipyard and premises, together with use of the patent slip, were leased to a boatbuilder, William Parkes, son of Joseph Parkes the Shropshire Union Canal Company Boat Inspector.

Parkes had previously managed the Dee Bank Shipbuilding Yard on the Crane at Chester, and built mainly flats, barges and canal boats in his Ellesmere Port yard, including Shropshire Union narrow boats, but he also built there four small, wooden two-masted tops'l sailing schooners. In 1864 he built the *Lorn* of Lancaster and in 1865 the *JCR* and the *Quickstep*. Two more were laid down, but only the 60 ton *Fanny Durant* was completed and registered at Liverpool in 1866 (a picture of this vessel is on the cover of Waterways Journal, N°. 15[36]).

In June 1866 William Parkes went bankrupt and the other hull was sold to be completed by others. By the time of the 1871 census, Parkes was living in West Derby, Liverpool, and was described as a 'shipbroker'. At the time of his death in Liverpool in 1894, aged 60, he was described as a 'ship and insurance broker'.

In 1863 Walker Parker built their last vessel at the Crane, the *Constance*, a two-masted schooner of 70 tons, which survived until 1875 when she was lost in the North Sea. Most of the Walker Parker seagoing vessels were sold by the company in 1870, when the land and buildings they leased at the Crane were also probably given up.

William Bishton re-appears again as a builder at Chester in 1865 with the *Daisy* constructed for the Davisons through 1866–7 while the last vessel, the *Imperial*, was completed in November 1868, also for Davison of Connah's Quay. During the period 1865–70, with the departure of William Parkes from the Dee Bank Shipbuilding Yard for Ellesmere Port, Edward Sanders was brought in as manager. Seemingly William Bishton rarely appeared at the Chester premises during the period, possibly because his various other businesses in the West Midlands were struggling financially, and he faced bankruptcy proceedings in 1868, 1871 and again in 1873.[37]

Edward Sanders had been born in about 1803 in Appledore, Devon. By 1841, aged 38, he was a shipbuilder living with his wife and six children by the dock in Bridgwater, Somerset. His eldest son, aged 14, was described as a 'sailmaker'. In 1851 he was living in Toxteth Park, Liverpool, employed as a shipbuilder with his son, John (18), also a shipbuilder, and another son, William (16), was recorded as being an 'apprentice shipbuilder'. The Sanders family certainly kept on the move and by 1861, aged 56, he was living off Bute Street in Cardiff with his second wife and daughter, Mary, aged nine. By 1865 he had arrived in Chester, where he was still living in 1871, employed as a 'shipwright', although iron shipbuilding on the river Dee in Chester had finished the previous year. Perhaps it was he who completed the barquentine the *Balogun* in 1870 at Chester, with the support of the shipbuilder William Allsup of Preston? In 1865, Sanders' second wife, Ann, launched the *Rosina* from the yard,[38] whilst his daughter Mary, born in 1852 in Cardiff, launched the schooner *Imperial* in November 1867, from the 'Dee bank Shipyard' as it was still known '... for an enterprising shipowner, James Fisher.'[39] No further information has been found about the career of the *Rosina*, although the press did say at the launch that she was named '*pro tem*'.[38]

By 1881, Edward Sanders and his wife were back living in Liverpool and was described as a 'retired shipbuilder'. He died, aged 79, in Bridgewater Street in Toxteth in 1883.

Although most of the Chester-built wooden schooners of the period 1855–67 period can be attributed to either Parkes or Bishton, the smaller sloops and flats built there during this period cannot be readily assigned to a particular builder. However, the Black Country connection, the canal related links and the similarity of vessels and their owners suggests that their businesses were operated in association and vessels built on the same site. Perhaps William Parkes was the manager on site in Chester for William Bishton, until he went to Ellesmere Port on his own account, and was replaced in Chester by Edward Sanders. Throughout the existence of the yard it seems likely that William Bishton held the lease of the site and provided the finance for building the vessels.

One interesting issue which appears several times in the Chester press between 1866 and 1870 are the claims by apprentices for non-payment in the Bishton yard. In April 1870 there were two cases, almost certainly a reflection of the financial problems that had developed in the various Bishton enterprises. It was reported that he was charged with refusing to pay Edward Mellish the 12s wages due to him.[40] Sanders appeared in court and an order was made for the payment of 9s which it appeared was the actual amount due. Later in the month, William Bishton was summoned for not teaching John Morrisey his trade.[40] Morrisey had been apprenticed in 1865, but the paper reported that his wages had not been paid, even though 11 apprentices under a foreman called Sanders, had carried on the business. John Morrisey said that he never saw his indenture after Sanders took over, and the complainant said he had rarely seen Bishton at the yard and that things were pretty much left to Sanders. In November 1869, it was stated that the schooner *Excellent* had been launched, which had perhaps taken eighteen months to build, but that the greater part of the work was done by the apprentices, with one or two journeymen working on her towards the finish. In reply to the bench, Mr Churton, a solicitor, said that he would do what he could to assist the lads in the way of getting them a Certificate of Servitude, something the Mayor suggested would be tantamount to a discharge on an indenture.

William Bishton lived all his life in the West Midlands. By the age of 20, in 1841, he was living in Dudley, already married with three children, and was described as a 'Canal Agent'. In 1848 the Birmingham & Liverpool Canal Company let out the haulage of barges by horse to a contractor, the same William Bishton, and he continued to hold the contract until 1866 by which time the SUR&CC were in charge and were showing interest in haulage by steam tugs on the main line of their canal.[41] Already, in 1863, Bishton was operating two steam tugs, the *Test* and the *Magnet* on the Liverpool to Chester trade and later that year the tugs were purchased by SUR&CC.

By 1851, William Bishton was living in Cannock Road in Wolverhampton, had a 300 acre farm and was describing himself as a 'farmer and railway contractor.' In 1861 he moved to Park Lane Farm in Wednesfield and was living there with his wife,

Priscilla, and six of their children. His business interests were very extensive, but in 1868, when he filed for bankruptcy, he was described as a 'Timber merchant, Boat builder, Butcher and Provision dealer also carrying on a business at Netherton near Dudley as a Chain tester and wharfinger, also carrying on a business in Chester as a shipbuilder and also at Rumbelows in Wednesfield and of Lapley, both in Stafford as a Farmer, Dealer and Chapman.'[42] He was discharged from bankruptcy in May 1869 and was able to continue with some of his businesses. In the 1871 census he was described as a 'timber merchant' and he continued as such, and as a 'general dealer', for the next ten years until his death in 1882 at the age of 63.

The last merchant vessel to be completed on the Dee at Chester in 1870 was officially built by William Allsup, a well-known shipbuilder based in Preston. The *Balogun*, a 201-ton barquentine is clearly shown in the Register as having been built at Chester, although Allsup built no other vessels there.[43] It is conceivable that she was on the stocks at the time that William Bishton filed for bankruptcy in 1868, and was completed for Kidd. In 1873 she was recorded as running between Liverpool and West Africa. By 1877 she was owned by Thomas Stanley Rogerson, who continued to operate her until 1883/4. She is recorded as missing, supposed lost, after sailing from Old Calabar on 13th May 1885 and was never heard of again.

Merchant shipbuilding on the tidal Dee at Chester finally ended in 1870, never to return.[44] Over 250 vessels were built on the Dee at the Crane Wharf and Roodee yards, many of the larger ones for Liverpool owners and merchants who no doubt were attracted over the years by better prices and the availability of shipyard capacity.

Notes

1. *Transactions of the Lancashire & Cheshire Historical Society,* 1941.
2. See www./liv.ac.uk.cmi/books/florida. html.
3. *Chester Chronicle,* 30th May 1857.
4. Extract from www. humberpacketboats.co.uk/packetboats.
5. *Chester Chronicle,* 8th August 1857.
6. *London Gazette,* 11th February 1859, regarding 22th July 1858.
7. T. B. Maund, *Mersey Ferries,* Part 1, in Bibliography.
8. Roy Fenton, *Mersey Rovers*, in Bibliography.
9. *Sea Breezes Magazine*, vol. XVII, April 1933–January 1934.
10. Graeme J. Milne, *Trade & Traders in mid-Victorian Liverpool* (Liverpool, 2000).
11. Letter to *Sea Breezes Magazine,* vol. 14 from Captain W. M. Reid, December 1952. He had sighted the

dismasted *Gitana* from aloft on the *Edinburghshire* in April 1896. See also David Walker, *The Hungry Goose Line*.

12. *The Times,* 11th November 1861.
13. *The Times,* 14th February 1862.
14. *London Gazette,* N°. 1892, 18th July 1862.
15. *London Gazette,* N°. 1893, 11th December 1863.
16. Order made by the Master of the Rolls, 5th December 1863.
17. *Chester Chronicle,* 29th November 1862. This article also covers launch of *Robinson Crusoe*.
18. *Chester Chronicle,* 3rd October 1863 and *Cheshire Observer*, 30th October 1863.
19. F. C. Beazley, 'Four Liverpool Clippers', in *Transactions of the Lancashire & Cheshire Historical Society,* 1925.
20. *Chester Record,* 11th April 1863.
21. *Chester Record,* 9th May 1863.
22. D. P. Branigan, 'Launched on the Dee', *Cheshire Life* magazine, September 1971.
23. *New Zealand Shipwrecks,* 4th ed. (1972). See also 'Board of Trade Wreck report, 1897', Port City South website,Wellington, New Zealand.
24. *Liverpool Daily Post,* 13th February 1864.
25. *The Engineer,* 24th June 1864.
26. *Chester Chronicle,* 12th November 1864.
27. *Liverpool Mercury,* 2nd February 1864.
28. *Chester Chronicle,* 5th March 1864.
29. D. P. Branigan article in *Deesider* magazine, July 1975.
30. *Chester Chronicle,* 28th February 1857.
31. *Chester Chronicle,* 16th May 1857.
32. *London Evening Standard,* 27th August 1877.
33. *Chester Chronicle,* 19th April 1862.
34. *Gore's Liverpool Advertiser*, 16th May 1867.
35. *Glasgow Herald*, 6th January 1875.
36. *Waterways Journal*, vol. 15 article by T. Kavanagh on shipbuilding at Ellesmere Port publ by the Boat Museum Society.
37. *London Gazette,* 4th May 1869.
38. *Cheshire Observer,* 4th February 1865.
39. *Cheshire Observer*, 2nd November 1867.
40. *Chester Chronicle,*16th and 30th April 1870.
41. Extract from *The Boat Museum,* No. 81, article by T. Kavanagh.
42. *London Gazette,* 4th May 1869.
43. Liverpool Ship Registers, 1871, MMM RO.
44. No further merchant vessels were built in Chester. However William Roberts built yachts and pleasure craft in various locations; in the Dee Basin and at the Little Roodeye around the turn of the nineteenth century, including the paddle steamer *Firefly* for Assheton Smith. Her engine and paddles can be seen in the Merseyside Maritime Museum.

# 6

## Mining and Shipbuilding in Mostyn and Talacre

Perhaps, surprisingly, relatively few vessels were built on the river Dee nearer to the sea, where one would normally expect deeper water than upstream. In the fifteenth and sixteenth centuries vessels had operated from Mostyn,[1] but there was relatively little activity in the early years of the Industrial Revolution, until 1836 at Mostyn and 1838 at Talacre, when the local landowners and industrialists recognised the benefit of building their own vessels to carry goods to and from their local mines, quarries and other enterprises.

The Eyton family had settled from early times at Maes-y- groes near Cilcain. By the 1840s the family was operating extensive collieries in Flint and John Prys Eyton of Kinsale (Hall) near Mostyn was the first owner of the schooner *Edwen*, built by Edward Eyton at Mostyn in 1840. He in fact built at least seven vessels at Mostyn between 1838 and 1849, most of which were two-masted schooners, including the *Dispatch* of 1843, which is the only vessel built at Mostyn of which there is a known picture, but the image is so poor it is not worth reproducing.[2]

The most famous of the Eyton-built vessels was the *Taliesin*, a wooden, two-masted schooner built in 1842 but, unlike the others, fitted with a steam engine. She is the most interesting vessel to have built by Edward Eyton. Rigged as a schooner and of 74 tons, she was originally a paddle-steamer owned by four members of the Eyton family. John Prys Eyton was the largest subscriber with 28 shares, whilst Edward Eyton of Pentrefynnon, James Eyton of Mold and Robert Eyton of Flint had twelve shares each. She was named after a famous twelfth-century Welsh bard and was almost 93' in length, with an engine room which occupied a length of 29' of her under deck space —a third! In later years she was lengthened to 114' and her engine room then measured 42'. The Eyton family owned a foundry at Mostyn and it was here that they designed a direct connecting type of engine 'combining extraordinary lightness with power and economy of space'.[3] They installed a pair of these 90 h.p. engines in *Taliesin* which was built for the

Mostyn–Liverpool ferry service. The engines each weighed about 15 tons and had long connecting rods, but no beams, and were only about 4' in length, so the cylinders must have been placed directly below the crankshaft. Moreover, this type of engine was suitable for both large steam vessels and shallow draughted river steamers which suggests they straddled the paddle shaft with the guides extending 'steeple-like' above the deck. Although it is not possible to be entirely certain about the engine layout, there is no question that the *Taliesin* was a powerful and fast-sailing steam packet. After her trials in June 1842, it was reported that the boat, which had been constructed rather wide (16' 4") with a view to towing and carrying cargo, and short so as able to turn in a confined space to suit the particular station, averaged a full 10 m.p.h. with upwards of 200 people on board. The newspaper report added that 'a much higher rate of speed will most likely be effected when the stiffness of the new machinery wears off by use.'[4]

The following May there was an eagerly awaited race between this beamy Welsh steamer and the crack Liverpool built paddler *Erin-go-Bragh.* The race was to be run from Liverpool as far as Hoylake, a distance of nine miles, which the unfancied *Taliesin* won by 'a fair mile'. A reporter wrote 'this decisive triumph reflects great credit on Messrs Eyton, the makers of the Welsh built engines of the *Taliesin*, as her hull is by no means so well modified for speed as that of *Erin-go-Bragh*.

The *Taliesin* further added to her growing reputation in late November 1843 when she sailed from Liverpool to Mostyn in the height of a gale and reached her destination in 3¼ hours. She was apparently the only vessel to make passage from the Lancashire port on that day, all other steam vessels which sailed being compelled to beat back for shelter.[5]

The *Taliesin* was lengthened in 1847 but was not destined to stay on the Mostyn service for too long. Perhaps the opening of the Chester–Bangor railway on 1st May 1848, with a station at Mostyn, made the vagaries of tide and the ferry service unattractive when compared with the railway? By this time Chester had been linked to Birkenhead by rail for eleven years. On 9th January 1848 the *Taliesin* was on passage from Liverpool to Rhyl when, near the Point of Ayr, she fell in with the wreck of the schooner *Dasher* of Killough, laden with oatmeal, entirely abandoned by her crew. Captain Hugh Jones of the *Taliesin* got a line aboard and towed her to the bank of the river where she stranded. He reported the affair to his employers, Messrs Eyton Brothers of the South Mostyn Colliery and details were transmitted to the owners of the *Dasher* and the Lloyd's agents in Liverpool. The *Taliesin* then attempted to tow the vessel into Mostyn on the following tide, but in the gutter the *Dasher* got onto one of the banks and could not be moved. Messrs Eyton then tried to save the cargo and eventually the family's own schooner, the *Dispatch,* was loaded with oatmeal worth £150. The remainder was plundered 'by a number of the lower classes which was a disgraceful act'.

While this off-the-cuff attempt at salvage may have been conducted in good faith, the fact that the incident was not reported to Mr Tarleton of Rhyl, the agent for the 'Receiver General of Admiralty droits', resulted in a summons being issued for Captain Hugh Jones and at Newmarket Magistrates Court he was fined £100, but the defence solicitor, Mr Eyton (probably James Eyton of Mold), said that he was a poor, illiterate man and had erred due to ignorance. As a result, the bench said that he could go to prison for twelve months, but would accept six as a suitable punishment. This case was considered by the press to be an important conviction under the Wreck and Salvage Act.[6]

*Taliesin* continued to run between Rhyl, Mostyn and Liverpool with the service regularly advertised, with different departure and arrival times at the two ports, dependent on the tides at Mostyn. In Liverpool, goods were taken on board at New Wall 2-Pier Head.[7] In 1850 she was sold to the Cardiff Steam Navigation Company for service on the Bristol Channel. In May 1858 she began to ply between Cardiff and Burnham-on-Sea following the opening of the Burnham Branch of the Somerset Central Railway.[8] Shareholders of the Somerset Central were informed that '... the great convenience thereby afforded for speedy communication between the West of England and South Wales and for the transmission of the agricultural produce of Somerset to that great market has secured for it a large traffic'.

In June 1853, the *Taliesin* again figured in the press, in one of those infamous incidents of steamboats racing one another and colliding.[9] She was coming up the river Avon in Bristol, approaching the Cumberland Basin, when her master refused to let the *Dart* (an iron paddle steamer built in Bristol in 1849 by G. Lumsell & Co.) overtake. The master put his helm down and, in doing so, the keel of the *Taliesin* caught the bank, canted her round, went stern on into the wall near Acraman's building yard, almost swamping two barges and sending a man overboard, smashing the jib boom and figurehead and ripping up a large portion of the stonework, thus putting the lives of 3–400 people at risk. One of her passengers wrote to the press describing the master's actions 'as shameful in crossing from side to side purposely to get into the suction of the *Dart* which was on the right side of the river.'

She was still running a Cardiff–Burnham service until 1860 when she was sold.[10]

Reverting to our story of the vessels built by the Eytons, Edward Eyton completed the two-masted schooner (also called locally a 'wherry') the *Dispatch* in December 1843. She was also owned by the Eyton family. After the deaths of the remaining Eytons in 1852 and 1856, the vessel passed into the ownership of James Timothy of Flint, a ship's carpenter, in 1858. On 28th October 1866 the wherry was carrying sulphur from Mostyn to Pentre when she foundered a mile off Mostyn with the loss of one of her two crew members.[11]

After the *Eva* in 1849 there do not appear to be any further vessels built by Edward Eyton, although he lived until May 1852. He did not marry, and in 1851 was described as a 'coal master', living in Brynford with his two unmarried sisters and three servants. His brother, Robert, who was born in 1806 and died in 1848 at Holywell, was also unmarried. In November 1849 the estate of Robert Eyton was sold by auction at the White Horse Hotel in Holywell, by order of the administrator of his estate. The assets were in seven lots (see Appendix 10) and included various shareholdings in eighteen different vessels and 3/16 of the shares in the Mostyn Foundry and shipbuilding yard. Of the eighteen vessels, three were those taken over when Sir Edward Mostyn died, and and at least eight of the others were built to the account of the Eyton family in Flint or Mostyn.[12]

In 1855 there was a resumption of shipbuilding on this part of the Dee estuary when Richard Rowlinson completed the three-masted barque *Sea Rover*, 234 tons burthen and109' in length, at Talacre Harbour according to her Liverpool registry. Owned first by Richard Rowlinson himself (who was a Liverpool shipowner and merchant), further references in Lloyd's and other sources say she was 'built at Mostyn'. She was running in the Mediterranean trade in1858–9, but by 1861 had been sold to W. Cliff of Liverpool, and was then trading to the West Indies. By 1863 she had again changed hands and was owned by D. Dymas of Liverpool and was running from Liverpool to Ceylon. She appears to have continued in this trade until the end of the decade when she again changed ownership and was running to the mainland Europe for G. H. Payne. Her entry in *Lloyd's Register* for 1870 is annotated 'wrecked'.

A very similar vessel was built at Mostyn in 1857 but the builder's name is not recorded. The three-masted barque *Orion,* also 109' in length and of 224 tons, was part owned by Elson Pringle of Southport (28/64). Again registered at Liverpool and owned by Pringle & Company in 1858, she was employed in the South American trade, but was sold the next year to S. W. Kelso, but continued trading to the same area and remaining with the same owner until 1868 when her register was marked 'burnt at Paraiba' ( north-east Brazil), 3rd October 1868.

Meanwhile, at Talacre, or most likely the area and site of the later wharf of Point of Ayr colliery, Sir Edward Mostyn, Bt., assisted by his land agent(?) and harbour master, John Dawson, began to seriously build ships. Between 1838 and 1842 they built at least seven vessels, the largest being the two-masted schooner *Fanny* of 125 tons burthen.

Sir Edward was the seventh baronet, but sadly died at the age of 56 in July 1841, just as he was reaching his shipbuilding prime. He was twice married and had thirteen children, but none of them carried on shipbuilding after his death. However, the end of the Mostyn family connection with Talacre did not come until the death in 1912 of Sir Pyers Mostyn, the ninth baronet, and Sir Piers Charles Mostyn, the tenth baronet in 1917, aged only 21, which compelled the trustees to sell the estate. The Mostyn estate is recorded in 1873 as comprising 4,184 acres, including lead mines, limestone quarries and the Point of Ayr Colliery. The Mostyn family had been involved as land owners in the area since William Mostyn (died 1605) had acquired, by his marriage to Anne, daughter of Henry ap Thomas ap Harry of Greenfield, the lands of Basingwerk Abbey.[13]

All the Talacre vessels built were owned 50/50 by Sir Edward and John Dawson, apart from the sloop *Mary* which was completed in 1842, after Sir Edward's death, and was wholly owned by John Dawson. Most of the jointly owned vessels were sold at this time to the Eyton family, including the *Caroline*, a 61 ton schooner, built by John Dawson in 1839, which was sold to John Prys Eyton of Llanerchymor and Robert Eyton of Flint.

Between 1838 and 1857 at least nineteen vessels were built at Mostyn and Talacre as shown in Appendix 2.

Notes

1. D. Thomas, *Hen Longau a Llongwyr Cymru* (Old Ships and Sailors of Wales), Cardiff, 1949.
2. Flintshire Records Office photographic collection PH/15/169.
3. *Chester Chronicle,* 21st January 1842.
4. Terry Kavanagh, 'Some early paddle engines on the Mersey', Liverpool Nautical Research Society, December 2001.
5. *Liverpool Mercury,* 30th November 1843.
6. *Caernarvon & Denbigh Herald*, 24th February 1849.
7. *Caernarvon & Denbigh Herald,* 22nd April 1848.
8. Robin Athill, *Somerset& Dorset Railway (Newton Abbot,* 1967).
9. *Monmouthshire Merlin*, 28th August 1853.
10. *Cardiff Times,* 22nd November 1859.
11. Royal Commission on the Ancient & Historical Monuments of Wales, September 2012.
12. *Chester Chronicle,* 2nd November 1849 and RCAHMW, September 2012.
13. Idloes Owen, 'Who were the Mostyns of Talacre Hall?' *Country Quest* magazine, February 1995.

# 7

# Wooden shipbuilding in Flint

When I first began the research for this book, my initial understanding was that Ferguson, McCallum & Baird had built a few vessels in Flint before moving to Connah's Quay in the early 1860s and that a few vessels were also built there in the mid-nineteenth century by David Jones. In fact, between 1828 and 1865, almost 60 sailing vessels were built in Flint by a variety of builders. Seven different names are listed in Appendix 3 as having built vessels there, which has subsequently made it difficult to determine today who was really responsible for financing and building particular vessels.

Local industry, associated with the Industrial Revolution and the need for imported timber, meant that in the 1830s Flint had become an important outport of the Port of Chester. In 1828, two timber dealers, Michael Parry and John Jones, had premises close to Flint Quay[1] and throughout the 1830s vessels were arriving there direct from Canada with timber cargoes. For example, the snow *Belle Isle* made several calls at Flint at that time. Today, it is hard to believe that vessels sailed from the east coast of Canada directly into Flint gutter and I am convinced that many of them discharged to lighters offshore.

In 1827 Thomas Eyton, a local colliery proprietor at Flint and Mostyn and the father of Edward Eyton who later built vessels at Mostyn (see Chapter 6), established a shipyard in Flint. The local press reported the launching of a new 'wooden schooner rigged flat' on 15th February 1828, named the *Flint Castle*; she was constructed for Thomas Eyton by shipwrights Andrew Green and Edward Evans. The launch was followed by a sumptuous dinner at the Royal Oak Inn. In 1829, Green and Evans built a further vessel for Thomas Eyton, the schooner *Beresford*. These vessels were built for shipping out coal exports from his collieries. It is likely that the name 'Beresford' was chosen because, at around this time, there was a Beresford Eyton who was a navy agent and broker in London who was bankrupted in 1849.

Shipyards in 1828 were not the sophisticated sites we were to see in the later Victorian period. There would have been a simple slipway on the bank of Flint gutter from which a vessel would be launched on a high spring tide. Additional features would have been a sawpit, a steam box, a boiler to provide the steam and maybe a shed. It is almost certain that the yard was sited below the end of the quay, on the east side of the dock and it was probably close to the start of the inlet from the foreshore.[2] In 1828, the dock was no more than 150 yards long from its entrance and a maximum of 40 yards width. It is interesting to note that Eddie Hogan says that 'in 1836 you could go sea bathing at Flint!'[2] The Industrial Revolution changed all that for ever.

No further shipbuilding seems to have taken place for Thomas Eyton after 1830, but in 1840 the brig *Malcolm* was built in Flint by Michael Parry, the local timber merchant and cooper.[1] Evidently in late 1839, he had employed the shipwrights Daniel Ferguson, James Baird and John McCallum, all of whom had come from Rothesay on the Firth of Clyde, and it was they who actually completed the *Malcolm*. On completion, she was classed A1 at Lloyd's for 12 years. Her dimensions have been estimated at 92'–95' in length x 23'–25' beam, with a depth of hold of 15'–16'. For the whole of her working life she was owned by Captain Malcolm McFarlane of Stranraer. At 224 tons 'old measurement' she had an eighteen-year career sailing on deep-sea voyages, for example sailing from Liverpool to Rio in 1845. Her end came in 1858 when she had sailed from London to the West Indies and was wrecked on French Reef, five miles off Key Largo, Florida on the night of 11th September, having previously loaded a cargo of fustic and divi-divi[3] at Rio Hacha by the mouth of the Rancheria river in the northern Caribbean region of Colombia. The wreck was sold at public auction on 16th September for $1,100, a considerable sum of money in 1858.

Today, it is difficult to establish how shipbuilding in Flint was organized during the 1840s; although the three Scottish shipwrights were living in the area, they are not named as shipbuilders until 1852 when they built (and owned) the sloop *Breeze*, a 36' 6" long vessel.

By 1851 ship's carpenter James Baird (34) was living in Castle View, Flint, with his wife Elizabeth, a local girl, born in Halkyn, and their four children.[4] In the same year, his fellow shipwrights Daniel Ferguson (34) and John McCallum (33) were living as lodgers in Prestatyn Village, 13½ miles from Flint. One wonders how they travelled to the shipyard each day – possibly by train as the new Chester to Bangor railway line had opened on 1st May 1848.

Meanwhile other shipbuilders began to appear in Flint. Paton & Company built a few small sloops in 1846–7. Between 1848 and 1851, first Thomas Hughes and then the firm of David Jones & Thomas Hughes, built wooden schooners and wherries. On Thursday, 24th May 1849, Jones & Hughes launched the *Lady Fielding*, a beautiful schooner.[5]

> She was baptized by Miss A. Lloyd, the amiable daughter of John Lloyd Esq of Pantgwyn near Holywell, who struck her with a bottle of good port. At 3 o'clock a most sumptuous and elegant dinner comprising all the delicacies of the season was prepared under the superior management of the worthy hostess, Mrs Edwards of the Oak Hotel for about 30 of the friends of the builders. The Chair was taken by Michael Parry, the vice by Mr Williams, porter agent of Rhyl, supported by Adam Eyton Esq. Whilst the male sex were regaling themselves(?) about 25 ladies sat down to partake of that delightful beverage 'infusion of the Chinese plant', prepared for them by Mrs P. Sanders of Flint.[6]

This report is interesting because it highlights the arrival of affordable tea as a socially acceptable drink for ladies and reminds us of the important influence of Michael Parry and the Eyton family in shipbuilding at the time. The vessel was first owned by Jones & Company.

In 1852, Thomas Mathias built the small schooner *Lady Helena,* again for Michael Parry and S. and C. Davison, a family later to become well-known as Deeside shipowners.

Launching vessels at Flint cannot have been an easy task. Certainly today one wonders how it was ever possible. The schooner *Robin Hood,* built in 1854, featured in a local rhyme quoted by the workmen at the shipyards there the '*Robin Hood* stuck in the mud, but *Little John* sailed straight on.'[7] We know that the *Robin Hood* was owned by James Treweek of the Anglesey shipbuilding family for almost all of her career until she was wrecked near Swanage in 1870, but the *Little John* of the rhyme is a mystery. Maybe the rhyme refers to the smaller (little?) wherry *John & Jane* built in 1848 at Flint by Jones & Hughes, or the 30 ton sloop *John James* built there in 1859. Or was there another schooner of that name which did not have a career long enough to warrant registration?

David Jones was to be of major importance in the expansion of shipbuilding at Flint. He too was a timber merchant and farmer who had grown up in Caerwys, a village 9½ miles away from Flint gutter, and we can assume that the timber import business led to his link with Flint. In 1851, aged 41, he was described in the census as a being a 'Farmer of 34 acres, employing 11 men', and living with his wife and children in North Street, Caerwys.

In 1855, David Jones built (financed the building?) of the square-sterned two masted schooner, *Miss Nightingale*[8] in which he owned 56/64 shares, the other 8/64 being held by John Valentine Harrison. The following year David Jones built the schooner *Kattie Darling* in which he was again a shareholder (24/64) with J. V. Harrison (32/64) and John Foulkes (8/64), a master mariner from Flint. The *Kattie Darling* was subsequently owned for many years by Edward Hughes of Flint (at least from 1872–95), but by 1920 she was registered in Cardigan, and at the time of her loss was owned by Robert Hill of Wicklow.

The *Kattie Darling* had probably the longest career afloat of any of David Jones' vessels, lasting until 1925 when she had a sad demise in the Mersey. According to MD&HB records, on 27th October 1925, after an incident in the river she was 'lifted and placed on Tranmere beach to be sold for breaking up' – for £5! Interestingly, the MD&HB contact at the time of her loss was 75-year old, Richard Ferguson the younger son of Daniel Ferguson, one of the original founders of Ferguson & Baird.[9]

In 1857, the schooner *Denbighshire Lass* was built by David Jones for Jones & Co. and registered in Beaumaris. Not a particularly remarkable vessel, she was to have a long hard life on the Irish Sea that lasted until 1926. By 1881 she had passed into the hands of the Reney family of Connah's Quay, who sold her in 1885 to John Fitzpatrick of Arklow, although the real owner was Kate Tyrell, one of the famous Tyrell shipowning family of Arklow and the first woman to captain a schooner on the Irish Sea. *Denbighshire Lass* was also to become one of the first vessels to fly the Irish Tricolor instead of the Red Ensign in 1921.[10]

Following the death of Kate Tyrell, the vessel was sold to U.K. owners and was lost on 16th March 1926 in an area of the Bristol Channel known as the Smalls. She sprang a leak in worsening weather, with gale force winds, and the crew were forced to abandon ship but were safely rescued by the GWR steamer *Reindeer*.

The trend of taking shares in the vessels David Jones built continued, and in 1859 he built and took all 64 shares in the flat *Price Jones* and 28/64ths of the schooner

*Mary*. In the same year he built the *John James*, a two-masted sloop, again owned by 'David Jones of Caerwys, timber dealer.'[11] He also took shares in the *Wepre Lass* (1860), *Caerwys Castle* (1861) and *Mary Jones* (1863) – Mary was the name of his sister. At the launch of the *Caerwys Castle,* the *North Wales Chronicle* of 4th May recorded that she was built by Ferguson, McCallum & Baird. By the time of his death in 1875 David Jones had moved out of the village of Caerwys to the Plas Cerrig estate, a couple of miles away.

Plate 26: The *Jane Porter.*

It is interesting too to see how those originally involved in farming and the timber business worked together in Flint at this time, both in shipbuilding and shipowning. In 1862 David Jones built the *Jane Porter*, a two-masted topsail schooner for Michael Parry (32/64) and Thomas Porter of Flint (32/64). Sadly she proved to be a poor investment, and was lost with all hands in November of the following year.

Not only did a timber merchant build a vessel for the account of another timber merchant, but in 1856 David Jones built the two-masted schooner *Isabella* for another shipbuilder and 16/64 shares are shown as being jointly owned by Ferguson, McCallum & Baird (FMB). At various times different individual members of FMB were shipowners in their own right. As we have seen, the sloop *Breeze* of

1852 was built by them and owned by Daniel Ferguson and James Baird. In 1858, Ferguson and Baird were the builders and owners of 40/64 of the schooner *Charles Edward*, (believed to be the first Ferguson & Baird vessel built at Connah's Quay) which was lost off Bardsey seven years later. She was owned by Ferguson & Company until 1863/4 when she was sold to Holt & Company who were her owners when she was lost off Bardsey in 1865. In 1859, FMB bought the flat *Margaret* from William Brierley of Parkgate, to be re-sold by them in 1863. Also in 1859 Ferguson & Baird were owners of the flat *St Helen's*. In 1861, FMB were the joint owners of the schooner *Isabella* built by David Jones at Flint in 1856.

Those who were in shipbuilding in Flint for the long term became part of the local maritime fraternity which developed there and, as we shall see later, even more so in Connah's Quay.

Michael Parry who was involved in Flint shipbuilding from 1843 until its final demise 22 years later, died in 1867 by which time his son, Alfred, had become involved in shipowning, taking over the *Alfred* (launched in 1865), the last vessel to be built at Flint, which was in fact built by Michael Parry[12] not David Jones as might have been expected. The following year, Alfred and Thomas Parry of Flint had the two-masted tops'l schooner the *Not Forgot,* built by Ferguson and Baird at Connah's Quay. Of the 56 vessels identified as being built at Flint, 33 were two-masted tops'l schooners.

David Jones also moved his shipbuilding business to Connah's Quay along with Ferguson & Baird, after the shipyard sites on Flint Gutter were gradually appropriated by the adjacent chemical works. David Jones, together with John Hooson, built his first vessel, the *Mag,* at Connah's Quay in 1858.[13]

Sometime in the late 1850s, John McCallum ceased to be involved in shipbuilding and became landlord of the New Anchor Inn on Holywell Road in Flint. Although he took no further part in schooner building, he was to remain in the Deeside area for the rest of his life.

We must remember that vessel ownership during these times was very often shared, each owner usually holding a number of '64ths'. In *Lloyd's Register* and the *Mercantile Navy List* the listed owner is often the manager or company secretary acting on behalf of the major shareholders. He/she may not, however, hold the majority of the 64ths.

In Flint at this time Michael Parry was the driving force behind shipbuilding and other marine related activity. As well as having FMB working for him he also had vessels built by both Jones & Hughes and Thomas Mathias, which poses the question of whether FMB also worked for these other builders? Michael Parry was elected mayor of Flint in 1848 and he was also the local agent for The Fishermen's and Mariners' Shipwreck Society. He also had shares in vessels other than those built at Flint, such as the schooner *Oulton* which had been built in Chester in 1820.

1853 saw the first vessel built in Flint by David Jones on his own. She was the *Britius*, a brig of 243 tons, o.m., loa 92'. On completion, she was also classed A1 for twelve years by Lloyds and owned by Michael Parry. She traded to the Mediterranean and Brazil and was supposedly lost at sea in the winter of 1864/5. She is believed to be the largest vessel to have been built in Flint.

In 1853, during an exceptionally high tide, a tidal wave broke through the embankment and created havoc, inundating all the shipyards and timber yards with 2–3 metres of water, causing an explosion in the local foundry and flooding the lower part of the town. Three vessels loading in the port were sunk. Eddie Hogan thought that the slipways at Flint were made in a trench with a coffer dam which was removed for launching on spring tides, and that the shipyard itself was only 1–1.5m above the high water mark.[1] Looking at Flint Gutter today it is hard to believe that ships were built there or that cargoes were loaded and discharged.

The shipbuilding activity must have taken place on the east bank of Flint Gutter,

Plate 27: Flint Gutter in 2014.

as the west bank consisted of land reclaimed from the river Dee where waste from ore smelting was dumped, later to become the waste tip for the Courtaulds works. In 1971 the author visited the site as Flint dock then lay within the factory site. Asking if there were any employees who still worked there who remembered vessels coming into the dock, I was directed to meet the man in charge of the tip. We set off in my car on an unmade road through a moonscape without vegetation and came down into a hollow (crater?) with a large soakway pipe sitting in the centre. The ends of the pipe had been boarded up and a door was fitted in one end and a stove-pipe chimney protruded through the top. Thinking it might actually be the home of Noddy or his friend, Big Ears, I knocked on the door to find my would-be informant cooking his breakfast with a mate! Indeed he did remember small vessels and barges going into the dock in the 1930s and even during the Second World War. To this day it is the most memorable setting for an interview that I have ever experienced! Now the whole area is green with vegetation and trees and there is little real hint of its lunar past.

No three-masted schooners were built at Flint, they came later with the move to Connah's Quay. Ferguson & Baird appear to have built their first vessel at Connah's Quay as early as 1858, although both Ferguson & Baird and David Jones continued to build vessels at Flint until at least 1864 when David Jones completed the *William Shepherd* a two-masted schooner for the owner of the same name, a firebrick manufacturer from Buckley. Two further two-masted schooners were completed at Flint in 1864, the *Florence Miriam* and the *Kate*,[14] although there is some uncertainty about who actually built them. Astonishingly, the last vessel built at Flint, the schooner *Alfred*, is listed in the registration documents as built by Michael Parry, for himself in 1865; when he died intestate in 1867, the ownership of the vessel passed to his son Alfred Parry of Flint. After 1895 she was owned in Newquay and was lost in 1910 after a collision off the Runnelstone.

By 1861 Daniel Ferguson was married with four children and living at Golftyn, (today part of Connah's Quay) and is recorded in the census as a 'Shipbuilder employing ten men and ten boy apprentices', one of whom was his eldest son, Archibald , then aged 17, an 'Apprentice ship's carpenter'. Similarly, by 1861, James Baird had had nine children, three of whom, Thomas, James and Walter, followed in his footsteps and became ship's carpenters and were to carry on the business into the early twentieth century.

Plate 28: The schooner *Mary Jones* as originally built with two masts.

The last of the vessels built at Flint to remain afloat was the schooner *Mary Jones*. She was built by David Jones in 1863. Originally an old fashioned style, two-masted topsail schooner, with a square stern, she later had a third mast stepped. She had her topsail yard removed in 1923 and an auxiliary engine fitted (a 60 h.p. Bolinder). In the late 1920s she came into the ownership of Captain William Shaw, brother of Hugh Shaw and son of Captain Humphrey Shaw. In February 1932 she was lost in the Thames estuary after the engine failed, her crew being picked up by the steamer *Foam Queen*.

Looking at the wooden schooners built in Flint it is interesting to note that three of the David Jones vessels served the coastal trade for an astonishing 69 years – the *Kattie Darling, Denbighshire Lass* and *Mary Jones*. Today's deep-sea vessels and shortsea ferries are thought of as long in the tooth if they reach the grand old age of 25!

Notes

1. Edward Hogan, 'The Streets and Lanes of Flint', unpublished MS, Flintshire Records Office (FRO).
2. Unpublished works 'The Streets and Lanes of Flint' and 'Notes on Shipbuilding at Flint', ably edited by the late Peter Bellis of the Flintshire Historical Society. Both works are deposited at the Flintshire Records Office.
3. Fustic, a wood of a tropical American tree of the mulberry family that yields a yellow dye. Divi-divi, a leguminous tree native to South America, the pods of the tree yield tannin.
4. 1851 Census return.
5. Lady Fielding was the wife of the Ninth Earl of Denbigh, a notable Roman Catholic convert who founded the Franciscan friary at Pantasaph.
6. *Caernarvon & Denbigh Herald,* 9th June 1849.
7. A short survey of Merchant Shipping, with special reference to the Dee, Shotton High School,undated and unpulished, FRO.
8. Chester Ship Registers, 1855, FRO.
9. Mersey Dock & Harbour Board (MD&HB) Wreck Book, 1925.
10. John Mahon, *Kate Tyrell, Lady Mariner* (Dublin, 1995).
11. Chester Ship Register, vol. 3, 1859, Flintshire Records Office.
12. Chester Ship Register, vol. 3, 1867, Flintshire Records Office.
13. *Chester Chronicle,* 13th March 1858, re –launch on 1st March 1858.
14. *Flintshire Observer,* 7th April 1863.

# 8

# Connah's Quay, the move from Flint and the Ferguson & Baird years

Until the arrival of Jones & Hooson in 1857, there seems to have been little activity at the port site which was to become Connah's Quay and only after the restrictions on using Flint Gutter came into being did it become the alternative port. The other development which boosted trade at the new port was the opening of the Wrexham, Mold & Connah's Quay Railway to freight traffic on 1st January 1866.[1] The export of bricks from the Buckley area, coal from the North Wales coalfield and the import of raw materials for the local metal, chemical and later, steel industries were to give rise to the establishment of the full range of maritime activities and occupations at Connah's Quay. Shipowners set up and expanded in order to service these industries, together with marine services, and there was a regular need for new vessels to carry the raw materials and products of these industries.

On Monday, 1st March 1858, the first vessel built at Connah's Quay, the *Mag*, a two-masted schooner, was launched from the building yard of Messrs Jones & Hooson.[2] She was designed and modelled by Mr Thomas Hooson and did great credit to his skill as a draughtsman, experienced persons pronouncing her lines as being very perfect.

> She is expected to carry well and be a good sailer. As this is the first vessel that was ever built at Connah's Quay it attracted a great concourse of persons from Flint, Bagillt and the neighbourhood, not fewer than 2,000 people being present. She was named 'Mag' by Miss Parry , daughter of Michael Parry, timber merchant of Flint and entered her new element in gallant style without hitch or accident, amidst the hearty cheers and good wishes of the assembled multitude. After the launch 40 sat down to a sumptuous dinner at the hotel, when several toasts were drunk and responded to. She belongs to J.Neale Lomax Esq of this city.[2]

Thomas Hooson had been apprenticed as a ship's carpenter in Flint, as was his older brother, John. By 1861, Thomas was a fully qualified ship's carpenter, aged 29, living in Wepre with his wife Elizabeth and their three-month-old son, also Thomas. By 1871, however, he had become a master mariner, and by 1881 he had a complete career change and become a greengrocer! David Jones was one of the two timber merchants who seem to have financed the building of many of the schooners and other vessels built at Flint until they were forced out to Connah's Quay by the chemical industries there. Little more is heard of Jones & Hooson after the launching of the *Mag*.

Ferguson & Baird also arrived in the 'Quay' in 1858, and were to remain there for the next 58 years. No other shipbuilder on the Chester River enjoyed such longevity; all the other operations being relatively short-lived – no more than 36 years (Abdela & Mitchell, Cortney & Mulvey). Bearing in mind that FMB had started working in Flint in 1839, the family members of Ferguson & Baird built vessels for a total of 66 years and were involved with the construction of at least 60 vessels, many of which had long and useful lives serving the trades around the coast of the British Isles. Apart from one instance, they only built wooden sailing vessels, most of which were two-masted tops'l schooners and flats, but also three-masted tops'l schooners. They were never to seriously embrace the new technology of iron or steam power which makes their lengthy career as shipbuilders even more remarkable.

According to Eddie Hogan it seems that the many Dee-built schooners were a compromise design between the schooners of the West Country and those of Lancashire and Cumbria. Like many of the Dee sailing coasters, the Lancashire built vessels did a great deal of trade on the Dee and the Mersey and its inland navigation. The Lancashire schooners' hull design was known as the 'Barrow Flat', with a round stern and a shallow draft, needing only about 9' of water when fully loaded, whilst a similarly laden West Country schooner needed 13' of water. The Deeside schooners were designed to accommodate the two traditions.[3]

Ferguson & Baird are probably the most important of the Chester River shipbuilders of the Victorian era, and it is a tribute to their skill and design that one of their vessels, the *Lizzie May,* has survived to the present day (albeit after costly rebuilding), but with a hull structure that is 70% original after 118 years!

James Baird died, aged 87, in1902, but his three sons, Thomas, Walter and James carried on the business, while the family also continued to own shares in vessels in the coastal trades, as did the Fergusons.

In the 1911 Census, Walter and Thomas Baird (aged 59 and 70 respectively) were described as ship's carpenters, although James, aged 68, was described as only a 'jobbing carpenter'. All three sons outlived the closure of the yard in 1917,[4] although at some point it had become the operation of 'A. Ferguson' only.

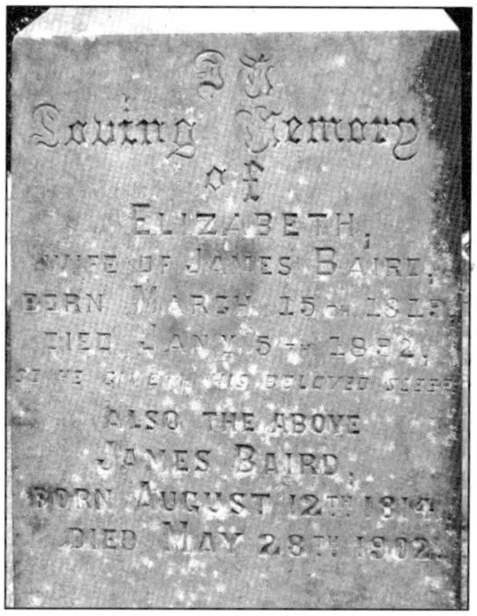

Plate 29. Baird grave headstone in Connah's Quay cemetery.

By 1871, Daniel Ferguson and his wife were living in Golftyn where he was described as a 'shipbuilder' and his youngest son, Richard, was a 'ship's carpenter', whilst his elder brother, Archibald was married and living by Connah's Quay Station. He was also a 'shipbuilder'. The Baird and Ferguson families were in fact living next door but one to each other at that time.

The Ferguson's cottage stood between what were the platers' sheds of the shipyard (in the time of Crichtons) and the higher ground at the head of the slipway. The cottage had been built at right angles to the river, and faced towards Shotton. The platers sheds were built just in front of the Ferguson's garden. The higher ground on the westerly side of the slipway, which slopes steeply to the river, was built up with stones to form a wharf, the top of which was lapped by the high water of the spring tides. This wharf was known as the Top Slip and vessels were built there and launched off at high water. The slipway, which can still be seen today, was cut out at a lower level than the Top Slip and sloped very gently down to the beach and into the river. On this slipway there was a cradle on rails, which could be run into the river at low water. At high tide, vessels could be warped into position on the cradle and pulled up the slip by means of a large windlass located on higher ground, above the head of the slipway. Originally, the windlass was turned by horses supplied by the local carter, John Griffiths, or by Tom Catherall, but later a steam donkey-engine was provided.[5]

Daniel Ferguson died in 1880, but his widow, Elizabeth (aged 75 in 1891) was described as 'The employer in a shipbuilding business' and Richard, her son, was employed (presumably by Mrs Ferguson), as the book-keeper. Her son Archibald was still living in the house by the railway station in Connah's Quay and was described as a 'Shipbuilder' and it seems he stayed with the family business up to its final demise in 1917.

At this point in the history of shipbuilding in Connah's Quay it is appropriate to comment on the fact that the three founders of Ferguson, McCallum & Baird –James Baird (87), Daniel Ferguson (67) and John McCallum (74), all lived to a good age. John McCallum probably left the shipbuilding business when they were still in Flint, but is listed as a shareholder in the *Isabella* which FMB built there in 1856. About 1878 he became the publican of the Quay House in Connah's Quay and spent most of his latter years in the town. In 1881, aged 60, he was still the publican at the Quay House, with his wife, Sarah, aged 39, and their daughter, Margaret, aged 18.[6] He and his wife were living at 7 Penllan Place in the Quay in 1891, by which time he had retired.[7] When Connah's Quay port was extended in 1886 it was John McCallum's wife who provided the repast for the celebrations at the Quay House. Sadly, in August 1895, aged 74, John was killed by a train on the line to Holyhead a little way from Connah's Quay station. At the subsequent inquest, his wife said that he liked to go and see the ships, but he had been in poor health for some time and was extremely deaf. At 3.30 p.m. she had escorted him across the track and told him not to come back until she called him, but clearly he became anxious and attempted to return.

As we have already seen, all three families had originally had an involvement in ship owning and building, similar to those of the early nineteenth-century Chester builders where the builder arranged the finance and built the vessel and then operated her until the right price was on offer.

In 1877 the first owners of the two-masted schooner *Mary Elizabeth*, built at Connah's Quay, included 16/64 shares owned by Daniel Ferguson, James Baird Snr and James Baird Jnr. Again, in the case of the *Chase*, built in 1878, 24/64 shares were owned equally by Daniel Ferguson and James Baird. In later years and up to the time of her loss in 1894, she was owned partly by Richard Ferguson. James Baird was also the first owner of the *Agnes Craig*, built in 1893. Yard N°. 48, the *Gordon*, was built in 1896 by Ferguson and Baird, and was owned by James Baird when she sank following a collision in 1914. Similarly, Richard Ferguson (aged 75) was listed as the agent of the *Kattie Darling* when she was wrecked in the Mersey in 1925.

Their shipowning activities seem to have been far from trouble–free, but may well have been typical of the experiences of schooner owners in the late nineteenth century. In 1893, *Agnes Craig*, a 99-ton topsail schooner they had built in 1884, ran aground near Bridgwater Lock on the River Mersey and James Baird was again listed as the owner.[8] Fortunately, she floated off on the next tide. However, the following year, Richard Ferguson was not so fortunate when the schooner *Chase*, 88 tons (built by Ferguson & Baird in 1878,) having been laden with coal on 15th February, sank about 500 yards NNW from the Formby Lightship after a collision with the S.S. *Falls of Inversnaid*. On 17th February the wreck was 'destroyed by blasting by MD&HB'[8] –a common fate it seems for wooden vessels that hindered navigation having sunk in inconvenient places in the Mersey.

Plate 30: The schooner *Lorne* of 1871.

It must be said that the regular groundings and losses of vessels were probably not unusual or peculiar to those vessels built by Ferguson & Baird; the hazards for sailing vessels must have been the same everywhere. But not all the vessels they built turned out to be good sailers. The two-masted top'sl schooner *Hilda* of 1893 was found to be a 'wet ship', inclined to dive bows under, and her foremast was taken out and stepped a couple of feet further aft which made her easier to handle. She often made voyages to mainland Europe and on one occasion took a cargo of dynamite from Rotterdam to Goole.[9] After being owned in Bridgwater for many years, she was sold to Swansea owners in 1918. In 1921 she was registered as an auxiliary, but was lost by fire at Strangford Lough the following year. There is no doubt that the two families established a very respected wooden shipbuilding business which continued to construct coasting vessels long after iron, steel and steam power had become the norm. It is astonishing that they continued to receive orders for wooden schooners after the turn of the century, but many of their vessels were built for Deeside owners and local manufacturers as well as Irish shipowners from ports that traded regularly with the Chester River. Hancocks (brick makers), United Alkali, Raynes (quarry owners), Thos Eyton (collieries), Michael Parry and David Jones (timber merchants) were all industrialists who bought their vessels. Also local shipowners such as Reney, Coppack & Carter, Edward Peers, Thomas Mathias Jnr, Charles Davison and Robert Foulkes, all ordered Ferguson & Baird vessels built in Flint or Connah's Quay.

Many of the two- and three-masted schooners built at Connah's Quay were to be lost due to bad weather, some very early in their careers and often in tragic circumstances. The *Glynne*, built in 1867, is thought to be the last sailing vessel to disappear after leaving the river Dee. Of 92 tons, she sailed under the command of Captain Sam Lawrence on 6th November 1890 and it is believed she fell victim to the storm of November 6/7th. Captain Lawrence was a prominent missionary of the British & Foreign Sailors' Society, and on 5th November, when the weather was already deteriorating, he held a prayer meeting aboard the *Glynne* at Connah's Quay.[3]

Plate 31: The schooner *Chase* of 1878.

Plate 32: The schooner *Duchess* of 1878.

Captain Lawrence's father, also a master mariner, was lost in similar circumstances three years later. *Mary Caroline* (1864), *Ernest* (1864), *Elizabeth Jane* (1875), *Chase* (1878), *Empress* (1885), *J. & A. Coppack* (1901), *Catherine Reney* (1901) and *Malvina* (1906) are all examples of Ferguson & Baird vessels which sank with loss of life. The *Empress* sank twice. In 1885, on her maiden voyage from Connah's Quay with a cargo of bricks to the Thames, she was run down by a steamer in Gravesend Reach. The crew was saved, the cargo was lost and the press reported the vessel was uninsured. She must, however, have been refloated as she survived until 1910 when she again sank in the Thames after a collision with the steamer *Marusa*.

The last sailing vessel built at the Connah's Quay yard was the *Malvina* of 1906, built to the order of the Falkland Islands Company. Only once in these twilight years did the yard build a new vessel, the barge *Nora Bate,* in 1911 for well known Mersey barge operators. The yard finally closed in 1917 when it was owned by A. Ferguson, the son of one of the original founders of the company. By 1920, the yard was building again, having been taken over by J. Crichton and it continued to construct vessels and carry out repairs until 1932.[10]

Only once after Ferguson & Baird was set up at Connah's Quay in 1858, was a vessel built there which was not constructed by them – in 1878 the press announced the launch of the *Duchess* for Charles Davison,[11] a local farmer turned shipowner. She was a two-masted topsail schooner, with pleasing lines. Mrs Davison performed the launch which was accompanied by cheering crowds and a 'salvo of diminutive artillery'.[12] It was said that the *Duchess* '... was the last wooden vessel to be built on the old shipyard alongside the quay wall.'[5] The name was chosen as a compliment to the Westminster family, under whom Mr Davison had lived for a number of years. The builder of the vessel is recorded as being Samuel Owens of Connah's Quay. In 1878, he was 27 years old and listed as a 'Shipwright'. Samuel was born in Hawarden, the son of William Owens, a shipwright and grocer, (who had himself been born in Pwllheli in 1809 and who, by 1871 was living in Chester). It is assumed that both William and Samuel had been employed as shipwrights in Chester where, after 1870, there were limited opportunities for newbuilding work. Samuel then moved to the Quay to try his luck there. Whether he worked on vessels for Ferguson & Baird is unknown, but by 1881 he and his family were resident in Liverpool and later moved to Tranmere, and he continued working as a shipwright until his death in 1904, aged 54.

As the picture shows (Plate 32), *Duchess* was a magnificent example of her type and she plied deep water for many years before entering the coastal trade and carrying china clay and scrap metal to Liverpool and Glasgow. A press report of October 1930 recorded that the *Duchess* had taken shelter in Ramsey harbour on a voyage from Southern Ireland to Glasgow. The article noted that the skipper had bought her six weeks previously, since when she had been windbound at Kingstown (Dun Laoghaire). Such were the joys of sailing a schooner under sail alone. At Ramsey, she struck a wooden pier, losing both her anchors, breaking her bowsprit and ripping planks out of the pier. After a career of 58 years, her end came in the Mersey in 1936 when she was caught in a gale and a violent sea dashed her against a sea wall, her hull was stoved in and she was broken up where she lay.

On only one occasion were Ferguson & Baird known to have built a steam-driven vessel. They may have only completed the hull which had been started in another yard, but in May 1881 they completed the *Hawarden Castle* for local owners, the Connah's Quay Alkali Co. She was a wooden screw steam flat, powered by two diagonal inverted direct-acting steam engines, made by W. E. Bates of Northwich. The engines had 17" cylinders and a stroke of 16" and provided 49 h.p. She was 78'

6" loa, of which the engine room occupied 21' 6". In 1886 she was taken over by local agents Coppack & Carter and they sold her in 1889 to William Rowland of Liverpool, who sold her again in 1892 to John Gibney the younger. He renamed her *Gleaner* and she was used for salvage work until, in 1931, she was sold to the Liverpool Derricking & Carrying Co. In January 1940 she was sold to Norwest Construction Co. Ltd. of Liverpool and, a few days later, on 24th January, was sunk off Preston Bar after a career of 59 years – not bad for a wooden vessel.[12]

In October 1885 there was a fatal accident at the Connah's Quay yard when Ishmael Dolben, a sawyer who had worked there for 15 years or more, was cutting a yellow pine board into strips. One strip caught in the teeth on the backside of the saw, snapping off about 6" which struck him on the cheek. He died four hours later in Chester Infirmary.

As well as building two- and three-masted schooners, Ferguson & Baird also constructed flats for local owners, the best known being the four 'super flats', built between 1887 and 1895 –the *Federation, Protection, Reciprocity* and *Fair Trade*– for J. W. Raynes, owners of the Llandullas quarry. These vessels all had bulwarks and bowsprits, and were largely employed by Raynes to carry limestone from the Llandullas quarry to West Bank in Widnes and they seldom ventured beyond the North Wales coast. After leaving the ownership of J. W. Raynes, they were employed around the Mersey and North Wales for many years, the *Protection* (having been

Plate 33: Jigger flats in the Mersey.

Plate 34: The jigger flat *Protection* (right), built in 1887, in tow of the *Angelo*.

fitted with a Kromhout engine in 1929) survived until 1948. Appendix 8 is a reprinted article about the *Protection* which appeared in *Sea Breezes* in December 1947, which gives the reader an excellent idea of life aboard a jigger flat.

A boat-building yard was set up by William Butler at the side of the Quay House Hotel in Connah's Quay. Butler came from a shipyard at Burton-on-Stather on the Humber where he had been a foreman shipwright. His son, William Morfin Butler, served his apprenticeship with Ferguson & Baird, and in 1896 joined his father in his business. In 1905, the workshop was destroyed by fire but was rebuilt by William Morfin Butler who then went into business on his own. Numerous vessels were sent to him for repair and during the Second World War, in business with his two sons, he built and repaired ships' lifeboats. This business eventually formed part of the Liverpool Lifeboat Pool.[5]

After the closure of Fergusons in 1917, the Connah's Quay site was taken over by J. Crichton & Co in 1920. They built a number of vessels there, the first two being the coasters *Kinnaird Head* and *Wearside* (1920). Crichtons also built their largest vessel, the 856-gross-ton *Allegheny,* for the Anglo-American Oil Co. at the yard in 1921, but mostly used the site for repair work and ship alterations. In 1923, they reconstructed the hauling-up slip and winch so that it could take coasters of up to 500 tons, after which the first job was the lengthening by 20' of the coaster *Red Hand* for John Summers. The coaster *Dyserth* was also converted to the hopper barge *AHC* on this slip, and lengthened by 20'. Crichton's closed the Connah's Quay yard in 1932.[*10]

Notes

1. Peter E. Baughan, *A Regional History of the Railways of Great Britain, vol. 11, North and Mid Wales* (Newton Abbot, 1980).
2. *Chester Chronicle,* 13th March 1858.

3. E. Hogan, 'Notes on Shipbuilding at Flint', unpublished MS, FRO, Ref. NT/1523.
4. A. H. Dodd, *The Industrial Revolution in North Wales* (Cardiff, 1951).
5. A short survey of Merchant Shipping with special reference to the Dee-Shotton High School, undated, unpublished MS, FRO.
6. 1881 Census.
7. 1891 Census.
8. MD&HB Water Bailiffs Record of Wrecks, vol. 2, Merseyside Maritime Museum Record Office, MD&HB/MS/4/1–4.
9. *Sea Breezes Magazine*, vol. XVIII, *Hilda* of Bridgwater.
10. *J. Crichton & Co., Shipbuilders*, see Bibliography.
11. *Wrexham Guardian*, 22nd June 1878.
12. Roy Fenton, *Mersey Rovers*, see Bibliography.

# 9

## Connah's Quay, some of its famous vessels

It is time to look at the lives and trading patterns of some of the more famous vessels built at Connah's Quay, particularly those which had lengthy careers, and see how they were typically used. Despite accidents and losses, five Ferguson & Baird vessels survived the ravages of the Second World War, which is a remarkable feat; no other wooden schooner builder in the U.K. had built as many vessels which survived for so long into the twentieth century.

*Earl Cairns,* 1883–1948 — 65years
*Agnes Craig,* 1884–1952 — 68 years
*Windermere,* 1890–1958 — 68 years
*Lizzie May* (*Kathleen & May*), 1900–to date — 118 years
*Sarah Lathom,* 1903–48 — 45years

During their careers these vessels were to carry many bulk cargoes and deadweight commodities such as coal, stone, clay, bricks and pit props in the coastwise and Irish Sea trades, cargoes that were hard task masters for ageing wooden vessels.

*Windermere* (Yard N°. 45), was a three-masted tops'l schooner, built in 1890 for Joseph Crosfield of Barrow. Measuring 104' 2" x 24' 3" x 11' 3" depth of hold, and having a gross tonnage of 174, she was one of the largest vessels built by Ferguson & Baird at Connah's Quay. When she first put to sea she had tops'l yards, but after 1927 only retained her original lofty topmasts. In 1948, she still did not have a wheelhouse, although she had been fitted with an engine by Captain Tyrell in 1927.

Captain C. A. Reney of Connah's Quay bought her in 1895 and she was again sold in about 1914 to Mr F. Tyrell of Arklow. He may have been impressed with the ship *Denbighshire Lass*, another Chester River schooner, that had been bought by a Tyrell family member many years earlier. *Windermere* was to remain in the ownership of the Tyrell family until 1956.

Plate 35: The schooner *Windermere* of 1890.

In the twilight years of their lives, vessels like the *Windermere* seem to go from crisis to crisis. In October 1945 she had grounded off Carnsore Point during a voyage from Preston to Dungarvan laden with coal; 30 tons had to be jettisoned and she refloated and later reached Rosslare. However, by November 1948, her topmasts had been shortened, bowsprit amputated and a wheelhouse added. In February 1954 she was again out of commission following a collision with the MD&HB sand pump dredger *Hilbre Island* near Pluckington Bank in the river Mersey on 6th February;[1] wooden schooners 104' in length and steel dredgers of 3,141 gross tons do not go together well and *Windermere* had to be taken into Birkenhead, dry docked and repaired at William Cubbin's yard in the West Float.

On 4th April 1956 she ran aground on Tuskar Point near Porthcawl whilst on a ballast voyage from Barry to Swansea to load anthracite for Arklow. After nine hours aground she was refloated by the crew and docked at Swansea. Despite reports of 'serious keel, rudder and bottom damage', temporary repairs were made and she loaded and sailed on 17th April.

She was sold in November 1956 to a Captain Locassis and a Mr Gibbs.[2] After an extensive refit at Harris's Appledore yard, she left Cardiff in June 1957 for the Mediterranean, her owners apparently intending to trade between French and North African ports. In January 1958, she was abandoned and presumed lost in the Gulf of Lyons, where her crew of seven was picked up by the M.V. *Montana* on passage to Genoa.[2] At the time she was trading under the Costa Rican flag and carrying a cargo of scrap metal. An almost exotic end under a foreign flag to a career spent carrying coal and other bulks across the Irish Sea —Garston, Swansea, Arklow, Dublin, New Ross, Barry, Cork, Whitehaven, Wicklow, Newport and, of course, Connah's Quay being visited regularly over her 68 years afloat.

The *Sarah Lathom* was built in 1903 as a two-masted flat/ketch and was another product of the yard which survived the Second World War, having a 48-year career, wholly spent around the sailing coaster ports of North Wales, Ireland and the Mersey. She was 80' 7" in length, 21' 5" beam with a depth of hold of 8', and a gross tonnage of 87. According to Eddie Hogan,[3] she was built to carry sheet iron from Messrs Summers at Shotton to Liverpool and Birkenhead for transhipment to deep sea vessels. She was considered quite modern for her time, with large hatchways, but according to Hugh Shaw, almost as soon as she was built, the contract for carrying the sheet iron was given to the railways. In 1913 she was involved in two incidents in the Mersey.[4] In February, she was in danger of dragging her anchor on to East Hoyle Bank when owned by Samuel Vickers of Shotton and was towed clear by the MD&HB vessel *Salvor* and given a clear course. In June 1913 she was again in trouble on the Mersey when, on 8th June, she was observed from the Hilbre Telegraph Station to be aground on West Hoyle Bank, with the tug *Overgarth* alongside – also aground! Fortunately both vessels were successfully refloated and the *Sarah Lathom* left in tow of the *Overgarth*.

In the early1920s she was fitted with a 28 h.p. Kelvin engine and was time-chartered to carry slack from the Point of Ayr colliery to Price's candle factory at Bromborough, when the creek at Bromborough was still tidal. At this time she was owned by Robert Foulkes of Connah's Quay, who was also her captain.[5]

In late 1946 she was sold by a Thomas Jones of Flint to owners from the north-east of England, and was under the command of S. Barnes of Sunderland.[6] A new engine had been installed in 1943 – a Kromhout, giving her a speed of 5 knots. Her running gear had been renewed in 1946. Philip Kershaw (writer of the 'Coastal Sail' column in *Sea Breezes* magazine for many years) had visited her in 1948 and found no record in her log of her ever having carried a damaged cargo. She had also recently gone from Stranraer to Mostyn in 27 hours and Connah's Quay to Belfast in 25 hours, but was no longer classed as a ketch as her mizzen sail had been dismantled and her jib-boom unshipped, 'but she was looking very smart'. In 1948[8] her cargoes had included: loading slate in Port Penrhyn, Bangor; carrying coal from Point of Ayr to Holyhead for the silica works, and taking bricks from Connah's Quay to Dublin. Sadly her refurbishment did not save her. In early July 1948 she sailed from Connah's Quay for Belfast with bricks.[7] A few hours out she met heavy weather, her sails were blown away, she started taking in water, her pumps were out of action and her engine failed. She reached Langness Point off the Isle of Man where she anchored. Shortly after, the Port St Mary lifeboat took off the crew, including her master, Mr Ralph Ashton of Blackpool and his wife. She foundered in deep water the same morning.[8]

The *Agnes Craig*, built as a three-masted schooner for the copper trade in 1884, was another great survivor. By 1889 she was operating out of Porthmadog and was described as being 'kept like a yacht-masts scraped and oiled, sails white, bright work all scraped and varnished and the deck spotless.'[9] In 1889–90 she sailed from Porthmadog to Papenburg, Harburg or Emden in Germany laden with slates. During this time she also called at London, Aberdeen, Swansea, Irvine, Portrush, Rochester and Runcorn. On a trip to Abbeville in France she was caught in a strong westerly

Plate 36: The *Agnes Craig* of 1884.

gale and a high tide at St Valery-sur-Somme and was in danger of landing on top of the piles to which she was moored.

Later in her career she was reduced to two masts and fitted with an auxiliary engine. Writing in *Sea Breezes* in 1947 Philip Kershaw gave an excellent description of how unforgiving the Irish Sea could be for this type of sailing vessel.

> In the early part of the year she had a hectic time trying to cross to Bideford from Belfast with a valuable cargo of grass seed. Sailing in early January she was straight away held up by bad weather and had to put back for stores after some days sheltering; a second time she tried to leave Belfast Lough, only to be forced to shelter for another week and to go back to Belfast for more stores. Finally she managed to reach Cobh, where the gale kept her almost a week. Another gale forced her into Arklow with a torn mainsail and in even more bad weather she arrived at Bideford with a torn foresail on March 8th – at the end of what should have been a one day trip. She was sailing at this time for Mr Kearon of Arklow. After this epic voyage she took bricks back to Ireland from Bridgwater, then crossed from Larne to Garston, before returning to Arklow.[10]

In 1947, Richard J. Scott also wrote for *Sea Breezes* magazine an excellent account of an Irish Sea voyage in the *Agnes Craig* (see Appendix 9 for the full article). She was to survive until 1952 when she was broken up at Arklow, a mere 68 years old.

The *Lizzie May*, is, of course the great Ferguson & Baird survivor. As I write, she is lying alongside the Canning Dock in Liverpool in immaculate condition, in excellent sailing order and can be visited or used for events on board. Jeff Grice and his wife Cindy, who manage the vessel on behalf of the Kathleen & May Heritage Trust, can tell you everything about the vessel. It is believed that 70% of the hull structure is original and it is thought that one of the reasons that she has lasted so well was the fact that Ferguson & Baird over-engineered the vessel in the sense that the hull is double –ribbed to standards laid down for Royal Navy vessels, with frames every couple of feet apart, rather than the usual spacing for this type of vessel. It is said that, when she was built in 1900 for the Coppack family of Connah's Quay, Ferguson & Baird put in the lowest tender and, although they were satisfied with the keel, framing, hog and timbering, Captain John Coppack (at that time the Lloyds's agent for the Port of Chester) took exception to a number of knees in the vessel.[11] These had already been passed by the surveyor, but Captain John insisted that all should be replaced. At first this request was refused but, rather than risk an issue in court, the builders duly replaced them.

The *Chester Chronicle* report of the launch is worth repeating:

Plate 37: The *Lizzie May* (*Kathleen & May*) of 1900.

> On Monday's tide, at the shipbuilding yard of Messr's Ferguson& Baird, the launch took place of a fine new coasting schooner. The event proved a great attraction and there was a large gathering to witness the proceedings, the ladies especially being prominent in their bright 'holiday' attire.
>
> The preliminary arrangements on the stocks were superintended by Mr Ferguson (Manager) and Mr Baird (foreman of the yard) and when the signal was given the ship glided gracefully into the water, amid the loud cheers of the interested spectators, who for fully an hour, had been on the tip- toe of expectancy. The cheers were re-echoed by those on board the ship and the new vessel entered the water under the most favourable auspices. The christening ceremony was prettily perfomed by Miss Elizabeth Ellen Coppack, the ship being named *Lizzie May* after the two daughters of Mr John Coppack who is the largest owner.[12]

Although built at a time when trade was booming, she was only to stay with the Coppacks until 1908. She is said to have cost £2,700, a figure which means very little today until we take account of the fact that in 1900 a shipwright earned about £1.25 per week. Under the command of Captain Tom Hughes she made her first commercial voyage in May 1900 from Connah's Quay to Rochester in Kent, carrying 226 tons of firebricks. In her eight years with Coppacks she sailed nearly 40,000 miles and carried 24,786 tons of cargo from salt to stones, from galvanized iron to gunpowder.[13]

In September 1908 she was sold to Martin J. Fleming of Youghal, County Cork for £1,700. Not long after, she ran aground on the Goodwin Sands while carrying a cargo of cement, but was refloated and towed to Dover, where her cargo was transferred to barges for re-shipment. Eventually, after temporary repairs had been carried out, she left and after a difficult ballast voyage was towed into Appledore where she stayed until the end of January 1909. From then until 1939 she spent most of her time carrying coal from Lydney and Garston to Ireland, managing to have at least three collisions with steamers during the 1920s. In 1931, she had an auxiliary 80 h.p. Beardmore engine fitted, and her topsails taken down and top masts shortened. At this time she was bought by Captain William Jewell of Appledore and in 1945, when he died at the age of 77, his son Tommy took over as her owner-skipper and kept her trading until 1960 when he had passed the age of 65.

The Jewell family kept her sailing throughout the Second World War making many voyages through the dangerous Western Approaches and in 1943 she made her first voyage from Fremington Quay (near Barnstaple) to Crosshaven in County Cork, carrying china clay for the Carrigaline pottery, a trade in which she was to become well known in the later days of her trading career. Later that year her Beardmore auxiliary engine was replaced by a secondhand Deutz of 125 h.p. In March 1952, Captain Jewell ordered a new £3,000 diesel, a four-cylinder Crossley of 133 b.h.p.[14] For the next ten years she did very little, passing through the hands of various private owners until bought by the Maritime Trust in 1970. Under their ownership she was refitted and preserved afloat at Sutton Harbour, Plymouth as a topsail schooner which was where I first went aboard her in 1976.

In 1985–6 she was moved to London as part of a new entertainment and office complex at St Mary Overy in Southwark, on the south bank of the Thames. A drydock was provided in which she normally lay afloat, but which could be dried out for any hull repairs to be undertaken. The Maritime Trust failed to win funding to restore her and she left the Thames in 1996 and was taken to Gloucester, passed into private ownership and eventually in 1998 she was bought by businessman Steve Clarke of Bideford who fully restored her there to her 1900 specification. She was also fitted with a replacement auxiliary engine, a 400 b.h.p. Detroit diesel. Since that time she has visited various ports round the U.K. coast and has also been to Spain and France and also attended the Diamond Jubilee maritime event on the river Thames in 2012.

As mentioned above, she is currently berthed in Liverpool's Albert Dock complex

Plate 38: The *Kathleen & May* in Canning Dock, Liverpool 2016.

and is a truly magnificent example of her builders' work and today is considered to be the second most important preserved wooden merchant sailing craft in the U.K., second only to the *Cutty Sark*. She is indeed a beautifully proportioned example of the excellent workmanship which Ferguson & Baird put into their two- and three-masted schooners.

Unlike the *Cutty Sark*, the *Kathleen & May* is still afloat and anyone with an interested in historic vessels should make a point of going aboard her in Liverpool – it is a far better experience than reading about her here. Her hold (once two) and deck space is available for events where you are constantly surrounded by the wonderful craftsmanship. When I retired from the Port of Liverpool in 2012 after 43 years working there I was fortunate enough to be able to hire the vessel for a reception to thank all those people in the Port community who had enabled us to successfully bring back cruise vessels to the Mersey over the previous twenty years.

Plate 39: The *Earl Cairns* of 1884.

The *Kathleen & May* is currently for sale and it is hoped that she can be kept in the U.K. for another 118 years so that future generations can appreciate the workmanship and understand how the coastal trade of the British Isles was served by hundreds of these vessels for many, many years.

The *Earl Cairns* of 1884 (Yard N° 37) was one of a number of vessels built by Ferguson & Baird for J. W. Raynes, the owner of one of the limestone quarries at Llandullas on the coast between Abergele and Old Colwyn. She was launched on Tuesday, 10th April 1883, by Miss Thom of Hawarden. A three-masted schooner, she was owned by Raynes until at least 1907. By 1914 she had been sold to Hancocks (along with the *Earl of Lathom*) and then to owners in Ireland. After surviving the First World War she was fitted with an auxiliary engine in 1921. Still trading in the Bristol Channel area in 1940, she became a barrage balloon vessel at Falmouth, but at the end of the Second World War was deemed unsuitable for further trading and her register closed in 1945. (Plates 39 and Plate 40 show her with reduced rig in her later years and in her final resting place).

All the 'Earl' schooners built at Connahs Quay were to the order of J. W. Raynes. In 1882, the *Earl of Beaconsfield* was launched, followed in 1885 by the *Earl of Lathom*, which achieved fame when she was sunk without loss of life by gunfire by the German submarine *U-20* off the old Head of Kinsale in 1915. The *U-50* was supposedly the submarine that sank the *Lusitania* on the same patrol.

In considering the interesting vessels built by Ferguson & Baird it would be wrong to ignore the last sailing vessel they built, even though she had only a

Plate 40: The *Earl Cairns* of 1884, laid to rest.

relatively short life. In 1906, the yard launched, off the top slip at Connah's Quay, the two-masted auxiliary schooner *Malvina*, built for the Falkland Islands Company, 66 years after Ferguson & Baird had launched their first vessel at Flint which had also voyaged to South America. A blunt-bowed carvel built, fore and aft rigged vessel, 93' in length, the *Malvina* was fitted with a 4 cycle, 4 cylinder petrol auxiliary engine developing 65 h.p. and giving a speed of 4–5 knots.[15] She arrived in Port Stanley on 11th June 1907, under the command of Captain Finch with a crew of seven. She was the first vessel owned by the Falkland Islands Company to be fitted with an auxiliary engine, and also the first vessel which the yard had built with an engine at the time of construction.

She was used for coastal service in the Falklands, delivering stores to outlying sheep stations and collecting their wool output for onward shipment to the U.K. She continued in this role until 9th May 1910 when she was wrecked in Reef Channel, West Falkland, off Saunders Island. At the time of her loss she was under the command of Captain Martz, a German. The Falkland Islands Company's tug *Samson* was dispatched from Port Stanley with a view to salvaging her, but this proved impossible so the tug took all the vessels stores, spars, sails, boat, anchor and cable and the engine and returned to Stanley with the crew all safe. The wreck was sold and broken up for jetty and fencing repairs on Saunders Island.[16]

Plate 41: The *Malvina* in the Falkland Islands.

At least two other vessels built by Ferguson & Baird also reached South America. The *Mary Garland*, a brig (108' loa), was built at Flint in 1854 and reputedly rounded Cape Horn and reached Callao, whilst the *Maggie*, a sloop built at Connah's Quay in 1867, was registered to be sailed to Montevideo where she was to be used for river purposes only. It is remarkable that such small vessels, of no more than 93' in length (which is only 20' longer than a standard canal narrow boat), were sailed across the Atlantic without any form of communication and no auxiliary power. One hundred and fifty years later, looking at the size of regular trading vessels on these routes, it is quite inconceivable that people even contemplated such voyages.

Notes

1. *Sea Breezes Magazine*, February 1954.
2. *Sea Breezes Magazine*, March 1958.
3. E. Hogan, 'Notes on Shipbuilding at Flint', unpublished MS. FRO, NT/1523.
4. MD&HB, Water Bailiffs Record of Wrecks, vol. 4, Merseyside Maritime Museum Records Office, Ref. MD& HB/MS/4/1–4.
5. *Sea Breezes Magazine,* letter March 1947.
6. *Sea Breezes Magazine,* September 1948.
7. 'Twenty-four fathoms deep, Sarah Lathom of Connahs Quay, Ralph Ashton's story. See *Maritime Wales,* No. 17 (1995).
8. *Sea Breezes Magazine*, June 1948.
9. Letter to *Sea Breezes Magazine* from Captain Evans of Melbourne, November 1949.
10. Coastwise in the *Agnes Craig* article in *Sea Breezes Magazine,* October 1947.
11. Tom Coppack, F.I.C.S., ed by C. V. & M. E. Waine, *A Lifetime with Ships* (Prescot, 1973).
12. *Ships Monthly Magazine*, vol. 15, N$^{o.}$ 1.

13. *Country Life* magazine, 7th September 1971.
14. *The Story of the Kathleen & May*, booklet published by *Ships Monthly* magazine in association with the Maritime Trust – Endlebury Publishing Co. Ltd., 1972.
15. Letter to the author, July 1977, from J. P. Lanning, of Launceston, Tasmania, a former merchant seaman who had served in the Falkland Islands schooners. Also letter to author from Mr V. H. Jeppersen, of Jeppersen Heaton Ltd, 1995.
16. Information sent to the author by Mr H. M. Milne, Stanley Manager of the Falkland Islands Company, 11th May 1977.

# 10

## Queensferry and Abdela & Mitchell

*Early Victorian shipbuilders*

Port facilities existed on the Chester river at Queensferry (originally known as Lower Ferry, then King's Ferry from the coronation of William IV in 1820 until the coronation of Queen Victoria in 1837 when it became Queen's Ferry) before the advent of shipbuilding. It was a ferry crossing on the route from Wales to Liverpool and was served by horse-drawn tramways bringing coal to the river for shipment to coastal destinations. The products of other waterside industries, such as Turner's Chemical works, were also shipped from there.

Prior to 1885, a few vessels were built, mainly schooners and flats, the earliest recorded being the sloop *Rossett* and the schooner *Honoratus*, built in 1836. James Boydell Jnr (1803–60), the agent for Sir Stephen Glynne, owner of the large Hawarden Castle estate and collieries, built these and other vessels while living at Dee Cottage (later Queensferry Hall) until about 1841. He undertook the construction of vessels on the bank of the river near to his home and was asked by local landowners to improve the ferry crossing, which he did by applying the principal of the 'endless chain'. This experiment was described in detail in the *Chester Chronicle*[1] of 1835 and was so successful that a road bridge was not built for another 60 years. Boydell moved to Stourbridge in 1840 to manage Sir Stephen Glynne's enterprises on his Oak Farm estate. Sadly, his enthusiasm for growing the metal manufacturing business there and sinking new mine shafts was not matched by his business acumen and common sense.[2] In 1848 the estate lost £267,000 in an economic crash which placed a great financial burden on the Hawarden estate, and which was only rescued by the wise stewardship of the later prime minister, W. E. Gladstone, when he married Sir Stephen Glynne's daughter, Catherine.

At least three further vessels were built at Queensferry by John Powell, a local timber merchant, between 1841 and 1852.

*The second phase*

Serious shipbuilding on a site some 250 yards west of the Lower Ferry, was not to begin again until 1885 when, after a 30 year gap, George K. Smith began the construction of small steamers there. In 1890, however, he was obliged to move the site of his yard east of the present-day position of the blue bascule bridge (opened in 1927) near the terminus of the Aston Hall Colliery railway, because Mr Hurlbutt, now the owner of Queensferry Hall, complained about the noise from the yard (the lane down to the river is still called Hurlbutt's Lane). It was said that their operations using metal in the structure of the ships created a high–pitched screeching sound.

The first reference to Smith & Co. building a vessel is in a newspaper report of 6th July 1888 on the completion of a steel screw steamer for passenger and cargo traffic on the Amazon.[2] This article also stated that this vessel was ketch rigged and stripped down with the superstructure packed inside her hold prior to being sailed to the Amazon by a Captain Brown. The same article also recorded that '... vessels constructed by the firm have at various times been dispatched to the Congo, the Levant and Spain, as well as a number of surfboats to other places.' In December of that year the *Ambas* was completed for use in West Africa, and in May 1889 another small steamer, the *Daisy*, was sent to Tunis via the French canal system, for Count Josef Raffo, partly for use as a pleasure craft, but also as a tender to his fishing fleet in the Mediterranean.

George Smith was a Scottish engineer from Aberdeen who had worked his way up the shipbuilding ladder. In 1871 he was living and working on Tyneside as a draftsman, ten years later he was described as a ship's draughtsman, living in Westhoe in County Durham. By 1891, he was living with his wife and five children at Station Cottages in Queensferry and was described as 'Manager of Shipyard'.

In 1893 a new company was formed to buy out Smith & Co., after the shipyard had been idle for some time. The new company, called the Queensferry Shipbuilding & Engineering Company (QSB&EC), concentrated on building small steamers and tugs. Its managing director was Charles Myers, the inventor of the Myer's patent propeller. In May 1894, Mrs Myers launched a vessel named the *May Queen*,[2] built for Crosbie and King for towing and carrying passengers on Lough Neagh, Ireland. She was moved upriver to the Sandycroft Foundry to have her engines and boiler fitted.

In 1897, the QSB&EC built three interesting vessels, under the supervision of a Mr Hanson, for service in the Isle of Man with the Douglas Steam Ferry Company. It is quite difficult today to visualize the need for some of the ferry routes which existed at the end of the nineteenth century and these three vessels were built to operate between the inner end of the Victoria Pier in Douglas and the inner end of the Battery Pier on the far side of Douglas Harbour, a distance of 450–500 yards. The actual steaming time, with letting go and mooring, would have been about three minutes. The fare was originally 1d, but was increased to 3d by the 1920s. These were double ended vessels with two propellers forward and two aft, with two rudders at each end of the vessel.[3]

Plate 42: The *Rose* and *Thistle.*

While these were under construction, there was a boilermakers and riveters strike. This was ended by Richard Cain of the Palace & Derby Castle Company who came over from the island and paid the next instalment so that the ferries could be completed in time for the summer season of 1897. The ferries only operated for six months of the year, but in the years before the First World War, between 500,000 and 750,000 people travelled on them each summer season. It is likely that, before a new breakwater was built in the 1980s, there would have been many days when easterly winds would stop the ferry operating, and there would probably not have been many trippers during periods of heavy rain.[4] A pre 1914 Ward Locke guide says that '... the most popular approach to the Head is by the steam ferry from the

Victoria Pier across the harbor [sic] to the Battery Pier. On fine summer mornings the ferries are quite inadequate for the conveyance of the waiting crowds. The Head was originally visited for its views but by the 1890s it offered an assortment of attractions, including the camera obscura, a revolving tower as well as the usual pierrot shows.'

The three boats were each certified to carry 350 passengers and in their heyday they regularly appear in photographs as being jam packed. There is no record of any accidents involving passengers and over-crowding on the sisters, and it has been estimated that at peak times as many as 10,000 passengers a day would have been carried by them. During the First World War the service was suspended, but the details of the ships' war service is unknown, other than the fact that the *Thistle* sank off Aberdeen on 23rd November 1916 whilst on Admiralty service.

The vessels became part of the resort development activities of Mr J. A. Brown, editor of the *Isle of Man Times* at the turn of the century, who was also involved in the Palace & Derby Castle Company which dominated Douglas entertainments for a long time.[5]

*Rose* and *Shamrock* resumed ferry operations in 1919, but in 1926 a new *Thistle* entered service, built by Yarwoods of Northwich, with a slightly larger capacity of 430 passengers. By the early 1930s *Shamrock* was being used as a floating landing stage at Battery Pier and she was sold for breaking in 1939, but her registry was not cancelled until 1942. The remaining two ships survived until after the Second World War which they spent at Ramsey, although they were taken to Londonderry where they were used to land US forces arriving on troopships.[5] The 'new' *Thistle* re-entered service in 1948, as did the *Rose* in 1949 after extensive repairs. The service finally closed in 1950 and the *Rose* was broken up in September 1953.[4]

Sometime after 1898 the QS&E Company failed, apparently following a controversy with the Admiralty due to the cancellation of orders in hand. Charles Myers was the patentee of an anti-cavitation propeller and reversing shields, termed a 'kitchen rudder'.[6] Whether this invention contributed to the closure of the business is not known.

In about 1906, it seems the yard became the Dee Shipbuilding Company which built a twin-screw steam yacht *The Halcon,*[7] and a series of dumb cargo barges for use on the Mersey until 1908 when Abdela & Mitchell first arrived on the river Dee, their first vessel built at Queensferry being the river steamer *Pepuhy.*

Plate 43: The *Pepuhy.*

Abdela & Mitchell continued with the programme of building barges for use on the river Mersey; between 1907 and 1915 at least 37 steel dumb cargo barges, ranging from 40–300 tons gross, were built for use in and around the docks on the river Mersey. Most of them (32) were built for the Rea Transport Company (including the ones operated for the Great Western Railway), well known tug and barge operators on the west coast of the U.K.. Many of these barges were still afloat in the 1960s and 70s, when they were 60 years old or more. By this time they had passed into the ownership of BCHS and were mainly employed moving grain from vessels discharging in Liverpool North Docks by floating pneumatic elevator to mills in Birkenhead and the South Dock system in Liverpool. In the 1970s this traffic declined rapidly as the imported grain trade changed to bulk carriers rather than general cargo vessels on liner services, and at the same time Royal Seaforth Grain Terminal opened which could discharge 70,000 dwt bulk carriers, serving three new mills served from the terminal by conveyor.

The GWR barges were much smaller (mostly 63 tons gross) which would mean a dwt of about 115 tons, and were used for moving goods from the Birkenhead rail-linked warehouses of the GWR across the river to Liverpool, to more GWR warehouses to enable the company to compete for domestic traffic with rival railway companies with direct access into the city.

*Abdela & Mitchell before the First World War*

Before continuing with a detailed look at some of the interesting vessels built by Abdela & Mitchell and its successors up to closure of the yard in 1930, it is necessary to establish how and why the yard was set up and the reason many of its vessels were built for overseas owners.

Abdela & Mitchell's head office was located in Manchester and they developed yards for boat and shipbuilding, firstly, at Brimscombe in Gloucestershire, in the 'Golden Valley' alongside the Thames & Severn Canal in 1900, and at Queensferry in 1908.

The yard at Queensferry which they took over was very basic and, in the period 1909–14, employed about 100 workers. It consisted of some slipways, a brick-built office and some corrugated iron sheds.

The founder of the shipbuilding side of the business was Isaac Jacob Abdela who was born into the Jewish community in Corfu. In 1875, when he was three months old, the family fled from Turkish persecution, settling in Manchester where they seem to have already had some family connections in the expanding cotton trade. One source states that other family members were believed to have gone to Brazil and France, whilst another says that others went to Egypt, Brazil and the USA.[8]

In 1891, when he was 16, Isaac was already at the Manchester Technical School where he studied engineering and naval architecture. His father, Jacob Elias, and mother, Meri, were then living with their six younger children and a servant at 5 Haywood Street in North Manchester. Jacob, aged 52, was described as an 'agent shipper to the east.'[8] By 1901, Isaac was being described as a 'naval engineer', aged 26 and still living with his mother and father.[9] Jacob E. Abdela was then described as a 'cotton merchant'. How Isaac came to be interested in buying a boatyard in Gloucestershire is unclear, but Jacob's family in Manchester had a wide range of business interests, mainly involving the textile trade and it seems that some of the interests of Edwin Clark & Co. were taken over by Isaac Abdela before 1901. The notice of the winding up of Edwin Clark & Co. was not published until January 1901, but three weeks earlier a local newspaper had published details of the purchase of the boatyard by Isaac J. Abdela & Co.[9] It is understood that Edwin Clark had been building craft at the Brimscombe site since 1885.

Shortly after the Brimscombe boatyard acquisition, Isaac J. Abdela & Co effected a merger with greycloth merchants, Mitchell & Co. of 311 Moss Lane in Manchester

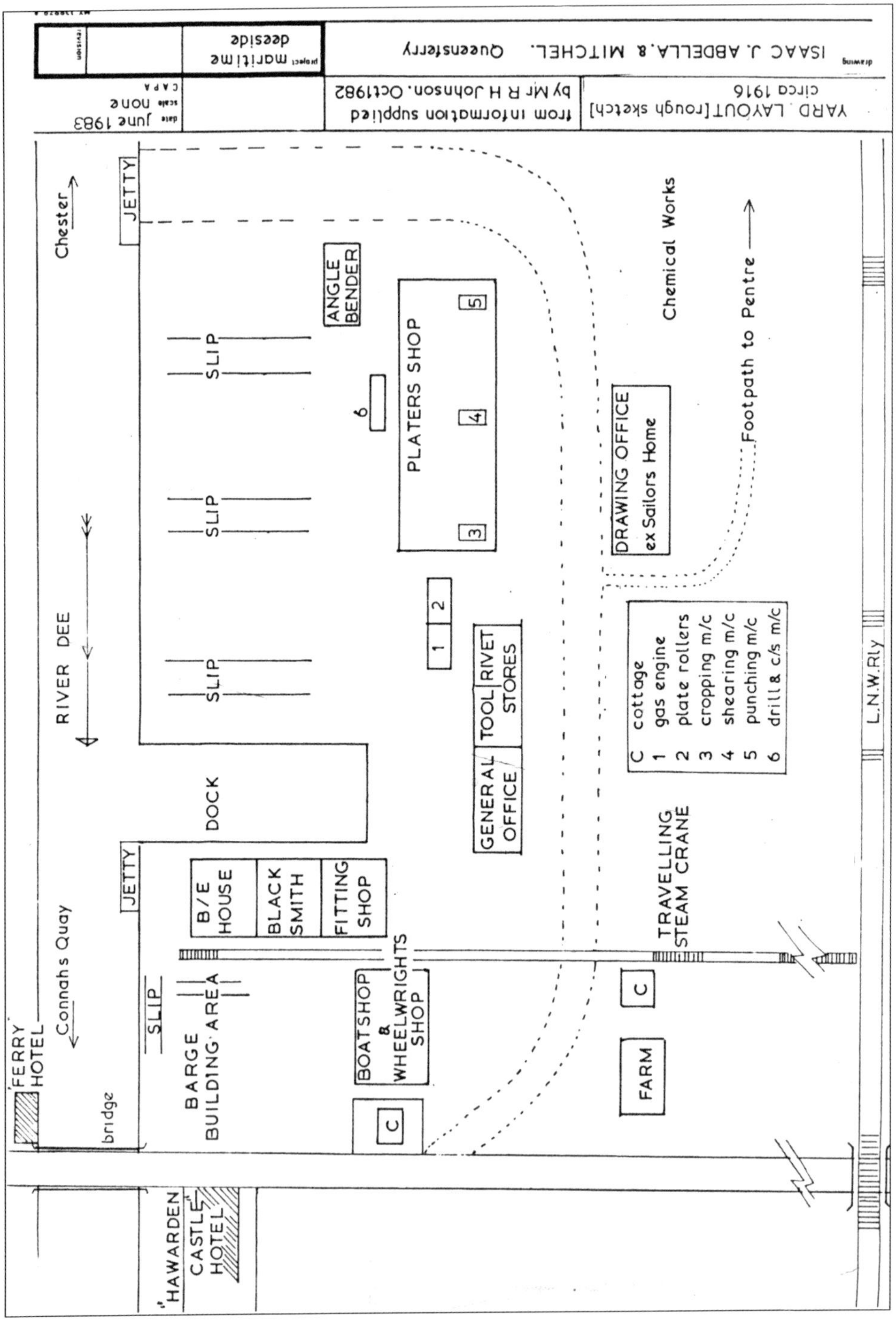


Plate 44: Plan of the Abdela & Mitchell yard.

Plate 45: Mr Earle and Mr Abdela.

to become 'Isaac J. Abdela & Mitchell Ltd.'. At the time of the merger, Isaac J. Abdela & Co. was described as a 'manufacturer of slippers, glass cutters and engineers of 45, Caernarvon St, Manchester', but at the 55 George St, Head office address they were described as 'shippers and agents'.

The new joint company operated the former site of engineers and boatbuilders, Edwin Clark & Co. at Brimscombe for the next 25 years. From 3rd April 1901, Isaac J. Abdela became chairman, with Demosthenes Tchaoussoglou (from Mitchell & Co.), as a director, and John Waterman Earle, formerly of Edwin Clark & Co., managing director of the new venture. Here they built small craft, surf boats, river steamers and canal craft, which went all over the world, especially to South America (particularly to the Peruvian Amazon) and the Nile and Niger rivers in Africa.

Although Isaac was a qualified naval architect, his visits to Brimscombe seem to have been infrequent –perhaps for a launch– and there is no doubt that Earle was the driving force in the boat building business. Isaac was well-qualified to have a hands-on role in the business, having spent three years at the Technical School in Manchester and then serving three years with Messrs Foden at Sandbach in Cheshire, the well-known makers of steam wagons, traction engines, small stationary engines and major steam engine installations.[9] Nevertheless, it is believed that John Earle did the design work for vessels built at both Brimscombe and Queensferry.

Clearly Abdela & Mitchell found that they were limited in the size of vessels that could be launched into the Thames & Severn Canal, or that could be taken to the Gloucester & Sharpness Canal (in deeper water, some nine miles away by canal) to be assembled. Some craft were sailed along the canal to London for shipment aboard deep-sea vessels. The restrictions on the size of vessel they could build led to the purchase of the Queensferry yard which they took over in 1908 from the Dee Shipbuilding Company.

The Queensferry takeover would have required increased capital, and a change in the list of directors may give a clue to the source. No directors list is available for 1909, but those from 1912–25 show that the directors were Isaac Jacob Abdela and his younger brother Joseph Jacob. There is no evidence of any continued interest by the former Mitchell directors. Abdela family tradition holds that Isaac Jacob Abdela, although acting as company chairman, was not the principal shareholder, so his younger brother may have taken this role.

*Pre 1918 vessel construction*

We have already mentioned the first vessels and barges which were built at Queensferry earlier in this chapter. Two tugs were built there in 1909 for the Société Anon Provençale de Remorquage of Marseilles – *Provençal 17* and *Provençal 19* (Yard N°. 182).

Plate 46: Tug *Provençal 19.*

A *Journal of Commerce* photograph shows the *Provençal 17* sailing on her delivery voyage from the Mersey. Perhaps the Abdela family relatives who had fled to France helped win this order. Further small steel and wooden launches and other craft followed in 1910, and in 1911 the company completed the 150' loa *Lobao*, (Yard N$^{o.}$ 311), a magnificent twin-screw river steamer. She was the largest vessel, both in terms of length and dwt, that Abdela & Mitchell built at Queensferry and her launching was entrusted to Isaac J. Abdela's mother-in-law. It is interesting how the two yards worked together on this order; as with many of the craft built at Queensferry her steam engines were built by the Abdela yard at Brimscombe. In the case of *Lobao,* her steam launch was also built at Brimscombe, together with three similar craft. On 30th August 1911, the four 25' pinnaces, strapped together, were logged going through the Gloucestershire canal system. There are photographs of four such launches on the quay at Queensferry, with the larger vessel in the background, and one assumes they made the whole journey to Queensferry via the canal system. Again, the Abdela relatives who had fled to Brazil, may have been the reason why so many vessels were built at Brimscombe and Queensferry for South America and Brazil in particular. For the voyage to Brazil, the *Lobao* was fitted with sails for her transatlantic crossing. The local paper describes her as 'a handsome screw passenger steamer which is intended for service on the river Amazon between Para and Manaus.' She was designed for the Amazon rubber trade, although the rubber boom was coming to an end by this time, and she was designed with three decks to carry both cargo and passengers. Registered at Para, she was owned by A. Lobao until 1929 when she became the *Mar del Plata,* under the ownership of Pablo Arena of Buenos Aires, and worked on the river Plate, finally disappearing from Lloyd's in 1944, although for the last year of her career she had been bought by Guillermo Martinez, of Buenos Aires. The South American market was very important to Abdela & Mitchell and both yards, particularly Brimscombe, built a variety of vessels which either sailed or were transported there as deck cargo. For many years, Abdela & Mitchell employed South American agents; E. A. Da Costa & Co. of 10–11G Exchange Buildings in Liverpool.

In 1912, the stern wheeler *Manoel Thomas,* with a 300 h.p. compound engine, was launched, again to go to Brazil. She was dismantled and shipped in sections, to be re-assembled using local labour at Teresina in the north-east of Brazil, to be used on the Parnaiba and Poti rivers.

Plate 47: River steamer *Manoel Thomas.*

In the same year, another stern-wheeler, the *Broughton* (Yard N$^{o.}$ 331), underwent trials on the Dee before being dispatched to Nigeria.[9]

The two iron canal tugs *Worcester* and *Birmingham*, which, as far as I know, are the only surviving examples of Abdela & Mitchell craftsmanship, were also built at Queensferry in 1912 for the Worcester & Birmingham Canal Company.[10] They seem to be the only iron vessels which Abdela & Mitchell ever built and were used for towing barges through Tardebigge tunnel. According to Tony Langford, Abdela's quoted for the order under their own name and also through an agent.[9] It is possible that the two yards competed with each other for this order, but the agent's offer won the contract. Today *Worcester* can be seen in all her splendour at the National Waterways Museum at Ellesmere Port, still operating with her original Bolinder

Plate 48: Model of the *Broughton.*

Plate 49: The *Worcester.*

engine. The hull of the *Birmingham* is displayed at Tardebigge Boatyard, close to the tunnel entrance where she worked. The only two iron-hulled vessels that were constructed at Queensferry are the only two of Abdela's vessels from the yard which survive, although it is known that the yard also built some iron pontoons the following year.

In 1912–13, a number of small coasters and barges were launched at the yard, including the first two vessels for John Summers & Sons, the steel manufacturer who had set up on reclaimed marshland at Shotton in 1896. Six of the 27 vessels listed as being owned by them between 1897 and 1967 were built at Queensferry.[11] The *Carita* and *Fleurita* were the first in 1913. The 103' loa *Fleurita* (Yard N°. 351), with a 46 h.p. Bolinder engine, was to have a long career with John Summers until after the Second World War when she was purchased by Coppack Brothers & Co. of Connah's Quay. They sold her in 1961 when

Plate 50: The hull of the tug *Birmingham*.

the Point of Ayr coal trade finished. She survived until January 1965 when she foundered in the North Sea . The slightly smaller *Carita* also stayed with the Summers' fleet until after 1947, and again survived until the 1960s. 1913 was a very busy year for the yard as six further barges were completed for the Rea Transport Company, and a further four for the Great Western Railway. The GWR barges were relatively small, only 63 tons gross, and it is likely that they were used to carry domestic goods brought by rail to Birkenhead and which required transhipping to and from Liverpool using GWR warehouses adjacent to Morpeth Dock,[12] using the Chester Basin across the Mersey in Liverpool, where the former GWR warehouse can be seen today.[13] For years the Great Western had tried all sorts of ways to gain rail access into Liverpool. After the First World War this business declined as road transport started to gain ground on the domestic freight market, and the barges were sold to other owners.

About a 100 employees worked at the Yard from 1908–18.

*Output during the First World War, 1914–19*

A further eleven barges for Mersey owners were built during the period 1914–15, including another six for the GWR.

A further coaster, *Sir William* (Yard N°. 355), was laid down in 1914, originally for Vernons, the flour millers, but bought on the stocks by John Summers and completed as the *Felita*. She was 98' in length and was to have a long career being still afloat in 1956 as the Swedish owned *Alvtank*. All three of the first coasters built by Abdelas for John Summers survived both world wars and lasted more than 40 years!

Also in 1914 they completed the tanker *Kingsholm* for William Butler of Bristol, for service in the Bristol Channel. She was sold in 1915 to Elder Dempster for service in West Africa, probably as a bunker barge, and renamed the *Ilesha.* She was lost off Bardsey Island on 8th August 1915, on her delivery voyage, where she can still be seen on the seabed.[14]

In 1915, a coaster was built for the Darwen & Mostyn Iron Company, based at Mostyn dock. The *Honor Storey* (Yard N°. 377) of 129 tdw and 85' in length, was also still afloat in 1956, owned in Bridgwater, Somerset by Peace & Co. by which time she was known as the *Parrett.*

In 1916, the tug *Sloyne* was ordered by the Alexandra Towing Company of

Plate 51: The tug *Palencia,* formerly the *Sloyne.*

Liverpool which was spreading its orders round various U.K. yards because of the pressure put on yards to deliver priority Admiralty work. It took twelve months for the *Sloyne* to be delivered, rather than the normal eight or nine.[15] She was, however, only in the Mersey fleet of tugs for a short time as she had been sold by 1920 to William Watkins of London and renamed the *Palencia*. Later in her career she was again sold to the Shell Company of Gibraltar and was still afloat there in 1964.

During the period 1915–18, Abdela & Mitchell spent most of the time building vessels for the Admiralty at Queensferry, including a number of dumb boom defence tanks/barges such as *BD49* and *BD50*, three larger barges for boom defence purposes, as well as two floating grain elevators, the *DD5C* and *DD6C*.

In 1918, Abdela's moved on to the building of seven Strath-type trawlers for the Admiralty, most of which were quickly sold to commercial interests as hostilities ended. These trawlers were typically 203 gross tons measuring 115' x 22', and armed with a 12-pounder gun. 148 were laid down in 1917–18,[16] and a further four were ordered from Queensferry, but cancelled. Although not used for their original purpose, they mostly served the fishing industry well and during the Second World War four of them served as fuel carriers, examination vessels and minesweepers. One of these, the *Robert Farecloth,* was sold in 1919 and renamed *Humphrey*. In 1928 she was purchased by a New Zealand fishing company and taken to New Zealand. In 1939 she was still owned by Sanford in Auckland and was requisitioned by the Marine Department and taken over to the Devonport Naval Base in Auckland, where she was fitted out as a minesweeper and armed with a 102mm gun, which took five weeks.

Plate 52: HMNZS *Humphrey.*

The government of New Zealand did not want a repeat of what had happened during the First World War when mines had been laid in their waters. To give the government more financial control, the *Humphrey* was purchased in November 1940 from Sanford for the sum of £22,500. Initially she saw little service, but in 1940 the German raider HKS *Orion* laid mines in the Hauraki Gulf, when *Humphrey* was being refitted in Auckland. On 19 June the RMS *Niagara* struck a mine and sank in the Gulf, famously taking with her a shipment of gold. *Humphrey* and other minesweepers then swept the approaches to Auckland and disposed of the remaining mines. In November 1940, the First Minesweeping Group was formed and, until early 1944, she was deployed sweeping the approaches to various ports including, Wellington, Lyttleton and Auckland. In early 1944, HMNZS *Humphrey* was sent to Wellington to be converted into a boom gate vessel, as by then 'Castle' class minesweepers were coming into service, but the project was abandoned as the war was coming to a close. In May 1944 she returned to Auckland and was sold back to Sanford, refitted and resumed her working life as a fishing vessel until 1954 when she was sold and dismantled in Auckland. By 1956 she had been hulked as a 'shingle bin' near Waikauri Bay, north of Kawau Island. In 1970, the hull was towed back to Auckland and finally scrapped, quite a career for a naval trawler that was no longer needed when built.[17] She managed to have a 52-year career and ended her days a very long way (14,500 nautical miles) from her Deeside birthplace.

*Post 1918*

In the 1970s when I began to research this book, I was able to meet and talk to a couple of former Abdela & Mitchell employees. Mrs Parks (née Fox) had been the short-hand typist at the Abdela & Mitchell Head Office in Manchester from January 1921 to June 1925, firstly at 55 George Street and, after the financial restructuring of the business, at Brazenose Street. The small staff there consisted of Mr Suffell (the company secretary), Mr Pettit (the book-keeper), a young boy clerk and Miss Fox. She understood that Mr Abdela had a Spanish mother and a number of brothers in the rag trade in Manchester. At the time she was there, the family was living at 79 Palatine Road in Manchester. She remembered him as a big man who became very excitable when the brothers came to the office (one of whom had premises next door). She remembered that he had three children, the only boy (Fred) later joined the firm some time after Mrs Parks left their employ.

Mr Abdela was always a late riser, so Miss Fox did not start work until 9.30 a.m. –he always telephoned from his bed and arrived in the office about 11.30. In the 1920s, when Mrs Parks was working there, she recalled that the ship and boat-building business was depressed, with few orders. Mr Suffell took a reduction in salary and Mrs Parks was paid £2 per week, occasionally having to stay at work until 6 p.m. Another reason for the company not doing well at this time (1925) was a fire at the Brimscombe Yard, which, apparently, was not properly insured.

Despite the firm's financial problems, Miss Fox could honestly say that Mr Abdela was a good man who never had a wrong word to say to any of the staff the whole of the time she was there. He was most upset when the firm was put into voluntary liquidation in the spring of 1925 when it became Abdela & Mitchell (1925) Ltd., when someone put money into the company.[8]

In 1918, five vessels could be on the stocks at any one time and smaller craft were also sometimes built between the engineers' shop and the Queensferry bascule bridge. Ships were launched stern first across the river, and the slipways were fitted with hauling gear. Quite a few marine engines were supplied by Abdela & Mitchell themselves, manufactured at Brimscombe, but boilers and other fittings were bought in. To save money the company also ran its own trials on vessels and, for example, did not have the Bolinder engine people in attendance.

It is probably fair to say that the yard was run very economically. In 1920, one of the former Dee pilot's remembers that his father, a master mariner, was asked to take a cabin cruiser built at the yard through the canal system to Hull with his eldest brother. His father said he would do it for £20, plus expenses. However another retired captain said he would do the job for £10, plus expenses. The cheaper quote was accepted, but en route the cabin cruiser's stove got smashed and the retired captain stayed in the best hotels, making the bill £10 plus £110 expenses![18]

The working hours at the end of the First World War were 06.00–17.00 hours, with an hour for lunch. The yard at Queensferry was thought to be very old-fashioned for the time. At Christmas 1918, when Charles Catherall (whom I met in November 1971), started work at 'Abdullahs' (as it was known locally) as a boilermaker, he remembered how old fashioned it was. The donkey engine which drove the machinery in the shipwright's shop was driven by an elderly man who had a white beard and a 'square-rigger' cap. The donkeyman's four sons also worked at the yard. In 1924–5 Charles Catherall recalled that the foreman, Mr Dillon, wore a leather apron, moleskin trousers and a cap. In 1924, at the time when Mr Catherall left to go to Crichton's at Saltney, he was earning £2 18s per week as an engineer, and the workforce had been reduced to about 30 people.

The equipment, such as presses and shears, was driven by an old gas engine which needed three men to start it. In the winter, Mr Catherall could remember snow coming through the windows on to the work benches in the corrugated iron buildings! Another ex employee, Mrs Nellie Hughes (née Owens), who lived locally all her life and who worked briefly in the office at Queensferry in the 1920s, also clearly remembered how old-fashioned and run down everything was.[19]

The yard had lots of staff changes and never seemed to get going again properly after the First World War. During the war Abdela & Mitchell had spent a lot of their time building building boom defence tanks rather than ships, which explains why there seem to be relatively few merchant vessels built at the yard between 1915 and 1918 and why they took a long time to complete.

An interesting result of the demands of war on the yard was the building of the *Warita* which was laid down before before the outbreak of war but, because of priority work for the Admiralty, was not actually completed until 1920. She remained at the yard without her engine and with a number of bottom plates only loosely bolted in place. Charles Catherall remembered boring out the stern tube using antiquated equipment and remembered the job being held up because the watchman employed at the yard lived in and had a large number of children, some of whom put sand in the cylinder of the donkey engine so that it stopped the boring out of the stern tube! He also worked on the other Summers' coasters, the *Eldorita* and *Indorita*. All three of these Summers' vessels were fitted with Bolinder engines made in Sweden and it is quite possible that the *Warita* was not completed because her Bolinder was requisitioned for use in the local munitions factory for the duration of the war. Eventually completed in 1919, she was taken over by John Summers and her maiden voyage took her from Summer's Wharf at Shotton to the Bristol Channel carrying 400 tons of steel plate. In Dale Roads, Milford Haven, she began to take on water (it is thought because rust had got between the bolted, rather than riveted, plates and not being sealed properly when later riveted up, and rust flakes worked out with the vessel's movement) and had to be beached in Dale roads for emergency repairs. She later returned to Cubbin's yard in Birkenhead where she was stripped down and re-riveted. She was to survive until 1968.[20]

In 1929, a fuel pipe fractured in Morecambe Bay and caused a fire which gutted the *Warita's* lifeboats, engine room, engineer's quarters and the captain's cabin. She had to be towed into Fleetwood and repairs were later effected at Barrow. In 1935, when she carried a skipper, mate, two engineers and two deckhands, her Bolinder engine was removed at Cubbin's yard at Birkenhead. In 1938, she returned to their yard for major repairs after tearing part of her bottom out on Barsalloch Point on Luce Bay, en route to Fort William with a cargo of basic slag.

Between 1940 and 1954, the *Warita* was under the command of J. W. Hopwood whom this author spoke to in 1971.[21] His sea-going career had started with John Summers as a deckhand on *Ogarita*, the pioneer Bolinder-engined vessel in the

Plate 53: The *Warita* in the ice – believed to be the river Dee.

Summers' fleet which was mostly employed carrying galvanized sheets from Shotton to their depot at Harrington Dock in Liverpool, or off-loading them overside to deep sea vessels there. He went with the *Warita* in 1946 when Summers disposed of their older vessels and she was sold. She was renamed the *Alfred Mason* on her purchase by Duff, Herbert & Mitchell Ltd. The Duff family of Faenol, Caernarfonshire had long connections with shipping through their slate quarrying activities at Llanberis, and one of the literary friends of the family was A. E. W. (Alfred) Mason, author of the best selling book *The Four Feathers*. Captain Hopwood said that when she was sold it was the first time that he had to read a chart at sea! Under her new owners she ran regularly from Garston to the Bristol Channel and was then taken on charter to Southampton gas works carrying coal from Blyth. She also took a cargo of empty tins to Crosse & Blackwell at Peterhead via the Caledonian Canal, where a man had to be sent ahead to prepare the locks. During this time she was drydocked at Port Dinorwic, which was owned by the Duff family.[21]

Sold again in 1954, the *Alfred Mason* was bought by Captain John Tyrell of Arklow and remained in his ownership until his death in 1967. Captain Hopwood left the ship at this time and returned to John Summers, where he continued as master of their *Staley Bridge* until 1966. The *Alfred Mason* was subsequently sold for demolition to Hammond Lane Foundries in Dublin in February 1968.

Certainly John Summers were enthusiastic about the use of Bolinder engines after their initial experiences with the *Ogarita* which had been built in South Shields as an exhibition vessel for the engine fitted by Bolinder's U.K. agent, James Pollock of Faversham in 1913. Captain Hopwood's view was that, once trained, ships' engineers could make them a very reliable engine. In 1920, following the eventual completion of *Warita*, two further vessels were completed at Abdela's Queensferry yard, the *Indorita* and *Eldorita*, both fitted with Bolinder engines – of 201 tons gross, they served the Summers' fleet until 1946, the *Eldorita* doing Royal Navy service as a victualling vessel at Greenock during the Second World War. In that year she was sold to Captain Hugh Shaw and his son, and was later sold again to the Colchester Shipping Company, R. S. Banyard, who already owned Abdela's 1913 built *Carita*. On 12th December 1966, after 46 years afloat, the *Eldorita* succumbed to a North Sea gale on a voyage to Rotterdam, after radioing for immediate assistance and reporting that she was listing badly with a flooded engine room. She sank 35 miles NNW of the Hook of Holland and the crew were rescued by a German vessel.[22]

Her sister vessel was more fortunate. Purchased in about 1947 by Coppack Brothers of Connah's Quay, the *Indorita* continued in the Irish Sea trade until 1969, often as, I remember, loading grain for Spillers for Belfast at the now infilled Canada Creek in the West Float, Birkenhead.

Laid up for sale in Egerton Dock, Birkenhead in 1969, she was sold for scrap to the Northern Slipway Company of Dublin, but the sale fell through and she was bought by John Hind, a naval architect. After a career with drab funnel colours, she suddenly sported a blue funnel with a gold Maltese cross and a black top. Then, in the spring of 1973, she made a trip under her own power up the Ship Canal to Manchester Marine Ltd. for repairs. Sadly it was to no avail, and she was subsequently sold for breaking up in Spain, being towed out of the Mersey by the Spanish tug *Punta Torres* on 21st March 1974.

1920 was a busy year for the yard and two coasters and two drifters were also completed. The *Cornish Trader*, 471 tons d.w. (see Plate 54) and the *Mary Nickerson*, 308 dwt. After a few years, the *Cornish Trader* was sold to Richard Hughes and became the *Cornish Rose*. In 1946 she was sold to J. P. Katsoulakos of Piraeus to become *Takis K*, disappearing from Lloyd's in 1955/6. The two steel drifters built

Plate 54: The *Cornish Trader (left).*

for the Admiralty, the *Foam* and the *Fogbreak*, were quickly sold into commercial service, but both were hired for Harbour Service duties throughout the Second World War.[16]

More interesting vessels were built in 1921 — the *Shell Mex 4* and *Shell Mex 5*— coastal tankers that survived the second World War, whilst a similar tank vessel, the *Aurora,* went to owners in Havana. The coaster *Coniston* was ordered by J & G Frew of Glasgow. Of 468 tons gross she was fitted with an engine from Abdela & MItchell, Brimscombe. In 1925 she became the *Solway Firth* of Northern Coasters Ltd., part of G. T. Gillie & Blair Ltd. of Newcastle.

After 1921 the Queensferry Yard seems never to have again enjoyed the success of its earlier years. There is no record of any vessels launched in 1922, and fewer than a dozen vessels were to be completed over the next ten years.

In 1923 only two vessels were completed, the small paddle steamer *Menna* was completed for Caernarfon Borough Council.[23] She may have been the smallest paddle steamer ever built for commercial service. Launched on 23rd June, by the Mayoress of Carnarvon, her length overall was a mere 80' and her beam over the sponsons 24', her gross tonnage was 76. Nine tenders were sought by the Borough Council, and the quote from Abdela & Mitchell was less than £5,000. She was designed for passenger and cattle carrying on the Tal-y-Foel ferry service across the western end of the Menai Straits from Caernarvon. The delivery voyage of the *Menna* proved to be an epic trip and Mr Abdela himself, accompanied by one of his two daughters set sail from Queensferry. When they were off the mouth of the Dee the weather got so rough that the paddles were frequently out of the water. Miss Abdela was ill and they had to put in to Mostyn where she was put ashore.

The ferry service only continued until 1929 when the vessel was sold to the James Towage Company of Westminster who renamed her the *Alumchine*. From 1933–62 she was engaged almost entirely in passenger and freight carrying in Milford Haven, running mainly between Neyland and Hobb's Point, passing into the ownership of Pembroke County Council in 1948. In her later career she was licensed to carry 216 passengers and four crew. She could also carry five cars.

When the *Alumchine* was replaced in 1962 by the M.V. *Cleddau King*, her original compound engine of 115 i.h.p. was still in situ and there were hopes that she would be the first paddle steamer to be preserved. However all attempts failed and she finally went to the breakers in 1965.[24]

Plate 55: The *Alumchine* (formerly the *Menna*) in her later years.

In 1923, the coaster *Cornish Merchant* was completed, a sister vessel to the earlier *Cornish Trader* of 1920. Like her, she was sold by Cornish Traders Ltd. of Falmouth to Richard Hughes, becoming their *Fowey Rose*. Of 470 gross tons she was fitted with a 74 h.p. Abdela & Mitchell vertical compound engine that gave her a speed of 8.5 knots.

On 5th July 1941, under the command of Captain Alfred Tyrell, she was bombed and sunk by German aircraft at a position approximately 20 miles SW of Govan's Head, Pembrokeshire, Captain Tyrell and seven of his crew being killed. In April of the same year, Captain Tyrell had been in command of Richard Hughes's *Dudley Rose* when she too had been bombed and sunk.

By this time the yard was really struggling to secure orders and in 1924 Abdela & Mitchell produced their last vessel, the barge *Penelope Paul*.

*Isaac J. Abdela & Mitchell Ltd (1925) Ltd.*

By February 1925, a resolution for winding up the company had been passed. As well as the decline in orders there had also been a fire at Brimscombe and speculation in steel stocks.[9] In November the new but short-lived company was given permission to use the company name and was formally registered in 1926.

Mr Abdela was still chairman, but Mr Walter Smith was now listed as one of the four directors. At Brimscombe, the new company built at least six vessels, but at Queensferry only the tanker *Energie* was completed in 1928.

The *Energie* (Yard N^o. 535, the previously recorded Yard N^o. being 463, the *Cornish Merchant*) was a coastal tanker with twin-screw Deutz oil engines. At 150' length she was the longest vessel built in Queensferry and was to have a long career. Ordered by Medway Oil & Storage Co. Ltd., she became the *Shell Welder* in 1952 and the *Rosia* in 1954, owned by the Shell Company of Gibraltar. After changing her name on two further occasions she became the *Comandante Ugo* in 1963 when she was owned in Naples by Gioachino Merone. She was still listed in Lloyd's in 1974.

Further financial problems arose and the company was forced to opt for the winding up procedure in October 1928.[9]

*Abdela-Mitchell Ltd (W. Smith)*

Walter Smith, who owned debenture stock, had applied to the Receiver over non-payment of interest by Isaac J. Abdela & Mitchell (1925) Ltd. when due, and the two yards then became part of the successful manufacturing firm Air Plants, which carried on and expanded a manufacturing ventilation plant at Brimscombe. Walter Smith's son, Sydney, had founded Air Plants in Leicester in 1930. At Queensferry, however, Walter Smith was able to complete two final vessels between 1930 and 1931.

The most important of these two vessels was the *Brightside*, a coaster of 476 tons grt built for the Eltham Shipping Co. of Liverpool (her Yard N^o. was 464, yet Yard N^o. 463 was *Cornish Merchant*, completed seven years earlier!). It is more than likely that the vessel was laid down in 1923 and not completed. She may have been a speculative build or economic circumstances may have meant that the owners could not afford to pay the yard. Fitted with an Abdela & Mitchell 69 h.p. vertical compound steam engine she was named after the house which Walter Smith owned in Leicester.[26] After two years she was sold to L. Knopp of Liverpool and again, in 1934, to the Fortis Steam Ship Co. Ltd. (T. H. Donking of Middlesborough, managers). She survived the Second World War, passing into the ownership of Robert Taylor and Sons and managed by G. T. Gillie & Blair in 1945.

On 24th September 1949, she became a total loss after running aground in thick fog a few miles north of Aberdeen in almost exactly the same spot as another vessel two years earlier. The crew were safely rescued after taking to their boat.

A barge was also built, or finally completed, in 1931, the *John Hickman*, for Spillers at Birkenhead. She remained afloat until the 1960s and was named after the Spillers company secretary who oversaw her registry for the whole of her career.

These vessels that were started and completed years after they were laid down are most interesting. *Warita* and possibly the *Indorita* and *Eldorita,* were not completed immediately because of the war, but *Brightside* and a 120' loa sectioned stern-wheel river steamer (Yard N$^{o.}$ 317), also started in 1914, was still on offer for sale by Abdelas successors in the 1930s.

Isaac J. Abdela had died in the early months of 1930 after retiring to the Fylde. According to Miss Fox, when the company was financially reconstructed in 1925, he was heartbroken and this misfortune could well have affected his health.

In December 1933 and January 1935, the firm of Abdela-Mitchell (W. Smith) offered Messrs W. J. Yarwood & Sons Ltd. of Northwich the plant that still existed at the Queensferry Yard, finally signalling the end of their operations there.[9]

*Thomas Lowe & Sons Ltd – concrete barges, 1940–2*

For the sake of completion with regard to the end of shipbuilding at Queensferry, I have included at the end of this chapter a few facts about the barges built there by Thomas Lowe & Sons during the Second World War.[26]

In September 1939, Thomas Lowe & Sons, civil engineering contractors of Burton-on-Trent, were engaged in the building of new county offices at Ruthin. This project was abandoned in 1940, and shortly afterwards they were engaged to build a barge building yard west of the Abdela & Mitchell site at Queensferry (where the new Queensferry road bridge stands today).

In March/April 1940 concrete foundations were laid with 12" x 6" pitch pine slipways bolted down on top. Mr Clarke told me that he went round most of the abattoirs in North Wales to obtain the tallow to grease them.[27] The yard was equipped with a Scotch derrick and a travelling crane.

Each barge was 100' in length, 20' beam and had to have a 3' draught over its entire length, when light. They were designed to carry 400 tons of cargo. They were used for storing grain on the Mersey, lightened from Atlantic convoy ships needing a speedy turnround. Once loaded they were anchored in the river and, when required, were towed to the appropriate mill for discharge.

The bottom of each barge was built up from a series of concrete girders that were joined lengthways. The sides were gunnited by blowing concrete on to a reinforced frame, and then trowelled up to produce the required finish. All surfaces were polished and finished to very fine Admiralty standards. When completed, each barge was tested for leaks by being loaded with 200 tons of pig iron on each side in turn. If barges were slightly out on draft, concrete was cut off or added as necessary. Even the cement used had to be rigorously tested before use. A 6" cube was made from each 10-ton batch from Earles, and taken to Liverpool University for testing. Each barge was fitted with its own anchor, stern and bow and had a hand winch and steel davit to lift the anchor. The hold had steel hatch combings with wooden hatch covers and tarpaulins.

Fourteen of these barges were built, some being launched sideways, others fore and aft. The first two built were not numbered, but later ones were numbered *FB 6–10* and *FB 30–36* inclusive.

The yard employed 65 people at its peak, but ceased to operate at the end of 1942. When the contract was almost completed, some process units were also built at the yard for a tannery in Bootle.

After the end of hostilities many of these barges, together with those built at Barrow-in-Furness and elsewhere, were surplus to requirements and after lying idle in the docks they became unseaworthy and they were towed out to sea and used to strengthen the training wall at the entrance to the Mersey in the 1960s.

An example of those built at Barrow-in-Furness can be seen today at the Boat Museum at Ellesmere Port.

Plate 56: The barges *FB6, FB8* and *FB10* fitting out.

Notes

1. *Chester Chronicle,* 25th December 1835
2. T. W. Pritchard, *A History of the Old Parish of Hawarden Parish,* chapter 11 (Wrexham, 2002).
3. Information from Ann Harrison, archivist, Manx Maritime Museum.
4. Much of the information in this section is from Captain Stephen Carter of the Laxey Towing Company. He worked on the very last Douglas Head Ferry in 1970, a 36 pax launch, *Speedwell.* He also worked with the men breaking up *Rose* at the top of Douglas Harbour. Also see www.isleofman.com/manxnotebook. and G. Kniveton, *Douglas Centenary 1896–1996* and *The Douglas Head Ferry,* and Stephen Carter, *The Port Soderick Boats* (2003).
5. Letter from R. J. D. Scott, son of former owner of the Douglas Head Pleasure Gardens, 16 November 1988.
6. Letter to *Sea Breezes Magazine* from Mr J. E. Myers, June 1953.
7. Letter from Brian Hilsdon, Secretary of the Steamboat Association of Great Britain to the author, 16th September 1973.
8. Information from authors meeting with Mrs Parkes (née Fox), former secretary at A & M Manchester, Flixton, 17th March 1973.
9. A. M Langford, 'The Steamboat Builders of Brimscombe (Part 2)', *Gloucestershire Society For Industrial Archaeology Journal*, 1988, pp. 3–20, Gloucester Records Office.
10. Cath Turpin, 'Tunnel tugs of the Worcester & Birmingham Canal', *Waterways Journal,* vol. 7, 2005, The Boat Museum Society.
11. Roy Fenton, *Mersey Rovers*, see Bibliography.
12. Tony Barrett, *Cheshire Shipyards.*
13. Mersey Docks & Harbour Board Yearbook, 1905.
14. Royal Commission on the Ancient & Historical Monuments of Wales, January 2010.
15. Tim Nicholson, *Take the Strain, the story of Alexandra Towing* (1990).
16. J. J. Colledge, *Ships of the Royal Navy, vol. 2* (Newton Abbot, 1970), see Bibliography.
17. Information supplied by the Devonport Naval Museum, Auckland, New Zealand, 2015.
18. Information from meeting with Mr J. R. Taylor, retired Dee pilot, September 1971.
19. Information from Mrs N. Hughes of Mancot, circa 1986, former office girl, Abdela & Mitchell, Queensferry.
20. Information from Mr N. A. Battisto, letter to the author, 16th March 1972 regarding the career of the *Warita.*
21. Information from meeting with Mr J. W. Hopwood, August 1971,former master of *Warita/Alfred Mason* who began his sea going career on *Ogarita.*
22. *Shipping Casualties & Deaths*, HMSO, 236. 1238, Patents Library, London.
23. *Paddle Wheels,* July–August 1962, the magazine of the Paddle Steamer Preservation Society.
24. www.kingswearcastle.co.uk/alumchine.
25. Letter from Brian Hillsdon, Hon. Librarian of the Steam Boat Association of Great Britain, 29th September 1973.

25\. Author's article for the Thomas Lowe & Sons biennial *News Review*, N°· 48, May 1973, (Burton-on-Trent).

27\. Information from meeting with Mr J. Clarke in July 1972. Mr Clarke was the General Foreman of the yard at Queensferry from 1940–2.

# 11

## Sandycroft and the early 'Iron Age'

Only two shipbuilders seem to have launched vessels at Sandycroft, but both were important pioneers in the development of iron shipbuilding in the U.K.

The first vessel built at Sandycroft was the wooden paddler *Kingfisher* in 1830 when John Rigby II (1794–1852) opened an extension of the family iron foundry that was already established there, becoming the first iron shipbuilder in Wales. Following the construction of a number of wooden vessels, the first new-build iron vessel from Sandycroft was probably the Mersey ferry *Star* in 1845.

The Rigby's had started their foundry business in nearby Hawarden in 1770, when John Rigby (1742–92) was 28 years old. He was the son of William Rigby I (1711–91), a local carpenter and road surveyor.[1] John Rigby II, the shipbuilder, was the grandson of John Rigby I who had started the iron foundry, his father being William Rigby II (1763-1842), who was known as William Rigby Snr.

The Hawarden foundry was an early development of the Industrial Revolution –it should be borne in mind that Abraham Darby III did not complete the first cast iron arch bridge near Coalbrookdale until 1781, eleven years after the start of the Rigby business in Hawarden, and John Wilkinson did not build the first iron vessel at Broseley, Shropshire until 1787. John Rigby, the shipbuilder, was closely involved with other family members and their various business interests. In 1818 he married Catherine, the daughter of William Hancock, a major producer in the Buckley brick-making industry. The Hancock family was destined to become one of the largest owners of schooners built on the river Dee by Ferguson & Baird and others, ships essentially used for the shipment of bricks to Ireland and other coastal destinations. As early as 1811, the sloop *William*, built at Chester, was owned by John Rigby I, William Rigby I and William Hancock.

The Rigby family were also related to the Boydells (who as already noted were involved in shipbuilding at Queensferry during the period 1836–41) of whom three generations were land agents to the Glynne family, from whom land at Sandycroft was leased in 1830 by the Rigbys in order to set up the shipbuilding business. It would appear that the Rigbys were planning to be in the shipbuilding business for the long term as they took out a 50-year lease on the Sandycroft site in January 1836.[2]

John Rigby II, was a steam-engine specialist before he embarked on the building of ships. Between 1830 and 1847 he provided engines for numerous vessels that were built elsewhere. The earliest record of a Rigby marine steam engine seems to have been that supplied to the *St David*, built by Mulvey at Chester in 1824, '... this beautiful vessel, which as our readers are aware, is built expressly for the purpose of facilitating our communication with Wales, is to proceed down river to Sandycroft by tomorrow afternoon's tide in order to receive the powerful engine prepared by Messrs Rigby and Hancock. It is likely that the novel sight will attract the presence of a good number of people.'[3] In 1831 and 1835, Rigby provided engines for two Mersey ferries, the *Askew* and the *Alexandra* and was clearly developing a good reputation because, in 1838, he provided the engine for the ferry *Boxer,* launched in February 1838 by Alexander Lyle at Dartmouth, Nova Scotia. She was a fine paddle steamer fitted with a side-lever engine, 26" dia, 3' stroke, built by Rigby in 1835. The *Boxer* was sold in 1864 and her engine was transferred to another side-paddle ferry, the *Chebucto*, built by Cameron of Dartmouth, Nova Scotia in 1865. This ship continued to trade until 1892, by which time she must surely must have had a new engine. Somehow, a transcript of the specifications for building this engine has survived:

> The whole to be made in a substantial and workmanlike manner, and in power fully corresponding to the assigned force of 20 Horses rated agreeably to the calculations of Boulton & Watt, as it is intended to propel a boat of about 90 tons on a Ferry, she starting from either side every 15–20 minutes and running 1¼ miles. Boiler to be in two pieces with two furnaces to be placed conveniently for the management of one fireman.
>
> The paddle rings and arms to be sufficiently strong and well fitted to bear occasional contact with drift ice.
>
> The water in the harbour is uncommonly salt. Engine weight and boiler weight to counterbalance one another.
>
> A list of spare parts to be provided as requested.
>
> Copper pipes for all communications with the salt water, copper bolts for all fixings,

wrought iron boilers, wrought iron paddle shaft and cranks, two safety valves (one of these to be out of reach).[4]

In 1841, John Rigby II built and engined the *Guapicen*, a six-gun wooden despatch vessel for the Brazilian navy. It is believed that when she was broken up, her engine was transferred to another warship.[5]

As well as marine steam engines, John Rigby II built steam engines for a variety of onshore uses. In 1842 he built an engine for the Liverpool & Harrington Water Company. The steam cylinder worked a 9' stroke and weighed 19 tons. The beam/lever was 33' long and weighed 16 tons. At the time, this engine was a milestone for John Rigby, but the involvement with the Liverpool & Harrington Water Company may well have subsequently contributed to his downfall as an ironfounder and shipbuilder of some repute.

Although John Rigby continued to build vessels and fit their engines at Sandycroft through the 1840s, he also continued to supply engines and boilers for other shipbuilders. By 1842 the Sandycroft Ironworks had acquired a reputation for engineering innovation and an article which appeared in the *Polytechnic Journal* noted Rigby's association with a new patent propeller system invented by a Mr Edward Finch who was born in Dudley, Worcestershire in 1812, the son of John Finch, who had established the Liverpool foundry of Finch & Willey. In April 1841 he was granted a patent for '... improvements in propelling vessels.'[6] In April 1842, a sloop of 31 tons was constructed by John Rigby II, carvel-built with a square stern. This vessel was wholly owned by William Rigby II, presumably John's father. The experimental paddle system and a steam engine designed by Finch, were also fitted to the sloop called the *Lapwing*. The propulsion system was more akin to oars or sculls according to a reporter, who enjoyed the vessel's maiden voyage.[7] Instead of the conventional paddle wheels she had two 'plates' which were attached to the shaft and entered the water at an angle of about 40° and were most deeply immersed when the engine was at half stroke. These propelled the vessel along by 'impulses', somewhat similar to the way in which a boat is propelled forward by oars. It was stated that once the vessel picked up speed, the impulses were scarcely perceptible and, unlike a conventional paddle steamer, they did not produce a backwash; instead they just made small swirls in the water. In July 1842 the *Chester Chronicle* advertised,

... excursions along the Welsh coast from the Crane, Chester, landing passengers at Flint and Bagillt, to Mostyn, and weather permitting, to Rhyl. The *Lapwing* steamer, worked by Finch's propellors, under the command of Captain Rowland, will start from the Crane, Chester on Tuesday next, 19th inst at 08.30 a.m. on a trip of pleasure, and return at 9.30 p.m. Fare 2/6d, children half price. Wine, Spirits and porter to be had on board.' Similarly on Monday 22nd August a trip to Bangor from Chester was advertised, at a fare of 5/-, apply Captain Rowland, 4 Crane St.[7]

William Rigby II (or in reality, after his death, his son) sold the *Lapwing* to John Benson (of Paddington) and some other gentlemen who were directors of the Bahia Steam Navigation Company, in 1843. In 1844, the Register is annotated 'sold to Bahia'. At only 68' in length, and with an engine room 21' long, she can only have been used a passenger carrier. Did she ever reach Brazil (under sail?) and did she keep her novel propulsion system? We will probably never know. As the vessel was sold within two years of her launch, it must be assumed she was not as successful as hoped. Edward Finch, still working as an engineer, moved from Liverpool to Chepstow by 1861, where he was a a shipbuilder and engineer employing 76 men and 30 boys. He remained in Chepstow, building ships and bridge sections, until his death in 1873.

John Rigby's most prestigious order must have been for the engines of HMS *Fury*, a 'paddle sloop of war'. The hull was built by Sheerness Dockyard and completed in 1845. She was 1,124 tons builder's measurement and 190' in length. She arrived in Liverpool on 22nd February 1846 where her engines were to be fitted. In April 1848, a report appeared in the local newspaper which was an extract of a letter to John Rigby from Commander Willcox, dated 27th January, regarding H.M. steam sloop *Fury*:[8]

Our voyage from Rio occupied 72 days. The ship sails and steams very well, going 12 on the second cam of expansion with three boilers. It appears we have just arrived in time and our captain has lost no time in getting away having coaled and refitted everything we wanted in 48 hours. We hope to reach Hong Kong about 4th–5th February. There is no force there at present to carry out any very active measures, except a blockade of Canton. Our craft has turned out something more than creditable, her engines work admirably, she is a beautiful sea boat and I think the fastest steaming vessel of her class in the service, never requiring her full power. We have found, working expansively and saving half the fuel she averages 11.6 kn. There is a pretty good steam force now in China … .

She subsequently saw service in the Black Sea during the Crimean War and also the Far East where she destroyed pirate junks and villages. She served in the Royal Navy until 1864 when she was sold for private use.

In 1845, John Rigby, as the Hawarden Ironworks Company, undertook some further work for the Liverpool & Harrington Waterworks Company. They had previously done a great deal of work on engines, steam boilers and pumps, but never a tank. By September of that year they had completed an iron water tank in Liverpool that was capable of holding 250,000 gallons. It was a rectangular shape, measuring 71' x 24' 5", and there was no previous tank in Liverpool that was as big – building large tanks with a circular base for strength had clearly not yet been developed. It was constructed under the direction of Joseph Howell,the manager of the Hawarden Ironworks Company but, for reasons unknown, it was not filled until Christmas Day 1845 when the pumping engines (probably those built by Rigby in 1842) were set to work and on Boxing Day, when it was about two-thirds full, it burst, totally destroying two houses and drowning five residents.[10] After an initial inquest and an inquiry in early January, a verdict of manslaughter was returned by the coronor's jury on Joseph Howell with a deodand (a fine imposed by the Crown) of £100 on the tank. This verdict was subsequently thrown out by a Mr Justice Patterson and, in September 1846 at the Liverpool Assizes, the final outcome of the case was that Hawarden Ironworks was obliged to pay a claim of £2,456 (almost £220,000 at today's prices) to the Harrington & Liverpool Water Company for losses sustained by the bursting of 'the great iron tank'.[9]

Opinions at the Assizes differed as to the tank's structure and the suitability of the foundations. Interestingly, one person who gave evidence at the inquiry and again at the Assizes, was one John Grantham, surveyor and engineer, who was a few years later to be involved with the construction of a number of vessels at both the Cram yards. He believed the foundations were suitable but that the supporting stays for the tank had been wrongly positioned.

There is no doubt that this fatal accident harmed the reputation of the yard and threatened its financial stability. Williams Brothers, bankers of Chester, were clearly involved in the yard's operation at this stage as they were named as defendants and represented by Solicitors at the Assize court hearing.[3]

Despite these ongoing issues, in October 1846 John Rigby launched his largest iron paddle steamer at Sandycroft, the 209 ton *Forth*, built for the Duke of Buccleuch and Sir John Gladstone, the Liverpool merchant and father of William Gladstone, the future prime minister. Originally from Scotland, Sir John had bought the Fasque estate in Kincardinshire in 1829 and in 1839 William had married Catherine Glynne. As already noted, the Rigby foundry at Sandycroft was sited on land leased from the Glynne family, so that when Sir John turned his attention to specialising in transport and trade with India and China, there was a ready-made shipbuilding connection.

The *Forth*, one of three steamers built under the terms of an 1809 Act passed to promote the ferry across the Firth of Forth between Burntisland and Granton, was first owned by the Granton Harbour Company. The railway line to Granton was completed in 1847, after which there was a through connection by rail and steamer between Edinburgh and Perth. The ferry fleet was taken over by the North British Railway in 1862. When the ship was launched by the sister-in-law of Captain Dundas of Aston Hall, the tide was 20' 5", but on reaching the water the *Forth* remained stuck in her cradle and all the efforts of the steam tug *Cymro* were unable to move her.[11] On the next tide, however, she floated off perfectly. Despite the failure of the first launch, the celebrations went ahead to mark the occasion at the Hawarden Castle Hotel in Queensferry where John Rigby presided. It is interesting to note that other well known shipbuilders from the area appear to have collaborated in the building of the *Forth*, '... under the inspection of Mr Wilson, shipbuilder [see Chapter 2] formerly of this city' [Chester], but now in eminent business in Liverpool,' and Mr Mulvey [see Chapter 3] had undertaken the ship's carpentry work.[11]

By the time the *Forth* was running trials in 1847, the builders had been renamed the Hawarden Ironworks Company, and a newspaper article of the time stated that '... the engines having been designed and constructed by Mr Howell of Hawarden, the able engineer of that establishment, and we have pleasure in copying the following from the *Caledonian Mercury* of 25th ult.[12]

> The new steamer for the Burntisland to Granton ferry made her last trial trips on the 16th when she crossed with two full cargoes in 25minutes each time, at first some feared that she drew too much water – but we are glad to find there has been some serious error in her measurement – in fact she draws 2" less than one of the present boats. Her draught will not be affected by any deck cargo which she is required to stow and from her power of

engine she will prove as effective with a headwind or a side sea – she will keep her course straight across ... whilst others in an easterly gale must stand nearly down to Inch Keith.

The decision to bridge the river Tay and bring the North British Railway (NBR) directly into Dundee was taken in about 1870. It was a bold move, guaranteed to increase NBR traffic to the north and, while a bridge over the Forth was contemplated (the Forth Railway Bridge was not completed until 1890), there would be a period where a substantial increase in ferry traffic would need to be accommodated. In May 1868 the Board of Trade reduced the number of passengers authorized to be conveyed on the boats and additional passages had to be laid on.[13] From that date the total capacity of the passenger fleet was required to implement the service, and the career of the *Forth* was extended.

In an accident at Granton on 21st November 1872, the *Forth* was backing out from the pier, but was so crowded that the helmsman could not see astern and she collided with *Kinloch* which was entering the harbour. The *Forth* was badly damaged at the stern. At the ensuing enquiry it was found that she had been overcrowded and the company was fined £52 10s.

The vessel was re-furbished, and continued in service until 1876, and was then used as a coal hulk. In 1879, the bluff-bowed ugly-duckling of the fleet was sold to S. & H. Morton of Leith for £725 and for many years she lay derelict on the foreshore of the East Harbour at Granton.

The final vessel that can be attributed to John Rigby is, unusually a schooner, the *Gamon*, built in 1847. Little is known about her, but she appears to be the only ship of this type to have been built there.

Plate 57: The buildings at the Sandycroft yard which date from the Rigby era.

The works at Sandycroft and Hawarden were offered for sale on two occasions – in 1847 and again in 1853 – and it is believed that John Rigby closed the shipyard in the late 1840s, perhaps because of ill health.

By 1852 the shipbuilder John Rigby had died and nothing more is heard of Joseph Howell after 1851 – he had been described as the '*Forth's* engine designer and constructor' in 1846. By 1857 the Hawarden foundry was being operated by Leigh and Gilbert Howell. Gilbert Howell was a son of Joseph Howell Snr, and Leigh was possibly a nephew, born nearby at Kinnerton, who by 1871 was a foundry owner at Bagillt. Another son of Joseph Howell Snr, also called Joseph, aged 25 in 1861, was the engineer of a steam vessel at Holyhead, so the Howells carried on their family engineering tradition elsewhere. However, the historic Hawarden Foundry was still in business in 1907 albeit under the ownership of Ratcliffe & Son, but after 1847 no further vessels were built at Sandycroft until the remainder of the lease was taken over by George Cram in December 1853.[2]

The Rigby family's tradition of marine engineering also continued into the next generation. William, the only son of John Rigby to survive into adulthood, studied engineering and joined the staff of Robert Napier on the Clyde and was eventually promoted to manager, and married Jane, a daughter of the Napier family.[1]

George Cram took over the yard at the end of 1853, the same year that he completed his first vessel at Chester (the iron steamer *Amelia* built at the Roodeye yard.) He clearly felt that the demand for iron vessels was going to outstrip the available space at the Roodeye and that taking on additional land at Sandycroft would help him to secure orders for larger vessels. At Chester he completed two vessels in 1853, and a further six in 1854, which was quite an achievement from a standing start in a yard that had probably not been used since 1848 and then only for wooden shipbuilding.

Only two vessels were destined to be built by Cram at Sandycroft. The first was the *Winefred*, an iron, full-rigged ship, built for Sharples, Jones & Co of Liverpool. She was registered in Liverpool on 17th January 1855 with a tonnage of 1,359 and measuring 219' loa and almost 36' beam. She changed owners in 1856, but was transferred to the London registry when she was again sold in 1872.

She was described as '... an old-fashioned ship with a heavy square stern with big gallery windows in her saloon. She had outside chain plates for her shrouds and backstays and dead eyes and lanyards. For many years she was owned by Taylor,

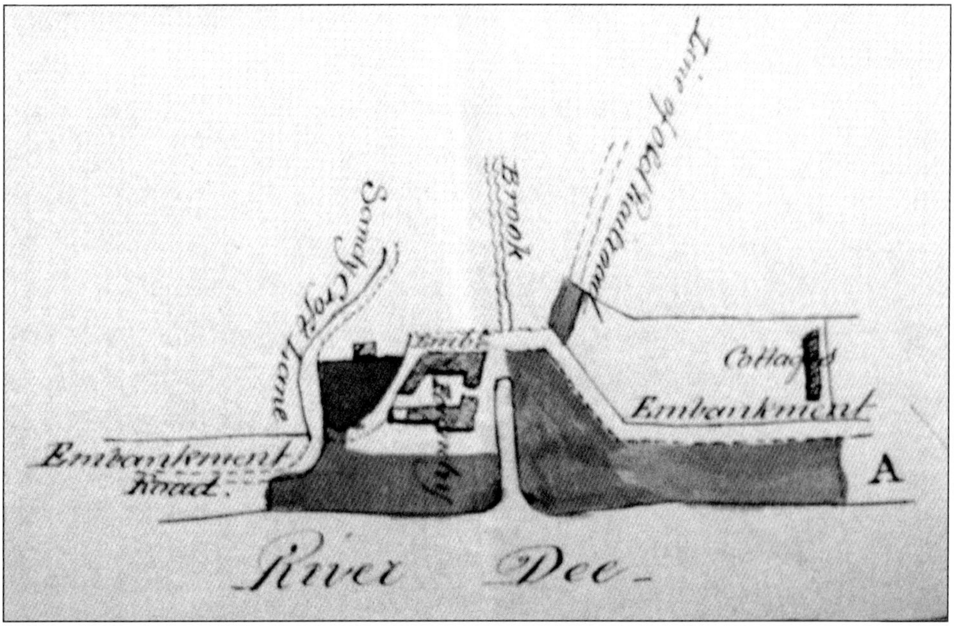


Plate 58: Layout of the Cram Yard at Sandycroft.

Bethell & Company of London and sailed in the Australian trade.' At her launch in December 1854 the *Chester Chronicle* reported:

> ... at noon a very beautiful iron ship of 1,460 tons register was launched from Mr Cram's shipyard at Sandycroft.[14] She belongs to Messrs Sharples, Jones & Co, merchants of Liverpool and is intended for the Australia or Indian trade. The vessel was named

Plate 59: The *Winefred.*

> *Winefred* by Miss Jenny Jones, youngest daughter of the owner. The ship glided off the ways in the most beautiful manner and was immediately taken in tow by steamer and arrived in Liverpool the same evening. Nautical judges consider her of superior construction and her lines are equal to any first class ship afloat. She has full poop and top gallant forecastle and her figurehead was greatly admired She is allowed by everyone who has seen her to be the strongest vessel ever built of iron.

The press report went on to say that she was the largest vessel ever built on the river Dee, and that it was understood that there was an even larger vessel now on the stocks at Sandycroft of 2,600 tons burthen, nearly as large again as the *Winefred*.

In 1894, forty years after her launch, the *Winefred* was sold to Finland, her new owner being J. W. Soderlund of Rauma. In 1900 she was sold again, to Armado Marius & Co. in Manaus, Brazil where she was used as a hulk.[15] Her ultimate fate is unknown.

Months before the launch of *Winefred* George Cram's financial problems had begun [as recorded in Chapter 4]. By June 1855, however, the press were able to report that the great iron ship at Sandycroft was approaching completion.[16] The *Royal Charter* was expected to be launched at the end of July. She had originally been laid down as an iron sailing ship for a Liverpool owner (it has been suggested that Henry Cram, George's cousin was one of those involved) but while on the stocks she was sold to Gibbs Bright & Company, the Liverpool Australian Steamship Company of Liverpool, who planned to run her to Australia in conjunction with the *Great Britain*. They had already bought the *Great Britain* in 1851 after she had been lying idle in Birkenhead for three years (her construction had begun in Bristol in 1839 and she had been completed in 1843, destined for the transatlantic service).

The Gibbs and Bright families were both merchants in Bristol. Robert Bright joined the Gibb's business in 1814, in which William Gibbs (later the richest commoner in England) also had a stake. After the death of George Gibbs Senior in 1818, the firm was renamed Gibbs Bright & Co. of Liverpool and Bristol. The Liverpool office, managed by the Brights, was involved in many aspects of shipping over the next 33 years, particularly ship sales, guano imports and liner agencies (for services to the West Indies, the west coast South America, America and Canada), but Gibbs Bright saw an opportunity to benefit from the rapidly expanding trade with Australia following the gold rush that had started there in 1851. It is estimated that 370,000 emigrants arrived in Australia in 1852 alone.[17]

Plate 60: William Patterson.

William Patterson, the naval architect, who had built the *Great Britain* in drydock at Bristol for Brunel, had first established himself in Bristol in 1823.[18] In 1831 he took ownership of the Wapping shipyard and drydock in Bristol that remained his until 1857. Patterson was employed by Gibbs Bright to re-design the *Royal Charter* on the stocks as a steam clipper and oversee her completion at the Cram yard as an auxiliary sailing vessel driven by screw. At the time he took over, only 75 frames of the mid-section of the hull had been erected.[19]

The *Royal Charter's* dimensions were length 320', 41' 6"beam and depth of hold 26' 6", with a measurement tonnage of 2,785 tons. She was almost 50% longer than the *Winefred*, the largest vessel previously built on the Dee, and was fully rigged with double yards and topsails. Her saloon could accommodate 50 first class passengers and was fitted with 28 state rooms, with double berths measuring 10' x 6' 4" in each room (her interior must have looked very similar to the excellent re-construction of the accommodation of the *Great Britain* which can be seen in Bristol today). When sailing she was to carry the same area of sail as the *Great Britain*. She had direct acting trunk engines, manufactured under their latest patent by Penn & Co. of, Greenwich, London, similar to those installed in the P&O steamer, *Himalaya*. The 'double acting' horizontal trunk engine was considered the latest in marine engineering technology and had already been utilised for two naval ships of the line the *Duke of Wellington* and the *Royal Albert*. One of these engines has been salvaged and renovated in Australia by the Western Australia Museum Service. HMS *Warrior*, built in 1860 and now restored at Portsmouth, was fitted with a more powerful version of the Penn trunk engine and a replica can be seen aboard the vessel today. *Warrior* was also fitted with a lifting screw.

Patterson also designed the *Royal Charter* with a two-blade lifting screw, similar to that to be fitted later to the *Great Britain* to make her more suitable for the Gibbs Bright Australian service. Today the thought of arranging for a lifting screw in an iron steamer seems quite unrealistic, but as screw propulsion was to provide only

Plate 61: The *Royal Charter.*

auxiliary power, then the drag of the propeller was felt to be too much when under sail alone. As you might expect, the mechanics were complex, but after a few teething problems with disconnecting the propeller shaft and actually lifting the screw on her maiden voyage, the crew became very proficient. A very impressive mock up of the *Great Britain's* lifting propeller can be seen at Bristol alongside this famous vessel.

At 320' in length, the *Royal Charter* was longer than the width of the straightened section of the Dee at Sandycroft at high water, which would be approximately 310', and she was 'launched diagonally into the river with her stern pointing upstream towards Chester; she had to be built and launched almost in line with the stream astern up the river so as to let her take the water in the same direction as the flood tide runs.'[20]

The launch was not reported until 4th August 1855,[20] saying that on the previous Tuesday

Plate 62: A lifting propeller as fitted to the *Great Britain.*

thousands of people had gathered for the great event 'despite the heavy making rain. From Chester, everything that could roll was on the road and everything that could float was on the water ... all were doomed to disappointment as the great vessel did not float!'

Three Liverpool tugs were in attendance, the *Rattler*, *Sampson* and *Pilot,* together with the steamers *Cygnet* and *Test,* and the great and good of the Liverpool maritime community.

> At one o'clock, just on the full and everything declared in readiness, Mr William Patterson, the builder (who had previously constructed the *Great Britain* at Bristol) gave the word, the daggers were soon struck down and the lady of Mr Samuel Bright dashed the bottle on the bow of the ship in a spirited manner and christened her *Royal Charter* and the noble looking craft began to slide slowly down the ways, she got more speed and then came to a dead stop. Daggers not being knocked away was the cause, the ship therefore slewed on the launchways. Efforts were made to tow her off but the hawsers snapped.

The launchway had in fact` collapsed at the lower end. The heavy rain encouraged the crowds to disperse, but 200 men were kept on to dig a channel and remove ballast and Mr Alex Bissett from the Liverpool underwriters was brought in to give advice. On Wednesday and Thursday she again refused to budge, and it was decided she would have to stay there until 30th August when the tide would give a depth of 21' 7".

Plate 63: Looking upriver from the launch site of the *Royal Charter* today.

She again failed to launch on 30th August and the inability to get her afloat quickly brought complaints about the state of the river Dee and the lack of water. This was a constant theme throughout the period covered by this book, there was never enough water and there were always enquiries and studies being undertaken, but it seems there was always insufficient money or equipment available to make an appreciable difference.[21]

> On Tuesday, 4th September, a further attempt to launch the vessel failed but on Wednesday, 5th September, with very little exertion, she floated almost off herself and the launch was greeted with hearty cheers and the event announced by the firing of guns. At one o'clock in the afternoon, at the time of high water the *Royal Charter* was taken in tow by three steam tugs and proceeded down the river on her way to Liverpool. She was gaily decorated and as she passed Queensferry and other places much cheering took place. By the time she got to Flint Castle the tide had ebbed considerably and on passing a corner where two channels meet, she took the ground and became safely embedded without any strain or shock. At the flood yesterday about 1 a.m. she again floated and at the return of the tide she proceeded.

By December 1855 she was ready and had been constructed with seven water tight compartments. The coal to be used was anthracite and it was anticipated that she would burn 22 tons in 24 hours to produce a speed of 9 knots with 76 revolutions. On her two day trial trip, which was extensively reported, she achieved 8 knots under steam only.[19]

Despite the press report that she 'became safely embedded' off Flint, at the enquiry subsequent to her loss in 1859 questions were inevitably raised about the suitability of her construction and the hull damage incurred on grounding. Captain Harris said that he had surveyed and repaired her in dock at Liverpool and believed that she had broken 33 or 35 of her flat angle irons, and bent her main keel amidships for about 12' fore and aft and the midship keelson was broken.'[22]

> It was a kind of tearing down the two sides. Three or four of the butts of the garboard streak amidships were strained. Three or four of the plates were bent, but not broken or rent. They were taken out and placed in the furnace and reset. I don't think we had any of the sideplates out as they were not injured. The bilge kelsons were not in at the

time of the accident, but were put in afterwards to strengthen the ship. There were three kelsons in when she was built. Four or five of the stanchions amidships were bent. Many of the rivets were started in the bottom but only in one place and none of the heads came off. Stronger plates were put into the main kelson, on the top sides for the space of about 40ft. The ship was properly and effectively repaired.

Some further strengthening work was put into the vessel at the end of the first voyage by Mr John Vernon, the Liverpool shipbuilder, a 'fore and aft stringer', as large and strong as it could be made – 'the largest I ever saw up to that time, no expense was spared and I was not limited to price.'

The maiden voyage of the *Royal Charter,* was announced – she was to sail for Melbourne direct on 17th January 1856.[23] Fares ranged from 16 to 60 guineas. She left on time with 260 passengers, but had to put back due to bad weather and was detained in Plymouth Sound to repair and strengthen her upperworks and 'leakage in her waterways', but this was quickly put right by carpenters re-caulking them. She arrived at Melbourne on 16th April, after a passage of 59 days from Plymouth, the fastest voyage yet made on that route. She was also said to be the first English vessel to have adopted the American sail plan of double topsails on each mast. There is no doubt that the *Royal Charter* was essentially a sailing ship and her engines were only to be used in light winds and to assist her in bad weather or on entering or leaving harbour. Her bunkers only accommodated 425 tons of coal. The *Illustrated London News* reported in 1855 that '... the coal to be used on board is anthracite which will make no smoke and will be consumed at the rate of 22 tons in 24 hrs to give a speed of 9 knots.'[20] This quantity of coal would have only lasted 19 days on a minimum two-month voyage, and coaling stations en route to Australia were not yet established.

Surprisingly, perhaps, the *Royal Charter* was described in the press as a well-armed vessel,[19] with 4 x 18-pounder, 4 x 24 pounder guns, and a large swivel gun in the forecastle, and a good number of rifles in the saloon.

She plied the route for the next three years without incident until the night of 26th October 1859 when she met her end off Moelfre, Anglesey, only 60 miles from her birthplace, a sad end for a pioneering screw steamer which was by far the largest vessel ever built on the Chester River.

As previously mentioned, at the subsequent Court of Inquiry, questions were inevitably asked about the construction of the vessel and whether this could have contributed in any way to her loss. William Patterson appeared before the court and gave a detailed description of her construction, giving a good insight into how these early iron 'steamers' were built and the materials used (see Appendix 11). Her appearance is that of a normal iron, three-masted sailing ship of the time, with the addition of a stovepipe funnel.

Respected Victorian engineers were well-known for over-engineering their creations and both the *Great Britain* and the *Royal Charter* were no exception to this practice. She was simply in the wrong place at the wrong time when she was lost, and the ferocity of the storm that night, on a rocky coast, would have resulted in the destruction of any wrought-iron hulled vessel.

As already noted, the Cram shipbuilding venture was already in financial trouble and, after the *Royal Charter* left Sandycroft for Liverpool in September 1855, no further vessels were ever built there.

Notes

1. Notes on the Rigby & Hancock families by H. Morris Jones, FRO N/T1708.
2. Aldersey Papers, the financial affairs of George Cram, Cheshire Archives, Ref. ZCR 69/33/10–20.
3. 'Grace's Guide to British Industrial History', www.gracesguide.co.uk.
4. See FRO N/T/1089.
5. *Chester Chronicle,* 22nd February 1985, article by Denis Branigan, and T. W Pritchard, *A History of the Old Parish of Hawarden* (Wrexham, 2002).
6. *The Civil Engineer & Architectural Journal,* vol. 4, e-book; list of new patents, April 1841, Peoples Collection, Wales.
7. E. J. Hogan, 'Notes on Shipbuilding at Flint' unpublished MS, FRO, Ref. NT1523.
8. *Caernarvon & Denbigh Herald*, 8th April 1848.
9. *Westmoreland Gazette*, 5th September 1846.
10. *Lancaster Gazette*, 3rd January 1846.
11. *Chester Chronicle,* 9th October 1846.
12. *Chester Chronicle,* 16th April 1847.
13. Ian Brodie, *Steamers of the Forth*, Part 1, see Bibliography.
14. *Chester Chronicle,* 23rd December 1854.
15. *Sea Breezes Magazine,* April 1984, letter from Lars Gronstrand of Abo, Finland.
16. *Chester Chronicle,* 9th June 1855.
17. goldoz.com.au.
18 www.engineerswalk.co.uk/wp.
19. *Liverpool Daily Post*, 14th December 1855 report on the first trial trip of the *Royal Charter.*
20. *Chester Chronicle,* 4th August 1855.
21. www.oldmerseytimes.co.uk. and T. W Pritchard, *A History of the Old Parish of Hawarden* (Wrexham, 2002).

22. *Chester Chronicle,* 26th November 1859 report on the Board of Trade Enquiry at St Georges Hall, Liverpool.
23. *Life and Death on the Royal Charter*, see bibliography.

# Appendices

Abbreviations used:

A & M – Abdela & Mitchell

BU – Broken up

*cds – 'Closing Down Sail' see Bibliography

(I) – Hull built of iron

LR – Lloyd's Register of Shipping

MNL – Mercantile Navy List

# Appendix 1: Ships built in Chester

| Year | Name | Builder | Type | Tonnage | Remarks/Owners |
|---|---|---|---|---|---|
| 1800 | *Active* | Troughton | Ship | 289 | Reg. Chester. |
| 1800 | *Pomona* | | 2mbgtne | 117 | 69' x 20' 3"x11' 6". Square stern. Reg. Chester. 1806 Reg. Whitehaven —owned by John Wilson, master mariner and shipbuilder. |
| 1800 | *Tom* | Troughton | | 144 | Owned by Jos and John Troughton. |
| 1801 | *Mary* | | Flat | 59 | Reg. Chester. |
| 1801 | *Union* | | Ship | 214 | Reg. Chester. |
| 1802 | *John* | | Flat | 51r | 63' 6" x 13' 6" x 6' 2". Reg. Liverpool. |
| 1802 | *Union* | | Galliot | 90 | Reg. Chester. 33% owned by Thomas Dixon with Joshua Lace, attorney of Liverpool and William Wales, merchant of Liverpool. |
| 1803 | *Mary* | | 1m Sloop | 86 | 47' 4" x 18' x 9' 7". Square stern. Reg. Newry. |
| 1803 | *Lord Forbes* | C.F. Cortney | Ship | 556 | 121' x 32' 6", 2 decks, 3masts. Built for Liverpool owners. In 1803 owned by Liverpool merchants William Forbes and John Carson, sold to London merchants 12 Oct. 1805. Largest vessel built at Chester before 1808. 1812–14 may have been running to East Indies. 1818 running London–India, owned by Parker & Co. 1843 owned G. Marshall of London. 1847 loading London. Out of *Lloyd's* 1855. |
| 1803 | *Active* | Troughton? | Ship | 303 | Reg. Chester. |
| 1803 | *Chester* | | Sloop | 76 | Reg. Chester. |
| 1803 | *Chesterfield* | C,F,Cortney | Ship | 396 | 111' x 29' 3". Reg. Liverpool. Square sterned ship, 3 masts, 1/1/2 decks with high quarter deck. At Kingston, Jamaica July1804. Owned by Fletcher Yates and Mathews January 1803. This vessel was lost near Rampside in November 1811. Not in register 1818. |
| 1803 | *Isabella* | C.F. Cortney | Ship | 306 | 93' x 28' 8". Square sterned. Built for Thomas Mathew and John Carson of Liverpool. |
| 1804 | *Active* | Troughton | Bgtne | 160 | Reg. Liverpool. |
| 1804 | *Fanny* | | Bgtne | 171 | Reg. Liverpool. |
| 1804 | *Harriet* | | Sloop | 28 | Reg. Liverpool. |
| 1804 | *Diligence* | | Brig | 191 | 1834 running Leith–St Petersburg. |
| 1804 | *Inquisitive* | | Sloop | 27 | Reg. Liverpool. O.N. 25703. 1872 MNL owned by Richard Williams of Liverpool. |
| 1804 | *Mary Ann* | | Ship | 174 | Reg. Liverpool. |
| 1804 | *Contest* | Cortney | Gun Brig | 178 | 80' x 23'. 10 x18 pdr, 2 x 12 pdr guns. Foundered December 1809 in Atlantic. |
| 1804 | *Defender* | Cortney | Gun Brig | 179 | 80' x 22' 5". Wrecked off Folkestone 14 Dec. 1809. |
| 1805 | *Corpach* | Cortney | Sloop | | Built for the General Account Commissioners of the Caledonian Canal. |
| 1805 | *Ann* | | 2mbgtne | 109 | Reg. Chester. LR 1829, running Liverpool–West Africa. |
| 1805 | *Bostock* | | Ship | 411 | 107' 11" x 29' 11". Built for Liverpool merchants Thomass Fletcher, Jos Brands, J.H. Mathew, Thomas France and Samuel Bole. Re-reg. 1817. |
| 1805 | *Fame* | Troughton | Ship | 327 | Built for Ritchie & Co. Reg. Greenock. |
| 1805 | *George* | C.F. Cortney | Ship | 234 | 88' 6" x 25'. Launched 1 Jul. 1805, the same day as the *Fame*. Intended as a 'Guineaman'. First |

| | | | | | |
|---|---|---|---|---|---|
| | | | | | owned by Samuel Newton, Thomas Mathew and John Carson (Newton later in partnership with Cortney) |
| 1805 | *Johns* | | Galliot | 81 | 61' 4" x 17' 8". Reg. Lancaster 1805. Re-reg. Dublin 1832. Later described as a schooner. 1853 LR owned S. Hudson of Scarborough –coaster. |
| 1806 | *John* | | Flat | 38 | 56' 8" x 13' 10" x 5' 6". O.N. 16437. 1836, bought by William Hughes of Rhuddlan. In 1872 MNL still reg. at Chester to William Hughes. |
| 1806 | *Betsey* | | Bgtne | 181 | Reg. Liverpool. |
| 1806/7 | *Friends* | | Ship | 352 | 99' x 28' 5". Square-sterned. Reg. Liverpool. Owned by John Litt of Liverpool and John Groom of Kingston, Jamaica. 1834 owned R. Long and running London–Halifax. |
| 1806 | *Heywood* | | Ship | 444 | 114' 3" x 30' 3". Square-sterned with quarter f'castle. Reg. Liverpool 1807. Built for Jos Bircham and William Ward. 1821 owned by Sir John Tobin. 1834 running Liverpool–West Africa. 1840 owned by Hamilton Jackson & Co., Liverpool. |
| 1806 | *Mary* | | Galliot | 108 | 69' 11" x 20' 5" x 8' 4". 2m, square-sterned. Reg. Lancaster 1806. At Liverpool in June 1806. 1834 described as schooner, trading Livperpool–Wexford, owned by Whittys. |
| 1806 | *Mary Ann* | C.F. Cortney? | Ship | 313 | 99' x 27' 3". Reg. Liverpool 1806 to William Forbes and William Peatt and others. Re-reg. London 1808. |
| 1806 | *Mersey* | | Ship | 357 | 103' 1" x 28' 6". Square-sterned,2 decks. Reg. Liverpool 1806. Built for Samuel Newton, Thomas Hayes and Thomas Graham. This vessel was burned at Port Royal Harbour in Jamaica (note in Register 29 Jan. 1827). |
| 1807 | *Caledonia* | C.F. Cortney | Ship | 446b | Launched 1 Oct. 1807. 114' loa x 30' 3". Reg. Liverpool. Square-sterned, carvel built. 1828 wholly owned by John Mottershead.1831 owned by Sir John Tobin. After 1837 owned by Thomas Bold and John Jackson Stanley. |
| 1807 | *Hope* | | Ship | 342 | Reg. Greenock. |
| 1807 | *Little Venus* | | 3m Sch | 131 | 75' 10" x 20' 2". Reg. Liverpool. First owned by William Taylor of Liverpool. Sold to John Leigh of Liverpool, 1809. |
| 1807 | *Phoenix* | | Ship | 490 | 121' 8" x 30' 4". Square-sterned ship, frigate built. Built for Thomass Fletcher, Jos Brooks Yates, J. H. Mathew, Thomas Frances and Samuel Poole. Recorded as loading for India 1820 in the *Asiatic Journal for Bengal*. |
| 1808 | *Ann* | | Ship | 226 | Reg. Whitehaven, 1811. |
| 1808 | *Telford* | Cortney | packet | | 29' x 15' 5". 1 mast. Sailing packet built for Ackerley & Fairhurst to carry passengers from Ellesmere Port–Liverpool. 1832 to John Evans and James Collister. Reg. Dublin 1833. 1848 LR owned in Peel. Owned in Arklow at the end of her career. |
| 1808 | *Fanny* | Cortney | Snow | 206 | Launched 5 Sep. 1808, intended for the coal trade Chester–Dublin. Reg. London 1814. |
| 1808 | *Nevis Planter* | Cortney | Ship | 519 | 123' x 31'. Reg. Liverpool 1808. West Indiaman, first owned by Liverpool merchants Roger Fleetwood Williams and Hayson Wilson. May be 3rd or 4th vessel of this name. |
| 1808 | *Spanish Patriot* | | Brig | 142 | 72' 8" x 21' 8". Reg. Liverpool July 1808. Owned first by four Liverpool merchants. Sold Nov. 1809 to two other Liverpool merchants. |
| 1808 | *Hooton* | | Sch | 119 | 1821 running Liverpool–Drogheda, owned M. Couchy. |
| 1809 | *Lady Warburton* | C. F. Cortney | Brig | 377 | 105' 6" x 29'. Launched 2 Feb. 1809 for the South American trade. Brigantine with flush main |

| | | | | | |
|---|---|---|---|---|---|
| | | | | | deck. First owned by Henry Clarke, George Tod and Robert Tod of Liverpool. Sold by them in Feb 1811. |
| 1809 | *Earl of Chester* | Cortney | Ship | 470 | Square-sterned ship with flush main deck. Launched 24 Oct. 1809. First owned by Henry Clark, George Tod and Robert Tod. 1829 owned by McCaul, running London–St Thomas. |
| 1810 | *Charles Mills* | Cortney | | 580 | In East Indies trade 26 Dec. 1810 —lost May 1822, Bay of Bengal. |
| 1810 | *John* | | Barque | 465 | 1834 owned Ellerby. Reg. London, running London–Sydney. Wrecked off Plymouth, struck Manacles, 3rd May 1855 (see Hocking). |
| 1810 | *Hope* | Troughton | Brig | 136 | O.N. 8093. 1857 owned by J. Bradford, Belfast. 1872 owned by Alfred Hine. |
| 1810 | *Harriet* | Cortney | Brig | 129 | Square-sterned. Reg. Liverpool. Intended for the Irish trade. 1829 running Liverpool–Liguria. |
| 1810 | *Minerva* | Cortney | Brig | 220 | Launched July 1810. Owned by Capt. Richardson, running Liverpool–London. 1820 LR owned by Cheese Co. running Liverpool–London. Not in LR 1821. |
| 1810 | *May* | | Snow/Ship | 396b | 109' 11" x 19' 4". Square-sterned, carvel built with 2 masts and tops'l. First owned by three Liverpool merchants, sold to three others. 1825–34 owned by Sir John Tobin. 1834 running Liverpool–Bombay. 1845 sold by Wilson & Son, Liverpool to Nicholson & McGill out of *Register* 1855. |
| 1810 | *Maria Crowther* | Cortney | Brig | 125 | Intended for Irish trade. Launched same day as the *Harriet*. Reg. Liverpool. Reg. de novo, Whitehaven in 1825. |
| 1810 | *Flint* | | Flat | 59 | 62 3" x 14' 8" x 5' 9". First part-owned by Thomas Dixon. 1828 owned W. Porter. 1828–1829 owned by Thomas Mather. Re-reg. Chester 1833. Lost off Prestatyn. |
| 1811 | *Alice & Amelia* | | Brig | 106 | Owned by Gregson & Co. Traded Liverpool–Dundalk/Dublin to 1827 when out of LR. |
| 1811 | *Margaret* | | Sloop/gal | 62 | Round-sterned. Reg. Liverpool. Owned by John and George Wilson, merchants of Liverpool, 1824. |
| 1811 | *William* | | Sloop | 76 | 58' x 19' x 9'. First owned by John Rigby, William Rigby and William Hancock. Still owned by Hancocks, lead smelters, in 1844. |
| 1811 | *Cornist* | | Galliot | 46 | 54' 7" x 13' 7" x 6' 8". 1 mast. 1836 owned by Thomas Williams, Red Wharf (16), John Owen (17) and six others. |
| 1811 | *Vere* | C.F. Cortney | Ship | 460 | 117' 5" x 30' 8". Built for France, Fletcher and Yates. Owned in Liverpool and Jamaica. 1828 owned 50/50 by Thomas Tobin and Charles Horsefall. Re-reg. London, 1838. |
| 1811 | *Douglas* | C.F. Cortney | Sch | 99 | Intended as packet and trader Between Liverpool and the Isle of Man. First voyage from Parkgate. 1834 owned Fleetwood, coasting. |
| 1811 | *Downshire* | | Sloop | 60 | 1834 owned by W. Lowry of Newry. |
| 1812 | *Dee* | | Snow | 316 | Running Liverpool–Barbados, owned Griffin & Co. |
| 1812 | *Highfield* | | Brigtine | 142 | 77' x 22' 6". Reg. Liverpool. Owned by four Liverpool merchants, including John Bibby.1834 owned by Bibby & Co, running Liverpool–Dublin. |
| 1812 | *Three Brothers* | | Brig | 117 | 69' x 20' x 10'. Owned by Thomas Dixon, timber merchant at Chester.1811–12. Brought timber from eastern Canada to Chester. Loaded at Miramichi and St John. By 1831 owned by Baile, may have been a cheese ship. |
| 1813–5 | *Lee* | | Snow | | 51' 2" x 13' 2". Reg. Liverpool? |
| 1813 | HMS *Cyrus* | Cortney | 6th Rate | 464 | 116' x 30'. Sloop-of-war with 20 guns. Launched 26 Aug. 1813. Sold 23 May 1823 to Bennet & Son. |

| | | | | | |
|---|---|---|---|---|---|
| 1813 | *Clarendon* | Cortney | Ship | 431 | 110' 4" x 37' 7". Reg. Liverpool. Owned by five merchants including Thomas Fletcher, Jos Yates and John Mathew of Liverpool and Thomas Francis of Bostock & Samuel Poole of Waverton. Still afloat 1834. |
| 1813 | HMS *Levant* | Cortney | 6th Rate | 464 | 116' x 30'. 2 x 6 pdr, 20 x 32 pdr guns. Sloop-of-war launched 8 Dec. 1813. BU Oct. 1820. |
| 1813 | *Amity* | | Brig | 188 | Reg. Liverpool 1829. LR running Liverpool–Bahia. 1834 running Liverpool–Mexico. Owned by Nicholson and McGill in west coast of South America trade for some years. Out of registration by 1855. |
| 1813 | *Lisbon Packet* | | Brig | 118 | Reg. Liverpool 8 Feb. 1813. Owned by John Johnson Hamilton, John Somerville Jackson and William Jackson of Liverpool. |
| 1813 | *John Shand* | Cortney | Ship | 470 | Launched 13 Sep.1813. Intended for West Indies trade. First owned by Sir John Gladstone in Liverpool. Sold to Fletcher & Son in 1818. Still running London–Jamaica. 1831 still owned Fletcher. Not in LR after 1831. |
| 1813 | *Amelia & Hannah* | | Sch | 81 | Listed in 1855. |
| 1814 | *Countess Liverpool* | | Pkt | 121 | Built for Capt Davies of the Holyhead Packet Station. 1855 LR listed as owned by J. Crumbie, running Newcastle–France. |
| 1814 | *Sarah* | Cortney | Brig | | Launched June 1814 for a merchant house in Belfast. |
| 1814 | *Frances Mary* | | Sch | 88 | 1834 owned Thomas Eyton of Flint, coasting |
| 1814 | *Limerick Trader* | Mulvey & | Brig | 150 | Launched same day as the *Sarah*. Copper sheathed. Single deck. Owned by Williams, Evans for the London trade. 1820 running Liverpool–Limerick. |
| 1814 | HMS *Mersey* | Cortney | 6th Rate | 451 | 108' 6" x 31'. Sloop-of-war. 18 x 32 pdr, 8x12 pdr, 2 x 6 pdr guns. Allocated to harbour service March 1814. BU July 1852. |
| 1814 | *Mary* | | Brig | 115 | O.N. 8749. Reg. 1872 Workington, owned by Robert Goves of Workington. |
| 1814 | *Wellington* | | Brigtine | 96 | O.N. 12618. In 1826 re-reg. to William Hancock and John Rigby of Rangemore, Staffordshire, merchant and partner. 1872 Reg. to Hugh McCartney of Maryport. |
| 1814 | *John Crowther* | Cortney | Brig | | 1820 running for Crowther to Quebec. 1825 owned by Battersby. |
| 1814 | HMS *Eden* | Cortney | 6th Rate | 451 | 108' 6" x 31' x 9'. Complement of 150 men. BU Portsmouth May 1833. Armament as HMS *Mersey* (above). |
| 1814 | *Ellen* | | Snow | 196 | First owned by Thoms & Co. trading Liverpool–Brazils, then 1820 owned by Jones & Co., trading Liverpool–Demerara. 1831–8 owned Capt J. Taylor in London–Rotterdam trade. Out of LR 1839. |
| 1815 | *Nelson* | | Brig | 209 | |
| 1815 | *Abeona* | | Brig | 138 | Running London–Antwerp 1818 LR. |
| 1815 | *Susanna* | | Brig | 142 | 1834, LR owned by Williams, London. |
| 1815 | *Catherine* | | Bn | 84 | 1855, LR owned by Guy & Co. |
| 1815 | *John* | Cortney | Bn | 108 | Launched 24 Apr. 1815 for Capt John Thomas. LR1853 owned by Junker running to to the Baltic. 1855 running Liverpool to Australia. 1857 still owned by Junker. |
| 1815 | *Tom* | | Snow | 160 | Square-sterned, carvel built. Reg. Liverpool, 1822. |
| 1815 | *Dee* | | Galliot | 45 | Reg. Liverpool 1816. |
| 1815 | *Ann* | | Brig | 165 | 77' 4" x 19' 8" x 12' 8". In 1833 owned by twelve people— main owners were J. Swainson and George Cram, trading as Swainson Cram. 1834 running Liverpool–London. Still afloat 1847. |

| | | | | | |
|---|---|---|---|---|---|
| 1816 | *Thomas* | | Bn | 96 | |
| 1816 | *Hibernia* | | Brig | 103 | 68' 6" x 18' 5"x 9' 11". Reg. Liverpool 1816, part owned in Teignmouth. Re-reg. Preston, 1827. |
| 1816 | *Shamrock* | | Bqtine/Bg | 99 | O.N. 6556. Launched 20 Apr. 1816. 1821 owned by John Lowe, merchant of Liverpool. 1834 owned by Dicksons, reg. Berwick, running Berwick–Hull.1872 Reg. Yarmouth, owned by Wells Barber, Great Yarmouth. |
| 1816 | *Swift* | Mulvey | Brig/Snow | | Launched June 1816 for Mr Herbert for the Brazil trade. 1825 running Shields–London. |
| 1816 | *John Craig* | | Brig | 102 | Square-sterned, launched August 1816. Reg. Liverpool. Owned by John and Edward Glynne of Liverpool. 1825 re-reg. Whitehaven. |
| 1816 | *Sarah Marianne* | | Brig | 194 | 1834 owned by J. Seymour. Reg. Whitehaven, running Maryport–Quebec. |
| 1816 | *Worrall* | Troughton? | Snow +tpsl | 153 | Later desc as a square-sterned brigantine. Part owned by John Troughton of Liverpool, merchant, and John Worrall and others. Lost off Newfoundland 1832. |
| 1816 | *John Troughton* | Troughton | Brig | 269 | 96' 3" x 25' 6". Reg. Liverpool, main shareholder John Thompson, minor shareholder Troughton. On Troughton's death in 1820, John Thompson took over shareholding. 1820s running Liverpool–Antigua. To Bahia 1830, still owned by Thompson.Vessel reg. de novo Newcastle 1839. |
| 1816 | *Lord Nelson* | Cortney | Brig | | Launched same day as the *John Troughton*. |
| 1816 | *Ann* | | Flat | 31 | |
| 1816 | *St Winifred* | | Sloop | 70 | 60' 2" x 16' 3" x 6' 10". Reg. Liverpool. Re-reg. Dumfries1826. |
| 1816 | *Hope* | Mulvey & Evans | Brig | 154 | 73' 10" x 22' 3" x 12' 4". 1830 two shares each owned by William Rigby and William Hancock, 38/64 owned by Thomas Herbert of Liverpool. Hogan says she was a cheese ship. Still owned by Herbert in 1834. Flush-decked vessel. Later owned in London? |
| 1817 | *Endeavour* | | Sloop | 35 | 48' x 13' 5" x 8' 1". 1836 owned by J. Price, Holyhead (16) and eight others. |
| 1817 | *Calcutta* | Cortney | Ship | 389 | 110' 8" x 28' 8". Reg. Liverpool. Had been on the stocks a long time as a brigantine before being sold to John & Robert Gladstone, merchants (64/64). Finally launched in January 1817. On 18 Mar. 1820, the rights of J. Gladstone were transferred by will to R.G. & Thomas Ogilvy. 1834 running Liverpool–Quebec. 1835 owned by Jos Williamson and John Banks. 1836 owned by Ashley Brothers, Liverpool stockbrokers. In 1855 owned by J. Rogers of London and running from Plymouth–Sierra Leone. |
| 1817 | *Unity* | | Brig | 98 | 1834 LR owned by Capt Williams. Reg. Beaumaris, trading London–Le Havre. |
| 1817 | *Lord Hill* | Goolden | Flat | 60 | 63' 3" x 14' 5" x 6' 2". Reg. de novo 1842. 1827 vessel reg. to John Shanklin, Richard Thomas of Brymbo and Thomas Balmer. |
| 1817 | *Margaret* | Goolden | Flat | 144 | 65' 4" x 14' 4" x 5' 9". Running Liverpool–Oporto 1820. Reg. de novo 1842. Owned as the *Lord Hill* by Shanklin, etc 1827. |
| 1817 | *John & Mary* | | Sloop | 22 | 36' 5" x 12' 3" x 6' 6". Square-sterned, carvel built. Re-reg Liverpool Oct 1831. 1841 owned by Liverpool Fish Co. (Thos Tobin, Michael Humble, shipbuilder, and John Crowther). 1847 owned by John Hughes, master. |
| 1818 | *William & Helen* | | Brig | 117 | 1834 owned by Whittle & Co., running London–Poole. By 1857 described as a schooner owned by Wakes & Co. and running Newcastle–Baltic. |
| 1818 | *Alice* | | Brig | 226 | 90' 4" x 24' 0½" x 15' 10". Reg. Liverpool. Up to 1830s owned W. Porter, traded worldwide. In 1829 LR recorded as running Liverpool–Valparaiso. 1835–9 owned Aspinal & Co., trading |

| | | | | | |
|---|---|---|---|---|---|
| | | | | | Liverpool–Sydney. |
| 1818 | *Martha* | | Brig | 203 | 82' 9" x 23' 9". Reg. Liverpool. Square-sterned, carvel built. 32/64 owned by William Rotherham and 32/64 owned by W. A. and G. Maxwell. Re-reg 1830, but Rotherham retained 32/64. |
| 1818 | *Mary & Ann* | | Sloop | 37 | 39' 9" x 13' 9" x 7' 2". Square-sterned, carvel built. Owned by Edward Hughes. |
| 1818 | *Belgrave* | Troughton | Brig | 146 | 74' 8" x 21' 5" x 13'. Reg. Liverpool. Square-sterned. 1834 running Liverpool–St Petersburg. |
| 1818 | *Helen* | | | | Cheese brig. 1855 LR. 1834 owned by Pope & Co., Reg. Waterford, as a 'coaster'. |
| 1819 | *Velocity* | Mulvey | Brig | 170 | Reg. Liverpool. Square-sterned. |
| 1819 | *Manchester* | Cortney | Brig | 144 | 71' 1" x 21' 8" x 13'. Launched 6 Oct. 1819, on the same day as *Velocity*. Reg. Liverpool. Square-sterned, carvel built. Running Liverpool–Oporto 1820. |
| 1819 | *Nottingham* | J Wilson jnr | Ship | 403 | 108' 10" x 29' 3". Reg. Liverpool. Square-sterned. 1828–9 running Liverpool–Jamaica. Not heard of after leaving West Africa in December 1837, when owned by Isaac Oldham Bold. |
| 1819 | *Catherine* | Cortney | Flat | 59 | Built for Shanklin & Co. for use on the Ellesmere & Chester Canal. |
| 1819 | *Liffey* | | Brig | 145 | 72' 7" x 22' 1" x 13'. Reg. Liverpool., Square-sterned. 1828 many owners. Partly owned by John Mottershead, shipbuilder. 1829 running Liverpool–Vera Cruz. Reg. de novo Whitehaven ,1833. |
| 1819 | *Dee* | Cortney | Ship | 381 | 105' 4" x 28' 9". Reg. Liverpool. Square-sterned, carvel built ship with a high quarter deck and forecastle. Reg. states this vessel was destroyed by fire off the coast of Africa 12 Jun. 1831. Vessel owned by Samuel Sandbach and others for the whole of her career, |
| 1820 | *Oulton* | Cortney | Brigantine | 76 | O.N. 1561. 57' 6" x 17' 1" x 9' 9". Named as a compliment to Sir J.G. Egerton. Intended as a general trader. In 1834 14/64 shares were owned Charles Davison of Shotton. Destroyed by fire off Holyhead, March 1858, on voyage from Chester. Believed to be last vessel built by Cortney to be afloat. |
| 1820 | *Douro* | | Brigantine | 147 | O.N. 92822m. 71' 8" x 21' 9" x 13' 8". Square-sterned, carvel built. Re-reg. Whitehaven 1832. 1834 owned J. Dawson. Reg. Whitehaven, running Whitehaven to Antigua. 1844 coasting, owned by Reid & Co., Whitehaven. 1847 still owned by Reid. 1850 in *Lloyd's* no voyage. |
| 1820 | *John Bogg* | | Brig | 157 | 1829 owned by Brotherston. |
| 1821 | *Southworth* | | 3m Ship | 350 | 98' x 28' 6" x 6' 8". Square-sterned. Launched 31 May 1821. First owners John Leigh, Edward Oates and David Sampson of Liverpool. Sold in 1821. Sailed for the Swan River, New South Wales, 8 Feb. 1829. |
| 1821 | *John & William* | | Sch | 88 | 56' 2" x 17' 2" x 10' 1". 1828 44/64 owned by William Thomas of Bagillt, master mariner. 1834 on voyage Gloucester–Glasgow. Re-reg. Beaumaris, 1843. |
| 1821 | *Albion* | Cortney | Brig | 116/150b | Launched 16 Aug. 1821 from the yard of the late Mr Cortney. 150t burthen. 1829 LR owned by Devereux. 1834 running Wexford–Newport. |
| 1821 | *Liverpool* | Cortney | | 406 | Launched 31 May 1821 after the death of Cortney. |
| 1821 | *Eliza* | | Sailing Pkt | | Sailing packet built on the banks of the Dee for service Ellesmere Port–Liverpool. |
| 1822 | *Sir Joseph Yorke* | Mulvey | Wood P.S. | 48 | 84' 8" x 16' 4" x 7' 3". Owned W.J. Joliffe and E. Banks of London. 30 h.p. engine by the Butterley Co. 1832 working in the Plymouth area. Reg. closed 1840, BU. |
| 1822 | *Lord Melville* | J. Wilson jnr | Wood P.S. | 137 | 112' 3" x 20' 11" x 12' 11". Two cylinder engine by the Butterley Co. Reg. closed 6 Sep. 1849, B.U. |
| 1822 | *Duchess of Leinster* | Sp | 25 | | O.N. 9273. Owned J. Mollance, Kirkudbright, 1872. |
| 1823? | *Perseverance* | | Sch | 77 | 1834 LR. Owned by Brenan & Co., Wexford, running to Wexford. |

| | | | | | |
|---|---|---|---|---|---|
| 1824 | *St David* | Mulvey | Sp rig P.S. | 75b | 72' 4" x 14' 10" x 6' 10". 20 h.p. engine and boiler by Rigby. Launched 13 Jan. 1824. 1825 owned Chester S.P. Co. 1828 owned by Hugh Williams of Woodside, innkeeper (64/64). Ran Chester–Bagillt. Broken up in Liverpool April 1832 |
| 1824 | *Belem Castle* | John Wilson | 2m Snow | 153 | 77 ' x 21' 9" x 13' 10". Subscribing owners, John Jones (32), Hugh Jones (7), Jos Yeoward (4). 'Vessel lost near this port Mar 1832.' |
| 1824 | *Robert* | | Brig | | 1829 LR. Owners Cram & Co., South Shields. |
| 1824 | *Camoens* | | Snow | 168 | Owned Martin & Co., Liverpool. 1834, running Liverpool–Oporto. |
| 1824 | *Snowdon* | | 2m Sch | 77 | O.N. 11825. 55' 8" x 18' 3" x 9'. Owned Alexander Kerr, victualler of Liverpool (16/64) and others in Scotland. Lost Hoyle Bank November 1831 with all the crew – letter from owner 1833. |
| 1825 | *Ellen Clare* | J. Wilson | 2m Brig | 174 | 80' 11" x 22' 2" x 13' 4". First owned by John Worrall, merchant (32) and Thomas Roberts, master mariner. Launched 2 Apr. 1825, towed to Liverpool by St David, packet. 1834 still owned by Worrall, running Cork–Liverpool. Reg. de novo 1842. |
| 1825 | *Lee* | J. Wilson | 3m P.S. Sch | 188/201 | 131' x 22' x 13' 6". Square-sterned, carvel built. Schooner propelled by steam. First owners William Fawcett of Liverpool, John Watson the Younger and Jos Robinson of Dublin. In the name of the Cork & Liverpool S.N. Co. 1829 listed as schooner with steam engine, owned by Dublin Co. running Liverpool–Dublin. 1836 owned St George S.P. Co running to Hull. Reg. Closed 9 Apr. 1851, BU. |
| 1825 | *Joshua* | John Wilson | 2m Brig | 177 | 81' 2" x 22' 3" x 14' 8". Owned first (64) by William Prowse, merchant of Liverpool. Vessel lost on the coast of Vera Cruz. Certificate delivered up 1831. |
| 1825 | *John Welch* | Wm Mulvey | 3m ship rig | 259 | 93' 1 x 25' 2" x 17'. Square-sterned, carvel built. First owned by John Welch, merchant of Liverpool (48), Thomas Hudson, merchant of Liverpool (8) and Thomas Woodhouse, master mariner (8). 1834 still owned by Welch, running Liverpool–Havana. Vessel totally lost on Hoyle Bank 29 Jul. 1836. |
| 1825 | *Loretto* | John Wilson | 3m Ship rig | 380 | First owner Havson Dutchman, John Woodhall of Scarborough and John Dutchman the younger. Vessel lost August 1827. Reg. delivered up 18 Feb. 1828. |
| 1825 | *Popplewell* | Wm Mulvey | 2m Sch | 77 | 55' 4" x 18' x 9' 1". Regd 20 Mar. 1826 to Joseph Jones of Northop (mariner), John Royle (builder) and William Edwards (iron founder). Square-sterned carvel built, male figurehead. Reg. de novo 12 Apr. 1836. |
| 1825 | *John Shanklin* | Wm Mulvey | Flat | 60 | Built for Shanklin Manley & Co. In 1925 SUR & CC sold the 100-year old vessel for further trading. |
| 1826 | *Ormrod* | J Wilson Jr | P.S. Sch rig | 77 | 79' 4" x 17' 5" x 9' 2", 40HP paddle wheels, single expansion steam engine. Square-sterned, carvel built. First owners John Sothern, John Askew, Annabella Davis (widow) all of Liverpool. Chartered 1826–31. Regd Goole, Jan 1834 extract from Transport Register from M. McRonald - BU17 Sep. 1856– Certificate from Liverpool Steam Tug Co. |
| 1826 | *Kingstown* | John Wilson | P.S. Sch rig | 71 | 91' 2" x 17' 0" x 10' 4". 60 HP single expansion steam engine. First vessel to run between Wexford and Liverpool. Built for St George S.P. Co. Reg closed 1845 BU. |
| 1826 | *Maria II* | John Wilson | P.S | 60/92 | 30 HP engine. Owned by Smith for Eastham–Liverpool ferry service. |
| 1826 | *St George* | John Wilson | Frigate type | 604 | 130' 9" x 31' 1". Launched by timber merchant, Thomas Green, towed to Liverpool for fitting out by the tug *Ormrod*, intened for South American trade but the company failed. 1834 owned by Acraman & Co, reg'd Bristol, running Bristol–Calcutta. |
| 1826 | *Maria* | Wm Mulvey | 2m Sch | 106 | 65' 3" x 19' 4" x 9' 6". Built for William Hancock of Aston Bank. |

| | | | | | |
|---|---|---|---|---|---|
| 1826 | *Mauncey/Mauney?* | John Wilson | 2m Brig | 176 | 78' 5" x 20' 3" x 14' 2" square-sterned, carvel built. First owned by John Jones (40/64), Thomas Kettleman (12/64), Liverpool merchants, and 2 others. 1834 owned by Viana & Co, Liverpool, running Liverpool–Lisbon. In 1840 owned partly by John &William Dawson, shipbuilders (8 shares each), and John Southell, spirit merchant of Liverpool. Re-registered 1843. |
| 1826 | *Cymro* | John Wilson | Wd P.S. Tug | 70 | O.N. 27009. 74' 9" x 14' 9" x 7' 9". 33 NHP, square-sterned, carvel built. 1845 engine room 26' 3" in length. In 1848 sold by owners in Dundalk to Thomas Evans, wharfinger, of Chester. Broken up 26 Jan. 1880. |
| 1827 | *Dairy Maid* | Wm Mulvey | Sp rig P.S. | 90/43.48 | 74' x 14' 8" x 8' x 8". 30 NHP. Engine room 25' long. Completed December 1827. Ran briefly from Chester–Flint. February 1842 sold by John Rigby to Charles Davison who in1850 sold her to Neil Brodie, a chemist from Prestatyn. 17 Jan. 1853 reg. closed, vessel lost. |
| 1826 | *Trader* | | Sch | 117 | 1834 owned Smith & Co of London – at London. |
| 1827 | *Chester?* | | | 117 | Afloat 1834. |
| 1827 | *Factor* | | Sch | 91 | O.N. 21516. 1834 owned Smith & Co of London, running Chester–London. 1872 owned by Charles Lovell of Weymouth. |
| 1827 | *London* | | Sch | 92 | O.N. 22466. 1834 trading Liverpool–London, regd London, owned by Lillwall. Ran Cork–Glasgow 1836. 1872 owned by Stephen Putland of St Leonards. |
| 1827 | *Sisters* | Wm Mulvey | Flat | 60 | O.N. 1982. 61' 2" x 13' x 5' 7". Certificate reg 24 May1827. 1836 owned by Charles Gamon, corn merchant. Owned by Thomson & Co of Liverpool and also by Neil Brodie of Prestatyn. |
| 1827 | *William* | J. Wilson & Sons | Sloop | 17 | 36' 4" x 10' 6". Square-sterned, carvel built. Certificate of Registry dated 1831. Bought 1832 by Thomas Humphrey, master mariner of Liverpool. Vessel left out of annual shipping list, 1870. |
| 1827 | *Liverpool* | J. Wilson & Sons | Flat | 62 | 65' 7" x 14' 5" x 5' 9". Certificate reg. 28 Aug. 1827. Built for Coffield & Son. In 1827 actually regd to John Johnston, Edward Tilston and James Smith, wharfingers of Chester. Vessel out of register 1840 – 'employed in Ellesmere & Chester Canal'. |
| 1827/8 | *Herald* | Wm Mulvey | P.S. | 174N | 130' 10" x 22' x 14' 5". 130 HP steam engine. Originally to be called the *Cork Packet*. 1828 owned by Sir John Tobin & John Watson (the younger) of Liverpool and Jos Robinson of Dublin. Re-registered Dublin, 1835. Later lengthened to 146' x 22'. Went ashore 1839. Reg. closed 1869 – 'vessel cannot be traced'. |
| 1828 | *Chester* | Wm Mulvey | Flat | 41 | O.N. 2378. 54' x 13' 9" x 6'. Round-sterned, carvel built. 1840 owned by the Trustees of Liverpool Docks. Regd 1840 cert of Peggy Mulvey executrix. Later used to carry stone and chains between Liverpool and Birkenhead under tow. Sold to J.Hornby &Sons, Holywell for £5,10th October 1930. Register closed November 1931. Used to carry stone blocks to and around Liverpool Docks for construction. |
| 1828 | *Halkin* | Mulvey | Sch | 108 | Intended for London–Chester trade. 1834 owned by Ellis & Co, regd Chester, running Sligo–London. |
| 1829 | *William Mulvey* | Wm Mulvey | 2m Brig | 161 | 78' 3" x 21' 6" x 14'. Square-sterned, carvel built. First owned by merchants and ropemakers with Thomas Jones (master mariner) (32/64). Reg. Liverpool to Daniel and Thomas Willis (64). 1834 owned by Moss & Co, Liverpool, trading Liverpool–Santo Domingo. Lost 15 Jun. 1835 at Mazatlan on the northern coast of Mexico. |
| 1830 | *Liverpool* | Wm Mulvey | Sch | 135 | O.N. 23324. 1834 LR trading London–Liverpool, owned J. Smith. Owned R. Paul, 1872 owned |

| | | | | | |
|---|---|---|---|---|---|
| | | | | | William Sandford of Gravesend. |
| 1831 | *Lapwing* | Wm Mulvey | 2m Sch | 93 | 66' 5" x 18' 5" x 10' 6". Launched 8 August. Intended for the Smyrna trade. First owners included Edward Osborne, block maker (32/64) and White & Philips of Liverpool. 1834 trading London–Lisbon.1840 owned by Ellis Martin Brodie & John Hamilton, trading as Brodie & Hamilton of Liverpool. |
| 1831 | *Water Witch* | Wm Mulvey | 2m Sch | 14 | 76' 1" x 18' 2" x 7' 9". Reg. Liverpool 25 Apr. 1831. First owned by four Liverpool merchants & William Mulvey. 1834 owned by Moss & Co of Liverpool, trading Liverpool–Messina. Reg London 1839. |
| 1832 | *Zephyr* | Wm Mulvey | P.S. | 103.35 | O.N. 4241. 113' 6" x 17' 3" x 10' 7". 70 HP engine by Fawcett of Preston. 1835 to St George S.P. Co of Dublin. 1857 owned W. Owen. Ran Liverpool–Barrow–wcs. Reg closed 23 Nov. 1885 – 'existence of vessel doubtful'. |
| 1832 | *Jane Prowse* | Wm Mulvey | 3m Barque | 200 | First registered to William Prowse (44), Joshua Prowse (4), Henry Miller Barclay. Built for South America trade. Re-reg. 1842. 1845–7 running to China. Out of Lloyds 1854. |
| 1832 | *Laidmans* | Wm Mulvey | 3m Barque | 360 | 97' 2" x 24' 6" x 17' 3". Square-sterned, carvel built. First owners William Laidman, merchant of Liverpool (16/64) & other members of the Laidman family. 1839 owned Henry Moore & Charles Moore (64/64) trading as Henry Moore & Co, Liverpool. Re-reg. 1842. |
| 1832 | *Sarah* | | Sp Ketch | 47 | O.N. 24098. 56' 8" x 15' 3" x 6' 8". 1872 owned J. Williams Parry. Wrecked Porth Ferin, Llŷn peninsula, 16 Sep. 1911. |
| 1832 | *John Watson* | Wm Mulvey | P.S. | 170 | Not registered. Launched 29 Jun. 1832 –party came from Liverpool by steamer, towed her to Liverpool after the launch. |
| 1832 | *Mary & Martha* | | Flat | 28 | O.N. 12389. 45' 8" x 14' 4" x 5' 5". B.U. 23 Apr. 1861 |
| 1832 | *Tower* | | Flat | 48 | O.N. 23904. 62' 2" x 12' 8" x 7' 0". 1845 owned by William & George Gibson, fishermen of Chester. They sold 32 shares to Neil Brodie of Prestatyn in 1849. |
| 1832 | *Eaton* | Moss | Sch | 47 | O.N. 22844. Built by Moss at Chester, lost 1919 (cds), but still afloat 1918 MNL. 1872 owned by Richard Owen of Bangor |
| 1833 | *Mary & Ann* | Wm Mulvey | 3m Barque | 212b | 91' 5" x 22' 9" x 15' 7". First owned by John Adams Bartlett (42/64) and Philip Whiteway (22/64). Regd de novo 1843. |
| 1833 | *Emily* | | Sk | 67 | Owned J. Gabriel 1857 'coaster'. |
| 1833 | *Smelter* | Wm Mulvey | Flat | 60 | O.N. 16493. 63' 9" x 14' 4" x 5' 8". Square-sterned, carvel built for Edward Samuel Walker. Still owned 1872 by S. E. Walker, leadworks Chester. MD & HB Wreck Book– 'laden with gravel, sank 380 yds from L6 red buoy 17 Feb. 1892 after beating over part of Burbo Bk–destroyed by blasting 19/20 Feb 18/92.' |
| 1834 | *Pelter* | Wm Mulvey | Flat | 45 | O.N. 16492. 62' x 13' x 6' 1". Square stern. Lifting bowsprit. Built for Edward Samuel Walker. Cert cancelled 2 Dec. 1870– 'vessel gone to inland navigation'. |
| 1834 | *Glynne* | Wm Mulvey | 2mSch | 103 | O.N. 5780. 69' 2" x 18' 9" x 11' 4". Launched 1 Oct. 1834. Cheese ship. Part owned by George Cram. He sold his shares in 1838 –2/64. Foundered off Land's End 22 Jun. 1861. Cert cancelled. |
| 1834 | *George* | Wm or T. Mul | P.Ssloop rig | 55 | 85' 4" x 16' 3" x 8' 5". Owned by Philip Laurence of Tranmere (64). Vessel laid up 1845, register closed 1865. |
| 1834 | *Bee* | Wm Mulvey | 3m bark | 233 | Launched 17 Apr. 1834 for the South American trade. A1 11 yrs Lloyds, owned by C. Duncan of |

| | | | | | |
|---|---|---|---|---|---|
| | | | | | Liverpool. 1 deck, square-sterned, carvel built. Later owned by William & Charles Hadfield. |
| 1834 | *Elizabeth Radcliffe* | Wm Mulvey | 3m bark | 222 | 93' x 23' x 15' 6". Squared-sterned, carvel built. Reg. Liverpool to William & Charles Hadfield. Intended for the Lima &Valparaiso trade. 1857 owned by J. Phillips, sailed to Hankow. |
| 1834 | *Fred* | | Flat | 39 | O.N. 16218. 1857 on the mud at Tranmere when re-registered. Reg. closed 1886. 1872 owned Thompson & Son of Liverpool. |
| 1834 | *Matilda* | Wm Mulvey | 3m bark | 318 | 102' 10" x 26' 6" x 17' 11". Square-sterned, carvel built. Owned William Rotherham of Liverpool (64). |
| 1835 | *John Royle* | Mulvey | 2m Sch | 98 | O.N. 25001. 67' 5" x 17' 9" x 9' 9". Original owners John Royle of Chester (builder), Joseph Jones of Wepre (mariner) and John Jones of Golftyn (stone mason). 1857 owned by Royle & Co, Newport. 1872 owned John Jones, Saltney. Square-stern. |
| 1835 | *Peggy* | | Smk | 35 | 58' x 13' 1" x 6'. Reg. Cardigan 1856, LR 1857, owned by Edwards of Cardigan. |
| 1836 | *Clive* | Mulvey | Flat | 88 | O.N. 78718. 1872 owned by James Barnes? of Liverpool. |
| 1836 | *Frances Barklay* | Wm Mulvey | Bark | 241 | 96' 5" x 23' 9" x 15' 9". Launched 2 Feb. 1836, delayed one day due to lack of water. Built for William Prowse of Liverpool, to be captained by his son. Intended for the South America trade. |
| 1836 | *Cestrian* | | Sloop | 27 | 42' x 13' 5" x 6' 3". Re-reg. Beaumaris 1843. |
| 1836 | *Queen Mab* | Wm Mulvey | 3m bark | 394 | O.N. 13600. 106' 7" x 24' 3" x 17' 9". Intended for the East Indies trade. Lost in 1865, main owner William Rotherham – see Livepool reg. |
| 1837 | *Ann Maria* | | Sch | 77 | Owned by Bithell. |
| 1837 | *Margaret* | Wm Mulvey | 3m bark | 270 | 96' x 25' 7" x 16'. Square-sterned, carvel built. Named by Mr Mulvey Jnr. First owned by William & Joshua Prowse & Henry Miller Barclay, William Prowse the Younger and William Radcliffe. Master Prowse the younger. Vessel lost on the coast of Brazil 08 Feb. 1840. |
| 1837 | *Lord Byron* | | Sch | 129 | O.N. 1089. Various owners 1857 Smith & Co, 1872 William Singleton of Drogheda, also 1881 owned by Thomas Barnes of Gloucester. |
| 1837 | *Dee* | | Flat | 31 | O.N. 28046. 63' 4" x 14' 2" x 5' 05". 1872 owned by either John Harden of Chester or William Smith. Broken up August 1897. |
| 1838 | *Pilot Queen* | Wm Mulvey | Dandy | 16 | O.N. 42567. 34' x 11' 5" x 6' .Pilot cutter built for William Hewitt & Benjamin Bennett of Wepre. 1872 owned J. Jones, Carnarfon 1839. |
| 1838 | *Victoria* | Mulvey | Stmr | | |
| 1838 | *Primrose* | Wm Mulvey | Flat | 51 | 58' 7" x 15' 4" x 6' 8". Round-sterned, carvel built. 22/64 owned by Edward Bate of Kelsterton, Robert Johnson of Liverpool (merchant) (12). Reg again at Chester 1851. |
| 1838 | *Clive* | Wm Mulvey | Stm p tug | 117 | 2 x 20 h.p. engines from William Fawcett. Built for the Ellesmere & Chester Canal Co. for towing flats and timber floats across the Mersey between Liverpool & Ellesmere Port. |
| 1838 | *Earl Powis* | Wm Mulvey | Stm p tug | | Believed to be an almost exact sister of *Clive*. |
| 1839 | *Cheshire Lass* | Wm Mulvey | 2m Sch | 138/125 | 72' 5" x 18' 4" x 11' 7". Square-sterned, carvel built. At the time of building there were 13 subscribers. Of these, 5 were cheese mongers or cheese agents. Owned Curtis & Co. Operated between London and Chester. |
| 1838 | *Temple* | Wm Mulvey | Flat | 55 | Sold by John Williams to John Davies, blockmaker of Chester –1855? |
| 1838 | *Margaret* | Wm Mulvey | Brig | 178 | 1842 owned S. Schauer, regd Leith. 1842 running Leith–Mauritius. 1852 owned J. Barr senior, LR listed 'missing'. |
| 1839 | *Pickwick* | Peggy Mulvey | 3m Ship | 343 | O.N. 1732. 107' 7" x 23' 8" x 18' depth of hold. Ran Liverpool–Valparaiso for most of her career, |

| | | | | | |
|---|---|---|---|---|---|
| | | | | | owned by Cornish. 1859 running from Swansea, not in LR 1860. |
| 1839 | *William Prowse* | Peggy Mulvey | ship rigged | 357 | 105' 3" x 23' x 17'. Standing bowsprit, carvel built, square sterned.1840 owned by William Prowse, Joshua Prowse, H. M.Barclay & Elizabeth Radcliffe (widow) all of Liverpool.' Wrecked on a rock off Valparaiso,. Letter to Registrar General 4 June 1850. |
| 1840 | *Amiga* | Peggy Mulvey | ship rigged | 350 | 102' 8" x 23' 2" x 17' 9". Square-sterned, carvel built, female figurehead. First owners Charles & William Hadfield (merchants), James Kenworthy (book-keeper) and John Dalrymple (master mariner). Reg. de novo 30 Dec. 1847 |
| 1840 | *Fanny* | | Sch | 115 | 1857 owned Strong & Co, sailing to South America. |
| 1840 | *Lycee* | Peggy Mulvey | ship-rigged | 467 | 140' 8" x 25' 5" x 19'. Carvel built, square sterned. First owner William Rotheham, Liverpool 64/64. Intended for the China trade. Supposed to have been lost on her voyage from Bombay–Liverpool. Letter from William Rotherham to Reg Gen 3 Oct. 1855. |
| 1840 | *Shifty* | Peggy Mulvey | Flat | 61 | O.N. 16448. 63' 3" x 16' 4" x 8' 1". Round-sterned. Thomas Smith Mulvey 16/64 on completion. Mulvey share sold at auction 1848. Lost on Canon Rock, Ireland, 10 Aug. 1865. See text re owners, including Yeowards. |
| 1840 | *Trap* | T. & W. Mulvey | Flat | 67 | O.N. 16447. 47' 9" x 14' 5" x 6' 8". Owned by the Mulvey brothers and others, including Yeoward. Thomas Smith Mulvey share sold at auction 1848. Lost at sea 1857? |
| 1840 | *Miner* | Sir E.Walker | Flat | 36 | O.N. 16497. 54' x 12' x 5' 5". Owned by several members of the Walker family. Sold into inland navigation trade**?**1870, cert. cancelled. |
| 1840 | *Charlotte* | Mulvey | Sp/ketch | 41 | O.N. 17025. 59' x 14' 1" x 6' 8". Round sterned, carvel built. First owned by John Royle (32). Owned David Jones of Golftyn, later William H. Lemon of Barnstaple. Lost at Clovelly 04 Oct. 1895. |
| 1841 | *Lead Works* | Sir E. S. Walker | Flat | 45 | O.N. 27007. 62' x 13' x 6'. Seven Walker/Walker Parker owners. Went into Irish trade –or inland 1870. |
| 1841 | *Ann Bridson* | T. & W. Mulvey | 3m ship | 358 | 105' 2" x 23' 6" x 18'. Square-sterned, carvel built. Owned by Prowses & Barclay & Eliz Radcliffe, running Liverpool–Valparaiso. Abandoned 29 Oct. 1859 off Mossel Bay. |
| 1841 | *John Christian* | Mulvey | 3m ship rig | | Launched 2 Sep. 1841, for the Chinese trade. |
| 1841 | *Sarah Davison* | | Flat | 30 | O.N. 27008. First owned by Charles Davison of Celyn, Flint. |
| 1841 | *Rhuddlan Trader* | | Flat | 26 | O.N. 24342. Owned by Henry Thomas of Llanfairmathafarn Eithaf, Anglesey. |
| 1842 | *Kitty* | T. & W. Mulvey | Flat | 44 | 57' 3" x 13' 3" x 6' 9". Rounnd-sterned, carvel built. Owned first by T. Mulvey (24), W. Mulvey (8) and Robert McKean (8). T. S. Mulvey share sold at auction in 1848. |
| 1842 | *Ann Mulvey* | T. & W. Mulvey | 2m Sch | 133 | O.N. 1923. Twelve owners include Thomas Smith Mulvey on completion. 'Cheese ship' October 1847, arrived Chester with 'London goods.' See text for more, including Yeoward 1853. T. S. Mulvey share sold 1848 at auction to John Henry Treweek of Amlwch. Lost 1887. |
| 1842 | *Ferret* | | Sch | 115 | Owned Owen & Co. |
| 1843 | *Templeman* | Thos Mulvey | 3m bark | 351 | O.N. 4311. 108' 7" x 23' x 17'. Built of oak & briar. Owned by Henry Barklay and William & John Prowse. 1857 running to Santiago, Chile. |
| 1843 | *Brewer's Hall* | T. & W. Mulvey | Flat | 20 | O.N. 25886. 49' 5" x 9' 9" x 4' 6". W. W. Mulvey named as master on builder's cert. Transferred to bank October 1843. T. S. Mulvey share sold at Auction July 1848, then re-sold to 'James Reney the younger' 8 Nov. 1849. 1872 owned by R. T. Rogers of Trefriw. |
| 1843 | *Firebrick* | T. S. Mulvey | Flat/ketch | 43 | O.N. 10580. 61' 4" x 13' x 5' 2". Round-sterned, carvel built sold to bankers. T. Smulvey share sold |

| | | | | | |
|---|---|---|---|---|---|
| | | | | | at auction 1848. 1848 sold to Charles Jones of Rhuddlan. 1872 owned by Owen Evans, Bryn Genarch, Caernarfon. 1 deck, 1 mast. |
| 1843 | *Roodeye* | T. & W. Mulvey | | 20 | 49' 5" x 9' 9" x 4' 6". Round-sterned, carvel built. Master on cert. is Thomas Smith Mulvey. |
| 1844 | *Earl of Chester* | T. Mulvey | 3m bark | 462 | O.N. 9136. 124' 5" x 25' 6" x 19'. Owned William Prowse, Jos Prowse & H. M. Barklay of Liverpool. 1856 altered from a ship to a bark. 1857 sailing London–Philadelphia. Wrecked near Holyhead, October 1867, Captain Nancollis and all aboard lost. |
| 1845 | *Jane* | T. Mulvey | 2m Sch | 65 | O.N. 1828. 63' 8" x 16' 6" x 8' 8". Regd Lancaster 3/ Nov. 1845 to Henry Walker of Ulverstone (16) and a number of other owners. Re-regd 1854 to John Atkinson and Edward Hall (miller). 1857 still owned by Hall & Co, Whitehaven. 1872 owned by William Park of Barrow. |
| 1845 | *Sarah* | T. & W. Mulvey | | | Owned by John Williams (banker) 9 Oct. 1845. |
| 1845 | *Dee Bank* | Walker Parker | Flat | | 61' 2" x 12' 9" x 5' 9". Cert cancelled 2 Dec. 1870, 'vessel into inland trade.' |
| 1845 | *Gwenddolen* | T. & W. Mulvey | 2m Sch | 85 | 65' 7" x 15' 3" x 9' 3". Round-sterned, carvel built. 64 shares owned by John Williams (banker) of Chester. Re-registered at Preston, 1848. |
| 1846 | *Jane* | T. Mulvey | Flat | 15 | O.N. 21035. 38' 1" x 12' 1" x 5' 6". Square-sterned. BU 1874. |
| 1846 | *Fume* | Sir E. Walker | Flat | 48 | O.N. 9803. 62' x 13' x 6' 4". 'Built by Sir Ed Walker at the leadwks.' Still owned Jos Walker, Parker & Co, 1872. Reg closed 2 Nov. 1916 – 'vessel B.U.' |
| 1846 | *Fox* | T. S. Mulvey | Flat | 27 | O.N. 1986. 48' 8" x 12' 3" x 5' 7". 64 /64 shares owned byThomas Foulkes of Shotton. To Isle of Man, reg. 1856. |
| 1846 | *Hematite* | | Flat | 25 | O.N. 6961. 1872 owned by D. Wilson/Wilkinson, Kirkudbright. |
| 1846 | *Transit* | Mulvey | Flat | 43 | |
| 1847 | *Betsey* | | Sch | 98 | Owned Jones & Co 1855. LR –could be built Sandycroft. |
| 1847 | *Punch* | T. S. Mulvey | Sch | 75 | T. S. Mulvey first owner. To bankers 1847. Sold 16 Mar. 1848 to William Beckwith of Douglas with the bank's approval. 1857 still owned by Beckwith. |
| 1847 | *City* | T. S. Mulvey | Flat | 46 | O.N. 16468. 56' x 14' x 7'. First owned William Hancock, Henry Craven and William Roberts of Aston. Vessel lost on 30 Oct. 1859. |
| 1847 | *Sarah Jane* | T. S. Mulvey | Smack | 52 | O.N. 16904. 64' 2" x 15' 6" x 7' 5". Round-sterned, carvel built. First owned by ten sharehldrs, including T. S. Mulvey and Robert McKean (iron founder). 1872 owned by John Jones of Curzon Park, Chester, later David Jones of Llandeiniolen. Reg. closed 17 Oct. 1898, vessel B.U. |
| 1848 | *Sir Edward* | Sir E. S.Walker | Sch | 98? | A1 12 years when built. First owned by three Walker family members. Built expressly for the lead ore trade, foreign & c'wise. 1857 owned by Walker of Liverpool, coasting. |
| 1848 | *Fanny Truss* | T. S. Mulvey | Sloop | 56 | O.N. 3148. 63' 7" x 16' 9" x 7' 6". 32/64 owned by T. S. Mulvey when built. T. S. Mulvey share sold at auction 1848. Round stern. MNL 1872 owned William Jones of Saltney. 1883 Ellis Hughes, Connah's Quay. Not listed 1885. |
| 1848 | *Rose* | T. S. Mulvey | Flat | | O.N. 12396. 58' x 15' x 5'. Square-sterned. 1872 owned by George Whittle of Chester. Wrecked at Hoylake in 1877. |
| 1850 | *My Lady* | Sir E. S. Walker | 2m Sch | 69 | O.N. 21967. 1857 owned by Sir Edward Walker, trading Chester–Continent. 1876 still owned by Walkers. 11 May 1910 sunk in collision in Mersey with *Balneil II*. Wreck destroyed by blasting. |
| 1852 | *Tower* | | 1m Flat | | Bought by James Fisher 1855. Lost 1866. |
| 1853 | *Cobre conv* | Cram | Sp rig stmr | 150/91 | O.N. 32206. 98' 8" x 13' 6" x 8' 9". Schooner-rigged with paddle wheels, originally built in Swansea, |

| | | | | | |
|---|---|---|---|---|---|
| | | | | | 12 Feb. 1849. Re-launched by Cram 19 May1853. Re -reg. Melbourne, Australia, 22 Nov. 1854. Sydney Harbour Ferry 1869–73. Sold to Newcastle as a tug, retired 1917. |
| 1853 | *Amelia (I)* | Cram | Stmr | 359 | O.N. 1985. First iron vessel built at Chester for Liverpool–Bristol service. 60 HP engine. Lost March 1857, St Govan's Head, Pembroke. |
| 1854 | *Helena (I)* | Cram | Scw Stmr | 188 | O.N. 4615. 137' x 17' x 10' 4" with bulk holds. Coaster owned by J. Meek. Also owned by James Haddock. |
| 1854 | *Golden Queen* | Cram | Stmr | 570 | Launched 24/ May 1853 for Van Hoey Smith of London. |
| 1854 | *Chester (I)* | Cram | Stm collier | 567/441 | O.N. 26251. 183' 5" x 26' 6" x 15' 2". 70 HP engine fitted at Sandycroft. For GI Screw Co, London with 3 bulk holds. In Lloyd's 1870. |
| 1854 | *Derwent (I)* | Cram | Stm Collier | 559 | 185' 4" x 25' 8" x 16' 5". For GI Screw Co. Launched six weeks after the *Chester*, on15 Aug. 1854. |
| 1854 | *Rosario (I)* | Cram | Bark | 268 | 131' 4" x 21' 2" x 12'. Launched 28 Jan. 1854. Main owner Jos Edward Robinson of Liverpool. Re -reg. as steamer. Out of LR 1866 as *Rosaria*. |
| 1854 | *Mino* | Cram | 3m Scw stmr | 559 | 199' 6" x 25' 8" x 16'. Launched March1854. Engine fitted in Liverpool. Vessel built for Paul Tintore of Barcelona. Lost in collision with *Minden*, March 1856. |
| 1855 | *Italia (I)* | Cram | Scw Stmr | 549 | 180' x 25' 3" x 17' 9". 80 HP 2-cyl compound engine. For Rubattino of Genoa. Hulked 1892, |
| 1855 | *Sardegna (I)* | Cram | Scw Stmr | 380 ud | 182' x 21' 7" x 12'. For Rubattino of Genoa. Scrapped 1895. |
| 1855 | *British Oak* | W. Bishton | Sch | 79 | O.N. 27017. 74' 4" x 19' 3". Round stern. Owned by Bishton until1866 then sold to Charles & Sarah Davison, still owned by Davison in 1872. |
| 1856 | *Gov Wodehouse* | | Lugger | 30 | O.N. 16884. Owned by T. E. Moss of Liverpool. |
| 1856 | *Eliza Bond* | T. Hughes | Sch | 71 | O.N. 18225. 1872 owned by Thomas Roper of Ulverston. Lost 19 Oct. 1907, Rosslare. |
| 1856 | *Chrystaline (I)* | Cram | 3m bark | 266.5 | O.N. 15389. 112' x 23' 5" x 13' 5". Elliptic stern. Running Liverpool–Africa 1856. 1857 to South America. F. H. Powell (24/64), Henry Cram (8/64). 1872 owned William McMaster of Liverpool. |
| 1856 | *Melfort* | | Sp | 36 | O.N. 15195. 1872 owned by Thomas Roger of Newland Furnace, Lancaster. |
| 1857 | *Deva (I)* | Roodeye S.B.Co. | 1 Scw Stmr | 279.9 | O.N. 16283. 130' x 21' x 11' 6". 40 HP screw. Launched Jan. First owned by W. C. Fosberry & others. Acquired by Goole S.S .Co Ltd, 1866, operating Goole–Ghent. Sold out of fleet 1870. Re-reg. as *Doon* 1877 at Glasgow. 1880 owned by Peter Barr of Glasgow +50 hp engine. 1889 to D. Rowan (marine engine builder) Clyde. Still owned D. Rowan Jnr in 1900. |
| 1857 | *Hagar* | Wm Bishton | Sch | 122 | O.N. 18862. 87' 6" x 21' 6" x 11' 2". Launched Jan. Counter stern. Transferred to Aberystwyth reg. 1859. First owned by Bishton, then Evan Jones of Newcastle, Cardiganshire, 1870. |
| 1857 | *Ann Sumner* | | Sch | 59 | O.N. 16679. 1872 owned by John Bell of Ulverston. |
| 1857 | *Cymbeline (I)* | Cram | Brig | 219 | O.N. 20535. 120' x 20' 8" x 12' 8". Built for Benjamin Bowring. Lost 1859. |
| 1858 | *City of Chester* | Wm Bishton | Sch | 87 | O.N. 21036. 77' x 20' 4" x 9' 5". Round stern. Intially owned by William Bishton & Wiliam Jones of Queensferry. Sold to Davison in 1861.Transferred to Beaumaris reg. 1897. Lost near Carmel Head 6 Apr. 1898 on voyage Swansea–Mostyn with cargo of burnt ore, wind condition S force 5. |
| 1858 | *Ocean Queen* | | Sk | 51 | O.N. 6997. 1872 owned by William Laugharne of Liverpool. |
| 1859 | *Eclipse* | Wm Parkes | Sch | 101 | O.N. 27902. 75' 5" x 18' x 9' 4". Round stern. First owned by William Bishton. 1861 sold to Davison. By 1877 owned J. Francis of Belfast. Listed in MNL until 1886. |
| 1860 | *Wayfarer (I)* | N. Cox | ship-rigged | 1321 | O.N. 28634. 212' x 36' x 25'. Maiinly employed in the Indian trade. Wrecked near Kilmore Quay 16 Jan. 1871 with a cargo of flint. |

| | | | | | |
|---|---|---|---|---|---|
| 1860 | *Ocean Spray* | W. Parkes | 2m Sch | 70 | O.N. 28048. 73' 5" x 18' 6" x 9' 4". First owner William Bishton. LR 1861 owned by W. Allsup. Regd Preston. Round stern. Lost at sea Mull of Galloway, 29 Mar. 1861. |
| 1861 | *Eastham Fairy II (I)* | Nath Cox | P.S | 125/115 | O.N. 42594. 125 'x 19' 2" x 7' 7". 60 NHP. Operating until c.1891. 60pax. Owned by H. M. Lawrence. |
| 1861 | *Swiftsure (I)* | | P.S | 115 | O.N. 42607. 125' x 19' 2" x 7' 7". 60 NHP. Owned by Henry Gough. |
| 1861 | *Cestrian* | Wm Parkes | 2mSch | 99 | O.N. 29490. 74' 6" x 21' 1" x 10' 5". Original owner was Parkes, then James Reney. 1872 owned by William Jones of Chester. Vessel wrecked 2 Mar. 1886 near Berwick on Tweed. |
| 1861 | *Hannah Coppack* | Wm Parkes | Sch | 50 | O.N. 44041. 69' 4" x 18' 1" x 7' 6". LR 1862 owned by the Coppack family of Wepre. Stranded with coal from Sunderland for Dartmouth, SE of Gunfleet Light outside Harwich, August 1877, still Coppack owned. |
| 1861 | *Royle* | Wm Parkes | Sch | 73.12 | O.N. 44042. 73' x 18' 8" x 9' 4". Elliptic stern. First owned by Royle, Parkes & Thomas Bennett Lost at sea off Tuskar Rock, 21 Feb. 1866. |
| 1861/2 | *Gitana (I)* | Nath Cox RIW | ship rigged | 1366 | O.N. 29626. 210' x 36' x 24' 9". 2 bulk holds. Owned by Charles Moore of Liverpool. 1872 Edward Bates, also R. W. Leyland. Ran 1862–96. |
| 1862 | *Emily Helena* | Wm Parkes | 2m Sch | 64 | O.N. 44045. 72' x 18' 2" x 8' 2". Round stern. First owner J. Reney of Connah's Quay –still owner 1872. 1874 to E. Owen of Bangor. Recorded as 'lost' in 1886. |
| 1862 | *Florie* | Wm Parkes | Bark | 273 | O.N. 44714. 117' x 24' x 15'. 1863 owned by S. Wylde, sailed Chester–S.America. Ran Liverpool–South America. 1872 owned T. & W. King, Liverpool. Lost at East London, Cape Colony, Dec, 1874. |
| 1862 | *Magnet* | DeeBank S.B. Co.? | Bark | 550 | Launched 19 April 1862 by Miss Mary Ann Parkes. Rudder smashed at launch –£100 cost. Believed to be same vessel as *Florie* above. |
| 1863 | *West (I)* | Nath Cox RIW | ship rigged | 998 | O.N. 45932. 193' 2" x 32' 9" x 21' 11". 2 bulk holds. First owner Coubrough Boyd. Reg. 25 May 1863. Went missing in North Atlantic after sailing from New York, 4 Feb. 1869. |
| 1863* | *Robinson Crusoe (I)* | Nath Cox RIW | ship rigged | 1163 | O.N. 45442. 202' x 34' x 23' 2". 2 bulk holds. Reg. Liverpool 1863 to James Beazley. Went missing on homeward bound to Liverpool, 1872 –identifiable wreckage off St David's Head. |
| 1863 | Floating Dock | RISB Co. | | | 100' x 60' x 17'. Built for Rose & Crowder of London for use in the London Docks. |
| 1863* | *Roodeye (I)* | Nath Cox RIW | ship rigged | 1036 | O.N. 47581. 198' 8" x 33' x 22'. 2 bulk holds. Reg. Liverpool 1863 to James Beazley. Operated 1863–75. Caught fire Manila 1875. |
| 1863 | *Constance* | Walker | 2m Sch | 70.14 | O.N. 44048. 75' 4" x 18' 5" x 10' 1". First owned Edward Claudius Walker, lead merchants, passed to Alfred Walker July 1869. William Shone junior owner 1872. Lost in North Sea 14 Oct. 1875. |
| 1863 | *Fanny* | Wm Parkes | 2m Sch | 73.72 | O.N. 44049. 74' 5" x 18' 8" x 8' 8". Owned Davison family. Wrecked in Coma Bay, near Ramsey, Isle of Man, 5 Oct. 1886. |
| 1863 | *Lily* | Wm Parkes | Sch | 93 | O.N. 47218. 80' x 20" x 10' 5". Elliptic stern. First owned by Charles Davison. Lost at Terschelling, Holland, 25 Oct. 1895. |
| 1863 | *North-East (I)* | Nath Cox RIW | ship rigged | 998 | O.N. 47506. 193' 2" x 32' 9" x 21' 9". 2 bulk holds. First owned by Coubrough Boyd. Went aground Cape of Good Hope on voyage from Manila–New York, December 1872, due to navigational error. |
| 1864 | *Cheshire (I)* | Nath Cox RIW | ship rigged | 1233 | O.N. 48843. 199' 5" x 34' 6" x 23' 5". One bulk hold. First owned by Boult, English & Brandon. Supposed lost on maiden voyage to Calcutta, 1865. Reg. closed January 1867. |
| 1864 | *Delmira (I)* | Nath Cox RIW | Sch 1872 | 380 | O.N. 48828. 134' 7" x 24' 3" x 15' 7". 1870 LR owned by Thomas Ismay, running Liverpool–South |

| | | | | | |
|---|---|---|---|---|---|
| | | | | | America. 1872 owned J. Benn of Melbourne. Lost Cape Palliser, New Zealand, December 1896. |
| 1864 | *Terpischore (1)* | Nath Cox RIW | Bark | 528 | O.N. 49854. 154' 6" x 27' 3" x 16' 8". First owned by David Attwool and others. Wrecked Cape Corrientes, near Buenos Aires, 1870. |
| 1865 | *Rosina* | Dee Bank | Sch | | 84' 6" x 20' 6" x 10' 8". Christened 'pro tem' by Mrs Sanders, launched into river full of floating ice. |
| 1865 | *Daisy* | Bishton | 2m Sch | 103.9 | O.N. 52637. 82' 1" x 20' 5" x 10' 6". Semi-elliptic stern. Built for Davisons, still owned by them 1872. |
| 1865 | *Pride of the Dee* | Bishton | 2m Sch | 86 | O.N. 52640. 74' x 19' 5" x 9' 7". Elliptic stern. First owners Craven of Buckley. and John Howard of Runcorn. Foundered off Dungeness 12 Nov. 1901. |
| 1866–8 | *Excellent* | Bishton | 2m Sch | 75.7 | O.N. 58207. 71' 8" x 19' 3" x 9' 5". Elliptic stern. First owner Henry Fisher of Wolverhampton. Sold 1869 to Glasgow owners. 1872 owned Andrew Brown of Glasgow, running to West Africa. 1877–83. Out of MNL1883. |
| 1866 | *Excelsior* | Bishton | 2mSch | 90/77 | O.N. 52645. 75' x 20' x 9' 8". Round stern. Built for Henry Craven of Buckley. 1872 James Coppack involved in ownership until at least 1890. Altered to ketch 8 Jul. 1902. Lost off Ardmore Point, Co. Waterford 21 Jul. 1917. |
| 1867 | *Imperial* | Bishton | 2m Sch | 107 | O.N. 58205. 82' x 20' 6" x 10' 4". First owner Henry Fisher of Wolverhampton. Sold to Davison 9 Nov. 1868. Lost off Perranporth, Cornwall 29 Dec. 1894. |
| 1870 | *Balogun* | J. & M. Allsup | Bgtine | 201 | O.N. 65893. 101' 1" x 24' 2" x 12' 7". 1872 owned by William McCoskey and later by Kidd of Liverpool. 1873 running Liverpool–West Africa. 1879 owed by T. Harrison & Co. of Liverpool. Vessel missing, supposed lost, after sailing from Old Calabar 13 May 1885 and not heard of again. |

# Appendix 2: Ships built in Talacre (Sluice) and Mostyn

**Talacre (Sluice)**

| Year | Name | Builder | Type | Tonnage | Remarks/Owners |
|---|---|---|---|---|---|
| 1838 | *Lucy* | J. Dawson | 2m Sch | 110 | 67' x 18' 3" x 10' 9". Re-reg. Dumfries 1844. |
| 1838 | *Sluice* | J. Dawson | Flat | 47 | O.N. 12437. 58' 4" x 15' 1" x 6' 4". Owned 50/50 John Dawson and Sir Edward Mostyn. 1881 owned by Thomas Prytherch, Amlwch. |
| 1839 | *Caroline* | J. Dawson | 2m Sch | 61 | O.N. 8694. 50/50 Dawson & Sir Edward Mostyn. In 1842 on the death of Sir Edward his shares were sold to John Prys Eyton of Llanerchymor, Flint, and Robert Eyton of Flint. Owned later by William Thomas of Amlwch. |
| 1839 | *Gronant* | J. Dawson | Flat | 54 | O.N. 10634. Owned 50/50 with Sir Edward Mostyn. In 1842 vessel was sold to the Eyton family. |
| 1840 | *Fanny* | J. Dawson | 2m Sch | 115 | 65' x 19' 6" x 12'. Half owned by Dawson and Sir Edward Mostyn. |
| 1840 | *Agnes* | J. Dawson | Flat | 40 | 50' x 15' x 6' 6", 1 deck, 1 mast. 50/50 owned by J. Dawson & Sir E. Mostyn 1842 sold to the Eyton family. |
| 1842 | *Mary* | J. Dawson | Sloop | 57 | 59' x 15' 8" x 7' 6", round-sterned, carvel built. 64/64 owned John Dawson of Gronant. |
| 1850 | *Wave* | T. Woodward | Flat | 24 | 44' x 12' 6" x 6' 4", 1 mast. First owner Thomas Woodward, re-reg. Beaumaris 1851. |
| **Mostyn** | | | | | |
| 1819 | *Lord Nelson* | | Smack | | 25' x 8' 4" x 4' 4". Reg. to Jos Connah of Mostyn 1826. |
| 1836 | *Sir Edward* | | 2m Sch | 59 | O.N. 8695. 59' 1" x 16' 9" x 8' 9". Lost 19 June 1875 near Point Lynas on voyage with slates Bangor–Silloth. Supposed cause of loss 'unseaworthiness'. |
| 1838 | *Lady Harriet* | E. Eyton | 2m Sch | 94 | Lost at sea, 28 Dec. 1857. |
| 1839 | *Maid of Mostyn* | E. Eyton | 2m Sch | 102 | 74' 9" x 17' 6" x 9' 8". Reg. built by E. Eyton of Pentreffynon, re-reg. Lancaster 1851. Owned by James Fisher, sold by him 1872, vessel marooned 1874. |
| 1840 | *Edwen* | E. Eyton | 2m Sch | 126 | 69' 7" x 19' x 12' 6". First owned by John Prys Eyton of Kinsale. |
| 1842 | *Taliesin* | E. Eyton | 2m Stm Sch | 74 | 92' 8" x 16' 4" x 9', engine room 29' long. Owned by members of the Eyton family. Rounded stern, carvel built. Sold by the Eyton family to J. H. Langley of Cardiff, 1850. Lengthened1847, she was then 114' loa with engine room 42' long. |
| 1843 | *Dispatch* | E. Eyton | 2m Sch | 28 | O.N. 13580. 54' 4" x 13' 4" x 4'. All shares first owned by Eyton family. Lost off Mostyn 28 Oct. 1866. |
| 1848 | *Sophia* | T. Mathias | 2m Sch | 79 | O.N. 8772. 62' 2" x 16' 3" x 8' 5". Launched in April 1848, intended for coast and foreign trade. First owners were four members of the Eyton family. Re-reg. Caernarfon Sepembert 1860. |
| 1849 | *Eva* | E. Eyton | Smk | 60 | Launched June 1849, intended for the coasting trade. Owned by John Prys Eyton of Llanerchymor. |
| 1855 | *Sea Rover* | R. Rowlinson | 3m Barque | 212 | 108' 6" x 18' 8" x 12' 8". First owned by Rowlinson, running Liverpool–Mediterranean. By 1859 owned by W. Cliff, still running to Mediterranean. 1863 to D. Dynas, then 1868–9 to G. H. Payne running Liverpool–Continent. LR 1868–9 annotated 'wrecked'. |
| 1857 | *Orion* | | 3m Barque | 224 | 109' 3" x 23' 4" x 13' 2". 28/64 owned by Elson Pringle of Southport. 1859 same trade to South America but owned by S. W. Kelso. Cert. cancelled November 1868, burnt at Paraiba 3 Oct. 1868. |

# Appendix 3: Ships built in Flint

| Year | Name | Builder | Type | Tonnage | Remarks/Owners |
|---|---|---|---|---|---|
| 1828 | *Flint Castle* | T. Eyton | 2m Sch | 72 | Launched Feb1828 for Thomas Eyton, colliery owner for shipping coal exports. Built by shipwrights Andrew Green and Edward Evans 1834, running Liverpool–Cork. Lengthened a year later by 15' 9" to 64'. Later meas 67' 6" x 17' 9" x 8' 8". Square stern. Lost at sea 30 Nov. 1863 on the Plough Rock, Belfast. |
| 1829 | *Beresford* | T. Eyton | Sch | 104 | 64 1" x 16' 1" x 11' 1". Built for Thomas Eyton of Mostyn. Ownedby John Pryce Eyton of Kinsale, Robert Eyton of Flint and James Eyton of Mold (also trustees of Henrietta and Sophie Eyton). Apparently lost at sea 1843. |
| 1840 | *Malcolm* | FMB | Bark | 240o, 238n | First vessel built by FMB. Classed A1 for 12 yrs. Reg. 1840 Stranraer, owned by Captain Malcolm McFarlane the whole of his life. Est 92–5' x 23–5' x 15–6'. Aug 1845 sailed Liverpool–Rio de Janeiro. 1858 wrecked on French Reef five miles off Key Largo Florida. |
| 1841 | *Annabella* | M. Parry | Sch | 86 | 63' x17' 1" x 10'. Owned by Michael Parry(28), Thomas Parry of Holywell (28) and R. McCleod ships' chandler, of Liverpool(8). 1843 sailed Liverpool–Newfoundland. Supposedly lost at sea 1845. |
| 1843 | *Experiment* | M. Parry | Flat | 51 | O.N. 10633. Round-sterned, carvel built by Michael Parry 64/64. Evidently lost at sea in 1859. |
| 1843 | *Platina* | M. Parry | Sloop | 36n | 43' x 13'. Owned by Michael Parry. Lost 2 Apr. 1853 nr Puffin Island. |
| 1846 | *Mary* | W. Paton | Sloop | 21 | O.N. 10670. 39' x 11' x 5' 2". Reg. 8 Aug. 1848. 30 Sep. 1848 transferred to Liverpool reg. by Agnes Paton, widow. |
| 1847 | *Ann* | D. Jones | Flat | 30 | O.N. 67968. 52' 6" x 14' 7" x 6' 1". Square-stern. Broken up, letter received by Registrar 11 Mar. 1891. |
| 1847 | *Thomas Green* | Paton & Co. | Sloop | 21 | 45' x 11'. Owned by Paton & Co. Reg. 8 Aug. 1848. Reg transferred to Liverpool 30 Sep. 1848 by Agnes Paton, widow. Used on weekly Flint–Liverpool service in 1850. |
| 1848 | *Industry* | T. Hughes | Sloop | 15 | 32' x 10' x 5' 1". Launched February 1848. Owned by Robert Eyton & Co., three Eyton shareholders. |
| 1848 | *John & Jane* | Jones & Hughes | Wherry | 37 | O.N. 1145. 59' 1" x 12' x 6' 2". Built by David Jones and Thomas Hughes for John Lloyd. Reg. 8 Mar. 1849. Later owned by Henry Ellis, Port Dinorwic (Y Felinheli). |
| 1849 | *Mary* | W. Paton | Sloop | | Round-sterned, carvel built. Sold by Thomas Smedley of Greenfield in 1852 to owners in Conwy, Richard Thomas, shipbuilder and Richard Williams, innkeeper of the Erskine Arms, Conwy. |
| 1849 | *Lady Fielding* | Jones & Hughes | Sch | 56/47 | O.N. 16470. 58' x 16' 3" x 8' 4". Owned by the Hughes family of Amlwch. 11 Aug. 1910 sailed from Swansea with coal for Llanddulas, Anglesey, wrecked 2miles east of Aberdaron, Llŷn Peninsula.*cds |
| 1851 | *Success* | Jones & Hughes | 2m Sch | 57 | O.N. 3382. 59' 6" x 17' 5" x 8' 2". Elliptic stern. Reg. 6 Mar. 1851, owned by M. Parry. Owned by Robert Williams of Amlwch 1881. Last vessel built by partnership of Jones & Hughes. Reg. closed 8 Aug. 1911, vessel broken up. Final owners Robert and Thomas Williams, Amlwch. |
| 1852 | *Lady Helena* | T. Mathias | 2n Sch | 52 | O.N. 20559(?). 61' 9" x 16' 2" x 7' 5". Elliptic stern. Built for Michael Parry and S. and C. Davison. Later owned by Patrick Campbell, Bangor. |
| 1852 | *Breeze* | F. & B. | Sloop | 19 | 36' 6" x 11' 3" x 5' 1". Carvel built. First owner F. & B.. Reg. D. Ferguson 7 Jan. 1852. Later owned by John Griffiths Caernarfon. Reg. closed 8 Nov. 1909. |
| 1853 | *Britius* | D. Jones | 2m Brig | 243o 219n | 92' x 20' x 14.' Cert. from D. Jones 24 Jan. 1853, A1 for 12yrs. Owned by Michael Parry and David |

| | | | | | |
|---|---|---|---|---|---|
| | | | | | Jones. Traded Mediterranean and Brazil. Supposedly lost at sea winter1864/5. May have been the largest vessel built at Flint. |
| 1854 | *Mary Garland* | FMB | Brig | 227n | O.N. 12920. 108' x 20' 2" x 13'. A1 8 years. Cert. 25 Nov. 1854 from D. Ferguson. Square-sterned, carvel-built. Shares also owned by McCallum and Baird. Re-reg. Liverpool 1862. Made voyage from Liverpool–Callao (via Cape Horn). After 1865 re-reg. in Guernsey. Traded as a collier out of Newcastle. James Garland of Cardigan part owner. |
| 1854 | *Robin Hood* | Probably FMB | Sch | 99 | O.N. 1680. 82' 3" x 20' x 11' 4". Owned J. Treweek. A1 12 years when built. Wrecked at Durleston Head near Swanage in 1870 when carrying clay for Runcorn. |
| 1854 | *Mary* | ? | Flat | 18 | |
| 1854 | *Anglesea Lass* | Probably D. Jones | Sch | 99 | 88' 8" x 18' 8" x 10 1". A1 12 years. Owned William Thomas of Amlwch. In Genoa 1857. Lost 23 Jul. 1866, wrecked near Marsden Lighthouse, Northern Ireland, carrying salt Liverpool–Baltic. |
| 1855 | *Miss Nightingale* | D. Jones | Sch | 101g | 83' 7" x 19' 3" x 10'. Square sterned. Owned by David Jones and John Valentine Harrison. 1855 sailed to Rio Grande. Vessel lost at sea in 1860. |
| 1855 | *Sarah Ellen* | FMB | Sch | 121g | O.N. 1398. 85' x 19' x 11' 6". 1869 reduced rig, then home trade only. Lost 22 Nov.1908, Penrhos Point, Holyhead Bay, in ballast. Final owner Thomas Morgan of Amlwch. Listed by *cds as built by 'McCallum'. |
| 1856 | *Isabella* | D. Jones | Sch | 81/65 | O.N. 14381. 75' x 19' x 10'. First owners16/64 were FMB. Richard Ferguson also shown as owner in LR. By 1864 master is a Reney and owned by Shone. FMB sold shares to Davison 11 Sep. 1865. Jan. 1898 reg. transferred to Padstow. 8 Mar. 1902 sailed Waterford for Penrhyn, Falmouth with oats; wrecked on the Manacles. Crewof four saved.*cds |
| 1856 | *Kattie Darling* | D. Jones | Sch | 67 | O.N. 12394. 70' x 18' 5" x 8' 1". Round stern. First owned by J. Valentine Harrison and D. Jones, later by John Harrington of Holywell. Owned by Edward Hughes of the Raven Inn at Flint, 1918. MD&HB wreck records list sunk 26 Oct. 1925 in Mersey. |
| 1856 | *Flintshire Lass* | D. Jones | Sch | 97.74 | O.N. 12395. 76' x 20' x 10' 1". Built for William Jones and Michael Parry, lost Wicklow Bank, 21 Jul. 1867. |
| 1857 | *Chester Trader* | | Flat (Sp) | 38 | O.N. 18860. 58' 6" x 16' 2" x 6' 6". |
| 1857 | *Cyril* | | 2m Sch | 59 | O.N. 18863. 67' x 17' 9" x 8' 1". First owned by James Davison of Connah's Quay, later by Charles Davison. Lost off Tuskar Rock, November 1894. |
| 1857 | *Three Brothers* | | Sch (?) | 32 | Reg. Liverpool, ownd by John Ball of Hoylake. |
| 1857 | *Gipsey* | D. Jones | 2m Sch | 72/56 | O.N. 12400. 74' 4" x 19' 8" x 9'. A1 9 years. Round stern. Part owned by David Jones, later John Hughes of Holywell. Reg. transferred to Belfast 28 Jan. 1816. Final owner Samuel Gray of Antrim. Sailed 6 Nov. 1921 from Dunmore, Co. Waterford in ballast for Connah's Quay. Stranded in Wexford Harbour, total loss.*cds |
| 1857 | *Denbighshire Lass* | D. Jones | Sch | 74 | O.N. 20559. 72' 4" x 18' 6" x 9'. A1 9 years. Owned by Jones & Co. LR 1881 owned by James Reney. During the First World War she was described as a ketch. 18 Mar. 1926 from Cardiff with coal, abandoned in heavy weather off Smalls, crew taken off by the GWR steamer *Reindeer*. *cds |
| 1857 | *Nina* | | 2m Sch | 76 | O.N. 12399. 66' 6" x 19' x 8' 8". Round sterned, built of oak and pitch pine. Initially owned by nine members of the Davison family of Queensferry. Owned later by Charles Davison of Connah's Quay. 1895 owned by Robert Thomas of Liverpool. |

| | | | | | |
|---|---|---|---|---|---|
| 1857 | *Mary* | | Flat | 18 | O.N. 18861. 62' x 11' 7" x 4'. Rebuilt at Flint in 1857. Round stern. Vessel foundered in 1860s. Only Bennett records this vessel. |
| 1858 | *Mary & Jane* | D. Jones | 2m Sch | 68 | O.N. 21038. 68' 9" x 18' 5" x 8' 2". A1 9 years when built. First owner D. Jones (28/64), sold to Edward Peers in February 1865. Abandoned, dismasted between Carmel Head and the Skerries 28 Dec. 1897. Later owned by John Owen of Porthmadoc. |
| 1859 (Sep.) | *John James* | D. Jones | 2m Sloop | 30 | O.N. 27904. 52' 9" x 14' 6" x 6' 6". First owned by David Jones of Caerwys, later owned by D. Williams of Newquay, Cardiganshire in 1895. Sailed from Newquay in ballast for Swansea in calm weather, swept by tide on to Skomer Island 13 Feb. 1902. Wrecked, two crew saved.*cds (also says built by FMB?) |
| 1859 (Sep.) | *Mary* | D. Jones | 2m Sch | 68 | O.N. 27901. 69' 6" x 18' 5" x 8' 5". First owned by David Jones (28/64) and Edward Peers. Owned later byHumphrey & Co. of Connah's Quay until 1875, then H. Foulkes of Connah's Quay. 1895 owned by A. Dilworth of Ulverston. Vessel lost 29 Jan. 1897. |
| 1859 | *Price Jones* | D. Jones | Flat | 23 | O.N. 27903. 53' 2" x 14' 9" x 4' 7". First owner David Jones, 64shares. Reg. in Cardigan 1861. |
| 1859 | *Pride of the Lake* | | | | |
| 1859 | *Pride of Wales* | | Flat | 21 | Owned by Thomas Cooper of Hoylake. |
| 1859 | *Sarah Beck* | | Sch or sloop | 35 | Owned by Mrs Margaret Beck of Hoylake. 1-masted vessel, fore and aft rigged. |
| 1860 | *Industry* | D. Jones | 2m Sch | 72 | O.N. 28045. 71' x 18' 5" x 8' 7". Michael Parry and William Roberts first owners. Sold between 1866–70, then owned by William Evans of Borth. Foundered in Portmadoc Bay 7 Dec. 1891. |
| 1860 | *Wepre Lass* | D. Jones | 2m Sch | 44 | O.N. 28049. 66' 1" x 17' 5" x 6' 1". Built for John Fox of Castle Hill, Hawarden, David Jones and Thomas Hewitt. Transferred to Caernarfon registry in 1872. |
| 1861 | *Caerwys Castle* | D. Jones | 2m Sch | 58 | O.N. 29489. 69' x 18' 4" x 8' 3". First owned by David Jones of Caerwys. 1862 sold to Isaac Hughes of Liverpool. Sailed from Laxey, Isle of Man, 12 Nov. 1875 with cargo of blende ore for Saltney. Posted missing after 40 days 29 Dec. 1876. |
| 1862 | *Jane Porter* | D. Jones | 2m T'sail Sch | 111 | O.N. 44044. 86' 3" x 21' x 10' 8". Launched 13 Jul. 1862 for owner and master, Thomas Porter of Raven Sq., Flint (32/64) and Michael Parry (32/64). Sailed from river Garonne 30 Nov. 1863 for Greenfield. Never heard of again. |
| 1862 (Nov.) | *Catherine* | F & B | 2m Sch | 79 | O.N. 44046. 71' x 19' x 9' 5". Round stern. Six shareholders initially who were not the builders. |
| 1863 | *Margaret Jane* | D. Jones (?) | Sloop (Ben.) | 34 | O.N. 44047. 62 'x 14' 9" x 6' 2". First owned by Mrs Ellen Evans of Holywell. 23 Sep. 1900 from Tal-y-Cafn with bricks for Caernarfon – sank alongside the Railway Pier at Conwy (Deganwy?), raised and condemned. *cds |
| 1863 | *Mary Jones* | D. Jones | 2m T'sail Sch | 113/96 | O.N. 44050. 90' 4" x 21' 7" x 11' 5". Square stern. First owners included David Jones (8/64) and William Jones, master mariner of Connah's Quay. Later altered to 3m sch. Owned by Thomas Hughes of Connah's Quay 1879, Edward Peers of Connah's Quay 1891. 60 h.p. Bolinder engine installed in 1923 and t'sail yard removed. Wrecked on Tongue Sand in the Thames estuary 20 Feb. 1932 with scrap metal for Grangemouth from London. Crew rescued by *Foam Queen*.*cds |
| 1863 | *William & Leigh* | D. Jones | 2m Sch | 63 | O.N. 47222. 67' x 18' 7" x 8' 3". First owner William Hancock, master R. Coppack. 1892 reg. Campbletown. Final owner Thomas J. Sharp of Liverpool (64). 25 Dec. 1929 reg. closed, vessel decayed. |
| 1864 (Mar.) | *Alexandra* | F & B | Sch | 88 | O.N. 47221. 79' x 20' 3" x 9' 7". First principal owner Enoch Lewis of Mostyn. Lost off Holyhead |

| | | | | | |
|---|---|---|---|---|---|
| | | | | | 29 Aug. 1869. |
| 1864 | *William Shepherd* | D. Jones | 2m Sch | 72 | O.N. 47219. 74' x 19' 5" x 9' 2". Classed A1 9 years. First owner William Shepherd of Buckley manufacturer of firebricks. Soon taken over by R. Catherall & Co. Final owners John McConnel and S. Chambers of Kilkeel, Co. Down. 2 May 1929 reg. closed after she foundered at the New Jetty, Connah's Quay, with a cargo of scrap metal. Broken up Connah's Quay. |
| 1864 (Dec.) | *Florence Miriam* | F & B | 2m Sch | 62 | O.N. 47225. 71' 7" x 19' x 8' .8". Built for William Jones (34/64) of Ulverston. 1877 converted to dandy. Owned by James Groves, Tooley Street, London in 1890. |
| 1865 | *Kate* | D. Jones | 2m Sch | 83 | O.N. 47224. 75' 6" x 20' 8" x 9' 7". Built for Davison Brick & Tile Works, Buckley. Carried about 160 ton cargo. 1895 owned in Borth. Lost off the Skerries 24 Jul. 1898. |
| 1865 | *Alfred* | M. Parry | 2m Sch | 84/74 | O.N. 52639. 79'x19'x9'.7". Round counter. Built by Michael Parry, first master Capt J. Vickers. Parry died 1867, taken over by Alfred Parry, his son. After 1895 owned in Newquay. Last vessel built at Flint. Converted to ketch before 1901. Lost September 1910 off the Runnelstone when run down by the schooner-rigged steamer *Pink Rose*, 334grt. Crew rescued. |

# Appendix 4: Ships built in Connah's Quay

| Year | Name | Builder | Type | Tonnage | Remarks/Owners |
|---|---|---|---|---|---|
| 1858 | *Mag* | Jones & Hooson | 2m Sch | 53 | O.N. 18864. First vessel built at Connah's Quay. Round stern. First owner J. N. Lomax of Chester. 1887 owned by Coppack & Carter. After 1903 owned by Mrs Ness of Liverpool. Reported to have a female figurehead. Sold to Norway in 1905. |
| 1858 | *Charles Edward* | FMB | 2m Sch | 65 | O.N. 21037. According to Chester Ship Register built at Connah's Quay. 69' x 18' 3" x 8' 5". Round stern. 40/64 shares. Owned by FMB together. Lost off Bardsey Island 30 Aug. 1865 after collision with Cunard steamer *Aleppo*, all aboard lost. |
| 1861 (Mar.) | *Elizabeth & Jane* | FMB | 2m Sch | 70 | O.N. 28904. Reg. Preston. By 1881 owned by J. Edwards of Amlwch. 1893 owned by John Mostyn of Amlwch. |
| 1864 | *Mary Caroline* | F & B | 2m Sch | 78 | O.N. 47220. 75' 5" x 20' x 9' 8". Round stern. First vessel launched down the new slip at Connah's Quay by FMB in February 1864. Stated by Hogan to be their nineteenth vessel. First owner Hancock of Hawarden and James Coppack. Vessel lost in St Georges' Channel between 8/10 Nov. 1877. |
| 1864 | *Mary & Martha* | F & B | 2m Sch | 90.5 | O.N. 47223. 81' 2" x 20' 6" x 10' 1". Elliptical stern. Origially built for six shareholders.Vessel missing, supposed lost 18 Feb. 1892. |
| 1865 | *Florence Emily* | F & B | 2m Sch | 81/67 | O.N. 52636. 73' 8" x 20' x 9' 1". Elliptic stern. Built for Hancock (42) and James Coppack (16). Launched April 1865. Lost 15 Dec. 1890. |
| 1866 (Feb.) | *Ann* | F & B | 2m Sch | 78 | O.N. 52644. 76' x 20' x 9'. Round counter. Built for William Shepherd and Timothy Catherall. In LR 1886–8. |
| 1866 (Jan.) | *Ernest* | F & B | 2m Sch | 63 | O.N. 52641. 73' x 20' x 9'. Round sterned, standing bowsprit. Vessel supposedly lost on Hoyle Bank 7 Nov. 1890. |
| 1866 (May) | *Padeswood* | F & B | 2m Sch | 80 | O.N. 52643. 77' 6" x 20' 5" x 9' 1". Elliptic stern. Built for William Hancock. Lost off Scomar by collision 30 Apr. 1876. |
| 1867 (Jul.) | *Mary & Gertrude* | F & B | 2m T'sail Sch | 93/70 | O.N. 58203. 78' x 20' 9" x 9' 9". Round stern. Built for Hancock. Transferred to Wexford registry 1891. Possibly broken up in 1930 (Hogan). Reg. closed 16 Jan. 1934 after long lay up. Last owned in Wicklow. Launched same day as the *Glynne*. *cds |
| 1867 (Jul.) | *Glynne* | F & B | 2m Sch | 91 | O.N. 58202. 78' x 20' 9" x 9' 9". Round stern. Built for Hancock. Lost in the storm of 6/7 Nov. 1890. Launched same day as the *Mary & Gertrude*. |
| 1867 (Sep.) | *Maggie* | F & B | | 31 | Sailed to Montevideo 'for river purposes only.' |
| 1868 (Dec.) | *Unity* | F & B | Sch | 63 | O.N. 58209. 68' x 19' 7" x 8' 7". Round stern. Built for eight owners of the Reney family. Sold to Amlwch 1900. Final owner, Hugh Jones of Caernarfon 19 Jan. 1910. Lost 18 Nov. 1910 on southern bar off Le Havre on a voyage from Eling, Soton to Caen with pitch. Crew of four saved. |
| 1868 | *Not Forgot* | D. Jones | 2m Sch | 67/54 | O.N. 58204. 68' x 18' 6" x 9' 1". Round stern. Built for Alfred and Thomas Parry of Flint. Owned by John Coppack of Connah's Quay in 1890 and in 1918 .Registry cancelled18 Jan. 1893 to be used as a lighter. Sold by Coppack & Carter to Richard Abel in1921. Condemned at Liverpool 1931 *cds says built by Jones?. Reg. closed 24 Jul. 1931. |

| | | | | | |
|---|---|---|---|---|---|
| 1871 | *Lorne* | F & B | 2m T'sail Sch | 85/66 | O.N. 58214. 77' 4" x 19' 1" x 9' 1". Round stern. Owned by four shareholders when first built, including the Reney family (?). Later owned in Aberystwyth and Cardiff. Foundered 10 Nov. 1919 50 miles NW of Roches Douvre, Guernsey en route Cardiff–St Brieuc with coal. Crew and master's wife rescued by trawler. *cds |
| 1872 | *Bessie Arnold* | | Sch | 129/113 | O.N. 58199. Yard N°. 28. 86' 6" x 22' 2" x 11' 6". 1881 owned by William Morgan, Duddon. Wrecked 28 Dec. 1908 on south coast of Arran on voyage Millom–Clydebank with iron ore. Only survivor was the mate who swam ashore. |
| 1873 | *Rosendale* | F & B | 3m Sch | 150/118 | O.N. 68229. Yard N°. 29. 92' 1" x 22' 6" x 12' 1". Built for Reney family. Sold 1913 and later owned by William Postlethwaite of Cumbria. Final owners in Arklow. Lost 15 May1918 on voyage Par–Mersey with clay. Collided with H.M. Trawler *Cyrano* off Trevose Head, North Cornwall. Crew of six saved. |
| 1875 | *Elizabeth Jane* | F & B | 2m T'sail Sch | 102 | O.N. 67996. 80' 3" x 21' 6" x 10' 5". Owned by Thomas Mathias Jnr. of Connah's Quay, later Humphrey Foulkes of Connah's Quay. Lost two miles west of Coastguard Station, Inch, Co. Cork 29 Sep. 1916 on voyage from Cardiff with coal. Crew of three lost. *cds |
| 1875 | *Comet* | | Dandy | 39 | Owned by Henry Isaac, St John's Fish Market, Liverpool. |
| 1875 | *Mayflower* | | Yawl | 39 | Owned by T. R. Atkinson of Liverpool. |
| 1877 | *Mary Elizabeth* | F & B | 2m Sch, salt | 113/99 | O.N. 76551. 87' x 22' 4" x 10' 4". Elliptic stern. First owners included Daniel Ferguson (6), James Baird Jnr (4), James Baird Snr (6), Thomas Mathias Jnr, of Connah's Quay, Hancock and Garratt families. Owned in Appledore 1918. Sold to US owner 1927 following arrest trying to run liquor into U.S.A. during the Prohibition era. *cds |
| 1878 | *Duchess* | S. Owens | 2m Sch | 109.62/86 | O.N. 76552. 85' 8" x 22' 7" x 10' 4". Built by Samuel Owens. Owned by Charles Davison of Connah's Quay. 1895 owned by Frederick Leigh Hancock of Hawarden. Lost in river Mersey 5/6 May 1934 on voyage Wicklow–Garston Light when she dragged anchors onto Taylors Bank and was beached at Tranmere after salvage by the *Vigilant*. Broken up. *cds. 'Seems to be a one off.'(H) |
| 1878 | *Chase* | F & B | 2m Sch | 109/98 | 85' 7" x 22' x 10'. Figurehead a crocodile. First owners included Daniel Ferguson (12) and James Baird (12). Later part owned by Richard Ferguson. Owned by Reney 1884–5. Lost in river Mersey15 Feb. 1894. |
| 1880 | *Nancy Jones* | F & B | 2m Sch | 108/95 | 82' 9" x 22" x10' 1". Elliptic stern First owners were local pilots and the Foulkes family. Lost 23 Jun. 1880 off Morecambe Bay, light vessel. |
| 1881 | *Earl of Beaconsfield (1st)* | | 3m(?) Sch | 114/99 | O.N. 84162. Yard N°. 36. Owned by George Raynes of Old Hall Street, Liverpool. 86' x 22' 6" x 10' 9". Reg. Plymouth1902 to William Lawry and Eugene White. Lost 12 Jan. 1905 in ballast Oporto–St John's, Newfoundland in Force 10 winds 35° 56' N, 39° 43W. Crew of five saved. |
| 1881 | *Hawarden Castle* | F & B | Steam flat | 95 | O.N. 76558. 78' 6" x 20' 8" x 9' 5". Built as screw steam flat with two diagonally inverted direct acting engines made by W. E. Bates of Northwich. 17" cylinder, 16" stroke, 49 h.p. Built for the Connah's Quay Alkali Co. and J. Coppack. Engine Room 21' 6" long. In MNL 1890s as steamer. Later the *Gleaner*. Vessel certainly completed by F&B, but not known who had started to build her. |
| 1884 | *Earl Cairns* | F & B | 3m Sch | 127/91 | O.N. 87826. Yard N°. 37. 93' 2" x 23' 8" x 10' 4". Built for J. W. Raynes. Owned in Fowey 1918. Auxiliary engine fitted 1921. On fire in river Mersey 1929. Barrage Balloon vessel at Falmouth during the Second World War. Reg. closed 19 Aug. 1947 – not worthy of repair. *cds |

| | | | | | |
|---|---|---|---|---|---|
| 1884 | *Agnes Craig* | F & B | 3m Sch | 99 | O.N. 88705. Yard N° 38. 94' 7" x 23' x 10' 4". First owner J. Craig. Owned by J. Baird in 1893. Later owned in Wicklow. 1938 altered to 2 masted auxiliary. Broken up Arklow 1952, gear stripped and allowed to go on the rocks to break up |
| 1885 | *Earl of Lathom* | | 3m Sch | 132/100 | O.N. 91172. Yard N° 39. 94' 5" x 23' 2" x 10' 4". Aground off Runcorn in 1889. First owner J. W. Raynes. Final owner William Hancock. Lost in First World War by gunfire from *U-20*, 15 May 1915 off Old Head of Kinsale. No loss of life. |
| 1885 | *Empress* | | 3m Sch | 120 | O.N. 88706. Yard N° 41. 94' 5" x 23' 2" x 10' 4". First owner Charles Davison of Connah's Quay. Later owned in Whitstable. Reg. Faversham 1886. Sunk 7 Aug. 1910 in collision with S.S. *Marusa* while sailing from London–Llanelli with scrap metal. Three crew saved and one lost. *cds |
| 1887 | *Faithful* | | 3m Sch | 132/103 | O.N. 88707. Yard N° 42. First owned in Connah's Quay by James Baird and others. Supposedly built of timber from Hawarden Park and one of her boats was used by Mr Gladstone at the start of the building of the new bridge at King's Ferry. Lost 22 Nov. 1921 sailing from Plymouth–Preston with clay. Wrecked on Splaugh Rocks, Wexford. Crew saved by Irish Lights tender *Ierne*.*cds |
| 1887 | *Protection* | | Flat | 67 | Owned by J.W. Raynes. Originally single-masted, later rigged as ketch. Fitted with 44 h.p. engine in 1929. 4 Oct. 1948 put on breakwater by Severn Bore. Broken up. |
| 1888 | *Fair Trade* | | Flat | 76 | Owned by J. W. Raynes. |
| 1888 | *Sandpiper* | | Dredger | | Reported in the press August 1888 that this vessel was built to help overcome channel silting in the Dee which was only 7.5' on high spring tide, and the Swedish and Norwegian timber trade was being diverted to Birkenhead. Press report September 1888 that *Sandpiper* had ceased dredging. |
| 1890 | *Reciprocity* | F & B | Flat/ketch | 89/75 | O.N. 97792. 79' 8" x 20' 2" x 8' 3". Owned by J. W. Raynes. Reg. Liverpool 1921 as Aux. 26 Aug. 1926 from Holyhead–Fleetwood in ballast, caught fire off Point Lynas and abandoned by crew. Scuttled by THV *Beacon* next day. |
| 1890 | *Windermere* | F & B | 3m Sch | 174/147 | O.N. 93420. Yard N° 45. 104' 2" x 24' 3" x 11' 3". F. J. Crosfield first owner. Owned by C. A. Reney in 1918. Later owned by the Kearon and Tyrell families in Arklow. Rig reduced and engine fitted in 1927. Sailed for Algiers in July 1957. Lost in the Mediterranean 1958. |
| 1892 | *Margaret Hobley* | F & B | | 119 | This vessel included as she was virtually rebuilt over a twelve-month period by Ferguson & Baird. She was originally built at Pembroke Dock in 1868 as a 2-masted t'sail schooner, but was rebuilt as 3-masted schooner. |
| 1893 | *Hilda* | F & B | Sch | 111 | O.N. 96284. Yard N° 46. 94' 8" x 22' x 9' 3". Built for W. Hancock & Co.. Sold to Swansea owners 1917. 1921 reg. as aux. 1 Nov. 1922 caught fire at Quoile Quay, Strangford Lough, total loss. |
| 1894 | *Maude* | F & B | Sch | 72 | O.N. 96285. Yard N° 47. 87' x 21' 3" x 8' 8". Built for W. Hancock. 7 May 1917 from Padstow–Manchester with clay. Taken by German submarine eight miles SW of Bardsey Island – sunk using scuttling charges. Crew saved. |
| 1895 | *Federation* | F & B | Flat/ketch | 87/87 | O.N. 105303. 79' 5" x 20' 7" x 8' 5. First owned by J. W. Raynes. Owned by A. E. Reney 1918. Lost 1923, but salvaged and renamed *Sutherlandshire Lass*. Final owner Hector Ross of Bonar Bridge, Inverness. Foundered 12 Jun. 1929 St Abb's Head, with coal from Blyth–Inverness. Crew of four saved. |
| 1896 (Apr.) | *Gordon* | | 3m Sch | 134/98 | O.N. 104471. Yard N° 48. 98' 6" x 23' x 10' 1". James Baird first owner. Final owner Jessie Jones (24) and eight others. Foundered 28 Jan. 1914 on voyage Penzance–London with clay, after colliding with S.S. *Webburn* off Royal Sovereign light near Hastings. Crew of five saved. |

| | | | | | |
|---|---|---|---|---|---|
| 1897 | *Winifred* | F & B | Ketch | 89 | O.N. 104472. Built for W. Reney of Connah's Quay. 104' 2" x 24' 3" x 11' 3". Converted to aux. 1907, 35 h.p. engine in 1918. Later owned by United Alkali, later ICI Ltd, Liverpool. Sold in 1949 to the S.S. *Pelter* Co. Ltd, of Liverpool. Final owners Zillah Shipping Co. of Warrington, William A. Savage as manager. |
| 1900 | *Lizzie May* | F & B | 3m T'sail Sch | 136/99 | O.N. 104473. Built for Coppacks of Connah's Quay. Sold in 1908 to Flemings of Youghal. Sold again in 1931 when 80 h.p. engine fitted. Still afloat 2018. See text for further details. |
| 1901 | *J. & A. Coppack* | F & B | Ketch | 95/80 | O.N. 104475. Built for Coppacks. Believed lost off the Cornish coast in November 1909 whilst on passage with coal Cardiff–Par. |
| 1901 | *Catherine Reney* | F & B | Ketch | 160 | O.N. 104476. 88' 6" x 22' x 9' 3". Built for the Reney family for use in the brick export trade. With Capt Crofts in charge on voyage from Connah's Quay–Belfast laden with bricks and fireclay, she went ashore at Donaghadee and was lost with all hands on 31 Dec. 1905. |
| 1903 | *Earl of Beaconsfield (2)* | F & B | 3m Sch | 167/141 | O.N. 104477. 105' x 24' 5" x 11' 5". Owned by Raynes family (16), William Marrow (12) and R. Hutton (12). 21 Jul. 1906 from Stranraer–Conah's Quay in ballast, was lost in collision with S.S. *City of Manchester*, five miles ENE of South Rock lighthouse, Co. Down. Crew of six saved. |
| 1903 | *Sarah Lathom* | F & B | Ketch | 87/70 | O.N. 104478. 80' 7" x 21' 5" x 8' 0". Built for W. Gough Thomas. 1918 owned by Robert Foulkes of Connah's Quay. Fitted with engine. Lost off the Isle of Man on 19 Jul. 1948. Final owner Ralph A. Ashton of Blackpool. |
| 1905 | *James O'Neill* | F & B | 3m Sch | 98 | O.N. 115120. Yard N°. 56. 91' x 22' 4" x 9' 7". Owned in 1918 by Kinsale Sailing Co., Cork. Described by Hogan as a 'fish carrier.' Final owner U.K. Sarnia Shipping of Guernsey. Sold to William Munn of St John's, Newfoundland and reg. there 1921–49. |
| 1906 | *Malvina* | A. Fergus | 2m fore & aft | | O.N. 124622. Launched off the top slip, fitted with motor and copper bottomed. Built for the Falkland Island Co.. Fitted with 65 h.p. engine – 5 knots. Fore and aft rigged, 2 masted. Wrecked on 9 May 1910 in Reef Channel, near Saunders Island, when returning from West Falkland with a full cargo of wool. |
| 1911 | *Nora Bate* | A. Fergus | Barge/flat | 49 | Built for ? Bates, Mersey barge owners. |

# Appendix 5: Ships built in Queensferry

| Year | Name | Builder | Type | Tonnage | Remarks/Owners |
|---|---|---|---|---|---|
| 1836 | *Rossett* | James Boydell Jnr | Sloop | 55 | O.N. 21425. Suitability in bad weather questioned in Hogan – see Flint Chapter 7 notes. Carvel built. 59' 7" x 15' 3 x 6' 9". 58/64 owned by James Boydell when n |
| 1836 | *Honoratus* | James Boydell Jnr | 2m Sch | 88 | 64' 8" x 15' 6" x 7' 8". Round stern. Lost at Bull Bay, Amlwch in October 1843. See Hogan Chapter 7 notes. |
| 1837 | *Anna & Maria* | James Boydell Jnr | 2m Sch | 77 | 67' 2 x 16' 5" x 8' 4". Sold by James Boydell Jnr to John Bennett, master mariner of Flint. |
| 1839 | *Skimmer* | James boydell Jnr | Sch | 150 | O.N. 31839. 84' 6" x 23' 6" x 8'. Round-sterned, carvel built. 64 shares, all owned by James Boydell. Certifiate dated 6 Apr. 1839. |
| 1839 | *Mersey* | James Boydell Jnr | Flat | 48 | 49' 5" x 13' x 5' 4". Rounded-stern, carvel built for Samuel Newton of Newton Lyon &Co., Croxton Park. |
| 1839 | *Skimmer* | James Boydell Jnr | Steamer | 76 | Converted to steam, new cert. 24 Oct. 1839. '…she is propelled by steam with an engine room 35' 7" in length.' Converted to sail 1846 (?). Shares – Boydell (43), Sir Stephen Glynne (6),W. E. Gladstone (1) and William Lyttleton (1). Sold in 1846 by James Boydell of Kingswinford and Charles Blaney of Plastêg to John Rigby of Liverpool, merchant. |
| 1840 | *Collier* | James Boydell Jnr | Flat | 49 | O.N. 16471. 59' 3" x 15' 5" x 7' 0". Round-sterned, carvel built. John Rigby of Liverpool also a shareholder. Owned by Rigby and Hancock. |
| 1840 | *Oak* | James Boydell Jnr | Flat | 39 | Co-partners Oak Farm Ironworks. |
| 1842 | *James* | John Powell | Sloop | 64 | Owned by John Powell, timber merchant. |
| 1848 | *Margaret* | John Powell | Sch | 89 | 68' 5" x 16' 9" x 9' 4". Owned by John Powell, timber merchant. 8 Jul. 1851 sold to John Williams, banker, of Chester. |
| 1851 | *Anne & Mary* | John Powell | Sch | 72 | Owned by 'the spinster daughter of John Powell.' Lost west of Skomer Island, 15 Nov. 1876. |
| 1888 | –?– | Smith & Co. | Screw steamer | | Built by George K. Smith for passengers and cargo on the Amazon. Sailed to the Amazon. Ketch rigged. Newspaper 6 Jul. 1888. |
| 1888 | *Ambas* | Smith & Co. | Steamer | | Built for H. M. Smith of Waterloo, Liverpool for service in West Africa. |
| 1889 | *Daisy* | Smith & Co. | Pleasure steamer | 17 | O.N. 96227. 48' x 10', for pleasure and serving fishing fleet. Built for Count Josef Rapallo. Sailed to Tunis via the French canal system. |
| 1890 | *Alerta* | Smith & Co. | Pleasure stemer | 9/29 | O.N. 98164. 51' x 12' 6". Similar to *Daisy*. Built for Wilson & Son, London. Probably built east of Queensferry Bridge after noise complaints. |
| 1890 | *Nora* | Smith & Co. | Pleasure steamer | 9/32 | O.N. 98186. Reg. London 1890 to James Watkin, 121 Fenchurch Street. Built of steel, 56' 6" x 12' 3". Later renamed *Foxhound*. |
| 1891/2 | *Reliance* | Smith & Co. | | 50/106 | O.N. 98323. 90' x 18' x 7' 6". Built of steel. Launched by Miss Smith for Messrs J. Beckwith of Colchester. |
| 1894 (May) | *May Queen* | QSB&E Co. Ltd | Pass. steamer/tug | 29 grt | 61' 4" x 12' 1" x 6' 7". Launched by Mrs Myers, wife of Charles Myers, MD, (inventor of the Myers patent propellor). Engines fitted at Sandycroft Foundry. Built for Crosbie & King for passengers and towing on Lough Neagh. 1897 *Lurgan*, Belfast. 1900 Port Talbot, then to Russia? A. M. Langford, Chapter 10 notes. |

| | | | | | |
|---|---|---|---|---|---|
| 1894 (Oct.) | *Monarch* | QSB&E Co. Ltd | Steam tug | 38 | O.N. 104192. 60' 7" x 14 'x 7' 1". Built for Grimsby fish merchants. Later *N°. 4* when purchased by Manchester, Sheffield and Lincolnshire Railway then Great Central Railway Co., then London & North Eastern Railway. |
| 1895 | *John O'Gaunt* | QSB&E Co. Ltd | | 51 | O.N. 84968. Built for Lancaster Port Commissioners. Later renamed *Escott*. 40 h.p. engine. |
| 1897 | *Rose* | | Passenger ferry | 52 | O.N. 95760. Built under the supervision of W. Hanson for the Douglas Steam Ferries Co., Isle of Man. |
| 1897 | *Thistle* | | Passenger ferry | 52 | Built under the supervision of W. Hanson for the Douglas Steam Ferries Co., Isle of Man. |
| 1897 | *Shamrock* | | Passenger ferry | 52 | O.N. 108856. Built under the supervision of W. Hanson for the Douglas Steam Ferries Co., Isle of Man. |
| 1897 | *Jubilee* | | Steam tug | | Built for U.K. owners. |
| 1898 | *Research* | | *Steamer* | | For work on the Klondike, for J. Waddington of Liverpool. |
| 1898 | *Hercules* | | River steamer | | For work on the river Amazon. |
| 1905? | *Belle* | Dee Shipb. Co. | Open steam launch | | |
| 1905 | –?– | | Launch | 8 | Steel 18 h.p. cpd engine – foreign. |
| 1905 | –?– | | Grab dredger | 200 | Steel. For the U.K. |
| 1905 | –?– | | Towing launch | 14 | Steel. 42 h.p. engine – foreign. |
| 1905 | –?– | | Motor launch | 4 | Wood. 8 h.p. engine – U.K. |
| 1906 | –?– | | Launch | | Steel. Shallow draught. |
| 1906 | –?– | | –?– | | Tw. Sr. triple compound engine. |
| 1906 | H.M.S. *Bulldog* | | Conv to barge | | 3rd Class gunboat, Ant Class, converted to barge. Sold by Royal Navy 16 Jul. 1906. |
| 1906 | *Boston* | Dee Shipb. Co. | Grain barge | 42 | O.N. 131355. For Grain Elevator & Automatic Weighing Co., Liverpool. |
| 1906 | *Tunny* | Dee Shipb. Co. | Barge | 166 | O.N. 124025. For Rea Transport Co. |
| 1906 | *Tarpon* | Dee Shipb. Co. | Barge | 169 | O.N. 124029. For Rea Transport Co. 100' x 21' 25" x 8' 65". Steel. Reg. cancelled January 1970. |
| 1906 | *Halcon* | Dee Shipb. Co. | Motor yacht | | 75' x 12' 5". Steel. Twin screw. Owned in Mexico. Lost by fire 1914/15. |
| 1907 | *Conger* | | Barge | 168 | O.N. 124085. For Rea Transport Co. |
| 1906 (Dec.) | *Crab* | | Barge | 168 | O.N. 124089. For Rea Transport Co. |
| 1907(Apr.) | *Pike* | | Barge | 168 | O.N. 124057. For Rea Transport Co. |
| 1907 | *Pilchard* | | Barge | 168 | O.N. 124062. For Rea Transport Co. |
| 1907 | *Agatha & Marie* | | | | |
| 1908 | *Francia* | Dee Shipb. Co. | Launch | | |
| 1908 | *Pepuhy* | A & M | River steamer | | First vessel built by Abdela & Mitchell. |
| 1908 | *Cary* | A & M | Sch (?) | 300 | O.N. 127065. For Rea Transport Co. 1918 owned in Bristol then *Lonsdale*. R. Abel sand barge in 1950s. |
| 1908 | *Grilse* | A & M | Barge | 170 | O.N. 14118. For Rea Transport Co. |
| 1908 | *Gurnet* | *A & M* | Barge | 170 | O.N. 124112. For Rea Transport Co. |
| 1908 | *Salvador* | A & M | Tug | 50(?) | 84' x 16' x 9' 1". For Brazil. |
| 1908 | *Provençal 19* | A & M | Tug | | Yard N°. 181. 220 h.p. CSC tug. Built for Sociéte Anon Provençale de Remorquage of Marseilles. Still afloat 1931/2. |
| 1908 | *Provençal 17* | A & M | Tug | | Yard N°. 182. 300 h.p. CSC tug. Built for Sociéte Anon Provençale de Remorquage of Marseilles. |
| 1910 | *Dory* | A & M | Barge | 125 | O.N. 131278. For Rea Transport Co. Later R. Abel *Fossdale*. |
| 1910 | | A & M | Steam sloop | | Yard N°. 302. Steel. 120, IHP. |

| | | | | | |
|---|---|---|---|---|---|
| 1910 | | A & M | Motor | | Yard N°. 303. Wood 6, IHP. |
| 1910 | | A & M | Motor | | Yard N°. 304. Wood 60, IHP. |
| 1910 | | A & M | Motor | | Yard N°. 305. Wood 50, IHP. |
| 1910 | | A & M | Sail | | Yard N°. 306. Steel. British. |
| 1910 | | A & M | Motor | | Yard N°. 307. Wood, 80, IHP. Foreign. Later *Princess*. |
| 1910 | | A & M | Motor | | Yard N°. 308. Wood 60, IHP. Foreign. |
| 1910 | | A & M | Steam | | Yard N°. 309. Wood, 70, IHP. Foreign. |
| 1910 | | A & M | Sail | | Yard N°. 310. Steel. British. |
| 1910 | | A & M | Steam | | Yard N°. 312. Wood, 30, IHP. Foreign. |
| 1911 | *Lobao* | A & M | River steamer | 272/534 | Yard No. 311. 149' 9" x 32' 1" x 12' 5". 2 x VC engines by A & M. Later *Mar del Plata*. |
| 1911 | *Laura* | A & M | Tug | | Steel. 100 h.p. compound tug. |
| 1911 | *Cod* | A & M | Barge | 133 | O.N. 131379. For Rea Transport Co. |
| 1911 | *Oyster* | A & M | Barge | 133 | O.N. 131380. For Rea Transport Co. |
| 1911 | *Plaice* | A & M | Barge | 133 | O.N. 131405. For Rea Transport Co. |
| 1912 | *Sole* | A & M | Barge | 133 | O.N. 131406. For Rea Transport Co. |
| 1912 | *Broughton* | A & M | River steamer | | Yard N°. 331. Compound stern wheeler. |
| 1912 | *Manoel Thomas* | A & M | River steamer | | 300 h.p. Compound stern wheeler. |
| 1912 | *Barbel* | A & M | Barge | 133 | O.N. 131456. For Rea Transport Co. |
| 1912 | *Bitterling* | A & M | Barge | 133 | For Rea Transport Co. |
| 1912 | *Worcester* | A & M | Canal tug | 50 | 45' x 6' 6". 50 h.p. Kromhout engine. For Worcester & Birminghan Canal Co. 2013 preserved at Ellesmere Port in working order. |
| 1912 | *Birmingham* | A & M | Canal tug | 50 | 45' x 6' 6". 50 h.p. Kromhout engine. For Worcester & Birminghan Canal Co. 2013 hull on bank at Tardebigge. |
| | –?– | A & M | Lighter | 250 | For Argentina. |
| | –?– | A & M | Lighter | 250 | For Argentina. |
| | –?– | A & M | Lighter | 70 | 50 h.p. motor. For Brazil. |
| | –?– | A & M | Lighter | 70 | 50 h.p. motor. For Brazil. |
| 1913 | *N°. 3 Newport* | A & M | Dock Hopper/ Dredger | 208 | O.N. 129327. For Newport Harbour Commissioners. Later James N°. 3 and Smiths Dock Hopper. |
| 1913 | *Pater* | A & M | Coaster | 141 | O.N. 135951. Yard N°. 339. 95' 1" x 18' 8" x 8' 1". 220 h.p. Plenty oil engine, twin screw. Built for James Fairclough. Reg. Runcorn. Later *Pioneer*. |
| 1913 | –?– | A & M | Tug | 20 | Yard N°. 340. 25 h.p. steam engine. For U.K. owners. |
| 1913 | *Fleurita* | A & M | Coaster | 171 | O.N. 124627. Yard N°. 351. 103' 2" x 22' 1" x 8' 3". 46 h.p. Bolinder oil engine. Built for John Summers. Foundered 29 Jan. 1965. |
| 1913 | *Carita* | A & M | Motor barge | 141 | O.N. 124626. 96' x ? x 7' 8". |
| 1913 | *Anchovy* | A & M | Barge | 130 | O.N. 135471. For Rea Transport Co. |
| 1913 | *Haddock* | A & M | Barge | 130 | O.N. 135495. For Rea Transport Co. |
| 1913 | *Hake* | A & M | Barge | 130 | O.N. 135472. For Rea Transport Co. |
| 1913 | *Sardine* | A & M | Barge | 130 | O.N. 135477. For Rea Transport Co. |

| | | | | | |
|---|---|---|---|---|---|
| 1913 | *Whiting* | A & M | Barge | 130 | O.N. 135500. For Rea Transport Co. Still afloat in 1979. |
| 1913 | *Whelk* | A & M | Barge | 130 | O.N. 135506. For Rea Transport Co. |
| 1913 | *3 GWR* | A & M | Barge | 63 | |
| 1913 | *4 GWR* | A & M | Barge | 63 | O.N. 135522. |
| 1913 | *5 GWR* | A & M | Barge | 63 | O.N. 135523. |
| 1913 | *6 GWR* | A & M | Barge | 63 | O.N. 135524. Later Nº 26. Bought by Richard Abel 1950s. |
| 1913 | –?– | A & M | Motor vessel | | Wooden. 95 h.p. motor. For Portugal. |
| 1913 | –?– | A & M | Motor vessel | | Wooden. 95 h.p. motor. For Portugal. |
| 1913 | –?– | A & M | Motor vessel | | Wooden. 95 h.p. motor. For Portugal. |
| 1913 | –?– | A & M | Motor vessel | | Wooden. 95 h.p. motor. For Portugal. |
| 1913 | –?– | A & M | Pontoon | | |
| 1914 | –?– | A & M | Pontoon | | |
| 1914 | *Sir William (Vernon)* | A & M | Pontoon | 96/170 | O.N. 137407. Yard Nº 355. 98' 1" x 21' 1" x 9' 6". Later *Felita*, *Tanker*, *Alvtank* (1951). Still afloat 1956. Sold on the stocks to John Summers. |
| 1914 | *7 GWR* | A & M | Barge | 63 | O.N. 135556. Later *Nº 7. Jos Rank.* |
| 1914 | *8 GWR* | A & M | Barge | 63 | O.N. 135560. Later *Nº 8. Jos Rank*. 1950s bought by Richard Abel. Renamed *Birkdale*. |
| 1914 | *9 GWR* | A & M | Barge | 63 | O.N. 135561. Later *Nº 9. Jos Rank*. 1950s bought by Abels 1950s. |
| 1914 | *10 GWR* | A & M | Barge | 63 | O.N. 135562. |
| 1914 | *11 GWR* | A & M | Barge | 63 | O.N. 135565. |
| 1914 | *12 GWR* | A & M | Barge | 63 | O.N. 135566. |
| 1914 | –?– | A & M | St Wh R St | 100 | Yard Nº 317. 119' 6" x 24' 1 x 5' 6". 280 h.p. twin tandem cpd engine by A&M. Vessel believed to be at yard unsold from before the First World War until 1930. |
| 1914 | *Kingsholm* | A & M | Tar tanker | 52/109 | Built for William Butler of Bristol for service on the Bristol Channel. Sold to Elder Dempster for service in West Africa as the *Ilesha*. Lost off Bardsey Island on delivery voyage 8 Aug. 1915. |
| 1914 | *Honor Storey* | A & M | Coaster | 129 | O.N. 137091. Yard No. 377. 85' x 21' x 8'. Built for the Darwen & Mostyn Iron Co. Later owned in Bridgwater by Peace Ltd. as the *Parret*. Still afloat in 1956. |
| 1914 | *BP1* | A & M | Tug | | O.N. 169384. 55' 7" x 15' 1" x 6' 2". Fitted with 45 h.p. steam engine. Owned by Benjamin Perry of Bristol, 1945. |
| | *Zambi* | A & M | Barge | 63 | O.N. 137475. For Lever Brothers. |
| 1915 | *Yumbi* | A & M | Barge | 60 | O.N. 137474. For Lever Brothers. |
| 1915 | *Dolo* | A & M | Barge | 46 | O.N. 137480. For Lever Brothers. |
| 1915 | *Bongo* | A & M | Barge | 46 | O.N. 137481. For Lever Brothers. |
| 1915 | –?– | | Coaster | | 160 h.p. Bolinder engine. |
| 1916 | –?– | | Coaster | | 160 h.p. Bolinder engine. |
| 1915–18 | *Sloyne* | A & M | Tug | 95 grt | O.N. 137528. Yard Nº 395. Later *Palencia*, William Watkins. Reg. London 1920. Later owned by Shell Co. of Gibraltar. Still afloat 1964* (SB Dec. 1964). |
| 1915–8 | *DD6C* | A & M | Grain elevator | | |
| 1915–8 | *DD5C* | A & M | Grain elevator | | |
| 1915–8 | *A473* | A & M | Boom defence | | |

| | | | | | |
|---|---|---|---|---|---|
| 1915–8 | *A474* | A & M | Boom defence | | |
| 1915–8 | *A106* | A & M | | | |
| 1915–8 | *BD49* | A & M | Dmb Bm | | |
| 1918 | BD50 | A & M | Dmb Bm | | |
| 1918 | *James Evans* | A & M | Trawler | 79/206 | O.N. 144461. Yard N°. 437. For Admiralty Strath type trawler. Sold 1922, retained name. |
| 1918 | *John Dupuis* | A & M | Trawler | 77/203 | O.N. 145029. Yard N°. 438. For Admiralty, Strath type trawler. Launched 29 Nov. 1917. Sold 1922 and renamed *Ravenna*. Broken up May 1952. |
| 1918 | *Henry Flight* | A & M | Trawler | /206 | O.N. 145018. Yard N°. 439. For Admiralty, Strath type trawler. Later *Yesso* (1921). Hired as A/P trawler Nov. 1939–Jun. 1940. Renamed *Arabesque* 1941 and used as fuel carrier 04/44-11/44. Broken up 1953. |
| 1919 | *Robert Farecloth* | A & M | Trawler | 94/206 | O.N. 143961. Yard N°. 440. 57 h.p. triple compound engine by A&M. For Admiralty Strath type trawler. Sold 1919, renamed *Humphrey*. Hired as M/S (RNZN) Sep.1939–Aug.44. Still afloat Auckland 1955/6, owned by Sanford Ltd. |
| 1919 | *John Elliot* | A & M | Trawler | 94/206 | O.N. 143265. Yard N°. 441. Later *Tom Jenkinson* and *Gillian*. Hired on examination service Aug. 1939–Aug. 1945. |
| 1919 | *Stephen Kenny* | A & M | Trawler | 93/205 | Yard N°. 444. Later *Witham*, Boston Deep Sea Fishing Co. Engined by A&M of Brimscombe. Hired as M/S Nov. 1939, fuel carrier in Second World War Apr.–Nov. 1944. |
| 1920 | *John Kennedy* | A & M | Trawler | | Admiralty Strath type trawler. Sold 1919. |
| 1920 | *Warita* | A & M | Coaster | 144/305 gt | O.N. 137097. Yard N°. 404. 127' x 24' x 10' 6". For John Summers and on stocks before the First World War. 320 h.p. Bolinder engine used in munitions factory. Sold 1946 to Duff, Herbert Mitchell and renamed *Alfred Mason*. Sold 1954 to Capt Tyrell of Arklow. BU 1968, Dublin. |
| 1920 | *Indorita* | A & M | Coaster | 99/201 gt | O.N. 144844. Yard N°. 408. 109' x 9' 9" draft. Bolinder engine for John Summers. Later to Coppack Brothers1946. Broken up 1974. |
| 1920 | *Eldorita* | A & M | Coaster | 99/201 gt | O.N. 145689. Yard N°. 409. 109 'x 9' 9" draft. Bolinder engine for John Summers. Later to Colchester Shipping Co, R. S. Banyard. Lost on voyage to Rosyth (Rothesay?)12 Dec. 1966. |
| 1920 | *Mary Nickerson* | A & M | Coaster | 308 gt | O.N. 140819. Yard N°. 414. 130' x 23' 1" x 9' 7". Built for Moffat Steam Ship Co. of Grimsby. Later *Snow Queen*. |
| 1920 | *Cornish Trader* | A & M | Coaster | 212/471 gt | O.N. 137210. Yard N°. 454. Later *Cornish Rose*, owned by Richard Hughes. 1946 sold to Greece. |
| 1920 | *S.W. Electra* | A & M | | | O.N. 147206. 119' 5" x 24' 1" x 5' 4". Owned A&M 1928(?). |
| 1920 | *Foam* | A & M | Drifter | 39/95 gt | O.N. 145552. Yard N°. 445. For Admiralty. Sold 1921, later *Starwort*, *Menna* and *Plough*. Hired on harbour service by Admiralty Sep. 1939–Mar. 46. |
| 1920 | –?– | A & M | Lighter | | |
| 1920 | –?– | A & M | Lighter | | |
| 1920 | –?– | A & M | Lighter | | |
| 1920 | –?– | A & M | Lighter | | |
| 1920 | –?– | A & M | Lighter | | |
| 1921 | *Fogbreak* | A & M | Drifter | 39/95 gt | O.N. 145547. Yard N°. 446. For Admiralty. Sold 1920, later *Craighall* & *Spes Aurea*. Hired on harbour service as *Spes Aurea* Oct. 1939–May 1945. |
| 1921 | *Aurora* | A & M | Crane barge | 423 | Yard N°. 461. 1931/2 owned by Cia Anglo-Cubana de Nav S.A. Havana. |

| | | | | | |
|---|---|---|---|---|---|
| 1921 | *Shell Mex 5* | A & M | C Tanker | | O.N. 145296. Yard N°. 460. Reg. London 1921. |
| 1921 | *Shell Mex 4* | A & M | C tanker | | O.N. 145194. Yard N°. 462. |
| 1921 | *Anchor* | A & M | Crane barge | 97 | O.N. 145076. Yard N°. 459. Owned by Gueret, Llewellyn & Merrett of Cardiff. |
| 1923 | *Coniston* | A & M | Coaster | 186/468 | O.N. 146261. Yard N°. 458. Built for J. & G. Frew of Glasgow. Engined by A&M, Briscombe. Later *Solway Firth*. SB Apr–May 1959. |
| 1923 | *Menna* | A & M | Passenger P.S. | 39/76 | O.N. 137061. For service across the Menai Strait. Later *Alumchine*, owned by James Towage 1929, then to Milford Haven. Laid up 1962 when passenger cert. expired. |
| 1924 | *Cornish Merchant* | A & M | Coaster | 183/470 | O.N. 146387. Yard N°. 463. 142' x 25'. 74 h.p. vertcompound engine by A&M. Later *Fowey Rose* Richard Hughes (1930). War loss July1941. |
| 1928 | *Penelope Paul* | A & M | Barge | 131 gt | O.N. 147285. Owned by Paul Brothers, Ipswich. Later *Chub*. |
| 1930 | *Energie* | A & M (1925) | Tanker | 433 gt | O.N. 160692. Yard N°. 535. Twin screw oil engine. |
| 1930 | *Audacitie* | Mr Smith | Tug | | O.N. 160699. Last heard of rusting in mud, Fingringhoe, Essex. |
| 1931 | *Brightside* | A & M | Coaster | 476 gt | O.N. 162324. Yard N°. 464. Built for Eltham Shipping Co. of Liverpool. Total loss September 1949 near Aberdeen. |
| 1931 | *John Hickman* | A & M | Barge | 138 gt | Reg. Liverpool. Owned by Spillers Ltd. |

N.B. Yard N^os^ 447–450 were Strath type trawlers cancelled at the end of the First World War – *Fulmination, Hertzian Ray, Inundation* and *Longswell*.

# Appendix 6: Ships built in Sandycroft

| Year | Name | Builder | Type | Tonnage | Remarks/Owners |
|---|---|---|---|---|---|
| 1824 | *St David* | Rigby & Hancock | Paddle steamer | 58 | 72' 4" x 14' 10" x 6' 10". Wood. |
| 1830 | *Kingfisher* | John Rigby | Paddle steamer | 120 | 77' x 16' 7 x 7' 8". 65 n.h.p. engine. Wood. |
| 1831 | *Askew* | Eng. by Rigby | Paddle steamer | | Wood. Built by Humble & Hurry. First owned by J. Rigby |
| 1835 | *Alexandra* | Eng. by Rigby | Paddle steamer | | Iron. Built by Hurry & Mylchrist. |
| 1838 | *Primrose* | John Rigby | Sloop | 69.9 | 58' 6" x 15' 6" x 6' 7". This vessel may, in fact, be the *Primrose* built by William Mulvey (see p. 217). |
| 1838 | *Boxer* | Eng. by Rigby | Paddle steamer | | Wood. Built in Nova Scotia. |
| 1839 | *Pernambucana* | Eng. by Rigby | Steam boat | | Built by Thomas Royden of Liverpool. Engines only by Rigby. |
| 1841 | *Princess Royal* | John Rigby | 2m Sch | 64 | 60' 1" x 14' 3" x 7' 5". Reg. indicates wood built. First owner John Rigby of Hawarden. 1844 sold to banker Thomas Peers Williams of Chester. 1854 sold by Thomas Peers Williams and John Williams to Henry White Lake (?) of Liverpool (64/64). |
| 1841 | *Guapicen* | Eng. by Rigby | Gunboat | | 6-gun wooden despatch vessel for the Brazilian Navy. |
| 1842 | *Sarah Davison* | John Rigby | Flat | 24.87 | O.N. 29005. 48' 5" x 14' 7" x 5' 3". Smk rigged, 1 mast. Vessel wrecked near Moelfre, 18 Aug. 1881. |
| 1842 | *Lapwing* | John Rigby | Sp. rig. steamer | 31 | 68' x 10' 9" x 6' 8". Square-serned, carvel built. 18 h.p. engine. Completed 5 Apr. 1842 for William Rigby (64/64). Ran trials round NW light at 29–30 Apr. 1842. William Rigby sold vessel in 1843 to John Benson of Paddington and others who were directors of the Bahia Steam Navigation Co. 27 Feb. 1844 'sold to Bahia'. Engine room 21' long. |
| 1843 | *Prince of Wales (1)* | John Rigby | Paddle steamer | 47/38 | O.N. 27016. 63' 7" x 13' 7" x 5' 3". Rebuilt 1843 sch rigged 40 n.h.p. Owned 1872 by Horatius Leigh Rigby of Hawarden. Later worked Rock Ferry–Liverpool. |
| 1845 | *Star (1)* | John Rigby | Paddle steamer | 92.24 | O.N. 24265. 90' 2" x 15' 4" x 8' 6". 45 HP engine, 140 pasengers. Owned by Willoughby 1855 and from 1873, Tranmere Ferry Co. Thought to be the first iron vessel built by Rigby. |
| 1845 | *Independence (1)* | John Rigby | Paddle steamer | 110 | |
| 1845 | H.M.S. *Fury* | Eng. by Rigby | Paddle sloop | | 190' x 36'. Bulldog-class paddle sloop. Ordered 19 Feb. 1844, completed 6 Jul. 1847. 515 n.h.p. giving 10.5 knots. Towed from Sheerness–Liverpool for engines to be fitted 1846. Sold 1864 to Castle & Beech. |
| 1846 | *Coulbourn* | Eng. by Rigby | | | Built by Thomas Pearson, Liverpool. |
| 1846 | *Birkenhead (1)* | Hawarden Iron Works | Paddle steamer | 132 | 100' 7" x 17' 1" x 10'. 130/60 h.p. Mersey ferry owned William Willougby. Survived to 1882. |
| 1846 | *Forth (1)* | Hawarden Iron Works | Paddle steamer | 209 | 114' x 26' 9" x 10'.4". 120 n.h.p. Trials run 1847, ordered by Sir John Gladstone of Fasque. |
| 1846 | *James Atherton (1)* | Eng. by Rigby | Paddle steamer | 108 | 116' x 16' 3" x 7' 6". Wallasey ferry built by Thomas Pearson of Liverpool. Broken up 1884. |
| 1847 | *Gamon* | John Rigby | Sch | 87/42 | For sale in 1847 and 1853. |
| 1854 | *Winefred (1)* | Cram | 3m ship | 1300/1468 | O.N. 24168. 213' 4 " x 34' 3" x 22'. Reg. 17 Jan. 1855. Clencher built on iron frames. Elliptic stern, 2 decks, 3 masts. First owners Henry Sharples & Owen Jones. Later John Taylor of Fenchurch Street, London. |
| 1855 | *Royal Charter (1)* | Cram | Screw steamer | | 320' x 41' 6". Launched 2 Jun. 1854. Lost 26 Oct. 1859 off Moelfre. |

# Appendix 7: RISB extract from *The Times*, 11th November 1861

The Roodeye Iron Shipbuilding Company incorporated under limited liability, capital £100,000 in 10,000 shares of £10 each, 10s to be paid on application, £2 on allotment and the remainder in calls not exceeding £2 10s at intervals of not less than 3 months each.

*Directors*

Admiral Sir Henry John Leeke KCB, MP — Chairman

George Bragington Esq, Deputy Chairman (banker and shipowner, of Torrington, Devon)

James Bancks Esq. (32 Bucklesbury)

Septimus Beardmore Esq, C. E. (27 Albion St., Hyde Park)

Nathaniel Cox Esq (Liverpool & Chester)

G. J. von Dadelszen Esq (Von Dadelszen & North, 158, Leadenhall Street)

Henry Fox Esq. (2 Royal Exchange Buildings)

Marine Engineer & Draughtsman — Mr E. C. Wheeler (late of Her Majesty's Dockyard, Devonport)

*Bankers*

Messrs Robarts, Lubbock & Co., Mansion House St., EC

Messrs Herries, Farquhar & Co., 16 James St., SW

*Brokers*

Messrs Crosley Bros., 30 Cornhill, London

Messrs Gasquoine & Chamberlaine, Liverpool

Messrs Hoyland & Co., Manchester

*Secretary pro-tem*

Mr H. W. Pearson

*Offices*

12 Gresham House (Old Broad St., London, EC)

The Directors have been enabled to secure the whole property at a valuation, the proprietor receiving the whole of the purchase money in shares. A minimum profit of 10% is calculated upon all estimates for work undertaken, the subscribers may confidently anticipate dividends of at least 20% per annum on the capital invested.

In the same edition of *The Times* is also the following in the classified advertising:

RISB Co. (Ltd.) Notice of Closing

Application for Shares in this Company must be sent to the Secretary by 13th inst.

H. W. Pearson, Secretary – address as above

# Appendix 8: *Fortunes of a Flat*
# (reproduced from *Sea Breezes*, December 1948)

# Fortunes of a "Flat"

**Many readers have asked what has become of the old sailing flats that used to trade into the Mersey years ago. This is the story of one of them—the oldest and the last to have her rig taken out—which is now trading as a motor barge**

## by John Sutton

THIS little ship was built at Connah's Quay in 1887, registered at Liverpool and named *Protection*. Her dimensions are 73.1 ft. x 18.1 ft. x 7.6 ft. When she was first built, I was told by someone who sailed in her as a boy, she carried one mast and a bowsprit and had a tremendous mainsail, foresail and staysail. She was noted for her heavy rig and for the weight of the cargoes she carried. She is supposed to have brought as much as 150 tons of stone from the Welsh quarries into Liverpool, the trade for which she was built. It was a common sight to see her in the old days coming in from sea loaded, her decks invariably awash; sometimes, in fact, the bulwark boards have had to be hammered off to allow the heavy seas she shipped to run off aft. That was in the days before she carried Board of Trade marks.

She must have carried thousands of tons of stone in her day from Penmaenmawr. Often she would run alongside the loading jetty and dry out on the ebb tide and be loaded while she was dry. Sometimes the weight of cargo must have been miscalculated, for it was a common experience for the decks to be awash before she lifted, and frequently the cargo was man-handled and dumped overboard in a frantic hurry to get her to lift. That was a thing which often happened in the days before these wooden flats were marked with a loadline. Sometimes when she has been on the beach waiting to load in bad weather, the heavy sea coming up the beach on the flood has made her pound the bottom with her sternpost enough to make you think she was going to break up any time.

In later years she was fitted with a new mainmast and also a mizzen and sailed as a ketch, and is remembered by a good many today as one of the old jigger flats, trading between the quarries, Fleetwood and Widnes and Runcorn carrying limestone, soda ash and other chemicals. In 1929 she was fitted with a two-cylinder hot-bulb Kromhout oil engine of 44 b.h.p., which gave her, under power alone in favourable conditions, a speed of as much as eight knots. Due no doubt to the fine lines of her hull, she took some "catching" when under sail and with the motor going full speed.

After a long and what must have been a very exciting career as a coaster, she was laid up at Sankey bridges, to which place she used to bring slates. She used to come up the Mersey under Runcorn bridge and lock in at Wooden lock, Widnes. There half of her cargo was discharged into a lighter and then she would proceed on to Sankey bridges, towing the lighter with her, as there was not enough water up the canal to go up at loaded draught. Sankey was as far as she could go inland as there is nowhere higher up where she could swing to make the return journey.

At this stage of her career she was owned by Messrs. Claire and Ridgeway, of Warrington, who used her for carrying the slates from the Welsh quarries for their business of builders' merchants. She was laid up there in 1936 due for a Board of Trade survey, but owing, probably, to the high cost of putting a wooden-built ship of her age through a survey, she lay idle until November 1937, when my uncle, Capt. S. Kirby, of Hale Shoal, bought her, and we ran her in the river trade, for which a Board of Trade certificate was not needed, until March 1948.

Her job during the 18 months prior to the Second World War was carrying grain, loaded in Liverpool or Birkenhead and taken to a mill at Frodsham. The route taken was up the River Mersey to Weston Point, a run which is noted for being "tricky" at any time owing to the channel through the banks shifting about so often. It was a common sight in the old days to see the sailing flats high and dry on the ebb tide. Many a flat has been broken up and washed into the bank with the strong run of tide which is encountered in the upper reaches of the Mersey.

After we had locked in at Weston Point—this was always done at high water, the journey having been timed to reach there just a little before—we would proceed up the narrow river to Frodsham. It is very shallow there, though wide in places, with a very narrow channel, sometimes running close to the bank on one side, then running over close to the other side, twisting and turning all the way to Frodsham—a risky business on a dark night. Often has the *Protection* run aground and had to wait for a big tide in the Mersey to overflow into Frodsham river before she could float clear.

Freights were very low those days and the *Protection*, being a bit leggy (deep-draughted) and the river being so shallow, the amount of cargo she was able to carry hardly paid her way. In 1939 and during the war she did a good job carrying chemicals from the I.C.I. works at Northwich and discharging them into the big ships at Liverpool, Birkenhead and Manchester. She also carried a lot of general cargo, including heavy cargoes of copper, lead and different kinds of ores, a trade to which she was suited owing to her having been strongly built.

There are quite a few little incidents I well remember from the war years. During the heavy winter of 1940 the old flat was left lying one weekend in King's Dock, Liverpool, loaded with a cargo of gunny bales for Northwich, and when we came back to her on Monday morning she was level to the bulwarks with snow, and my uncle and I had to dig our way in. It took us all day to move enough snow so we could work her. It can be understood that she did not sail that day.

Later, during the Christmas blitz of the same year, she was lying in Canada Dock when a number of incendiaries landed aboard and set her alight. We had quite a hectic time extinguishing the flames. Some of the incendiaries, in fact, went through the hatches into the cargo. She was loaded with bicarbonate of soda in bags at the time and quite a number of these were destroyed and the soda ran out and smothered the fire below. I am quite sure if it hadn't been for the type of cargo which she had, there wouldn't have been any *Protection* today.

It was during the early part of 1940 we decided to take all the rig off her, as it was often in the way while she was loading and discharging. Most of the time she was under motor power alone and we were carrying a lot of weight about for no purpose. Moreover, the motor always did its work well, invariably being driven at full speed and never giving any trouble, which is a lot to be said for that type of engine. She was taken up to the Old Quay dockyard at Runcorn and the masts, booms and gaffs, in fact, all the gear, stripped off her. What a shock we had and what a time it took us to get used to seeing her without her rig! Still, she proved much handier for the job she was doing, but the art of sailing her about had gone. I might add that at that time she was the only Mersey flat left with the rig, and also she was the only one left that was run by an owner-skipper.

Early this year William Adams and Company, of Newport, became very interested in her for a job they had working in the River Severn, and in March they bought her. Now the next question was: Would she be granted a Board of Trade certificate to allow her to make the trip down to Newport? Well, she had had a fortune spent on her over the years, and she really was in good condition in spite of her age and all that she had been through. She was put into Wellington Graving Dock for a survey and two months were spent fitting her out for the trip. No masts or sails were fitted to help her on the trip down; she was going to rely on the motor alone, the same motor which had been fitted new in 1929. She was given a new port of registry, the old taffrail which she had carried around all the years with "Liverpool" cut into it, was taken off and a new rail aft with the word "Newport" cut in was put in its place.

I was persuaded to go along as the engineer, and three more hands were signed on for the trip down, and if I had known as much then as I do now, I would never have stepped aboard her. I wouldn't do another trip like that for £100. The old flat was given a light loadline certificate just for the run down, with the stipulation that she must only sail during daylight hours. Well, with 50 tons of granite chippings as ballast, we locked out of Canada Dock on the day tide, May 25, 1948.

That night, about 10 p.m., we anchored in Red Wharfe Bay, and after a meal turned in. We were all soon turned out again, for just after midnight it came on to blow very hard from the N.E. She was on a lee shore and the anchor was dragging. There was only one thing to do, get

**The author at the "flat's" helm**

the engine started, heave up and put out to sea. Why we hadn't gone through the Menai Straits I don't know. Anyway, here we were, and we had to make the best of it. There was one thing the *Protection* was very good at, and that was rolling. She could roll the rails under with no effort. I was one who knew all about it. I have "had some" many times. Another thing she would never do, and that was drive head on to a heavy sea. She would ride the first one alright, but the next one "would catch her with her head down" and would come aboard and flood her fore and aft. The only way was to meet the sea with the port bow; no sea would come aboard worth talking about, but she would certainly jump around. It was quite impossible to go from aft to forward without the assistance of the lifeline which had been fitted round her, above the bulwarks.

She lay off Point Lynas the rest of the night, and all next day till the following evening, the engine "all out" and still the flat made no headway. The power wasn't there; she was having just about as much as she would take and getting nowhere. Eventually the wind eased a bit and we started to make headway. We reached the Skerries and stood in for Holyhead. We came in before a following sea, riding each wave like a duck, a wonderful relief after the punishment she had taken. Holyhead breakwater couldn't be seen for spray when we ran in, and were we all thankful to get into calm water and have a meal and a rest before starting on the next leg!

The following morning, Thursday, May 27, it dawned fine and clear. We had a short run to Bardsey Island and let go the anchor in a little bay to the south'ard of the island, in case the wind came hard from the nor'ard again. Two fishermen came off in a small boat and we bought half-a-dozen live lobsters and half-a-dozen large crabs; also we were able to get some fresh bread, eggs and milk, which were very welcome. We spent the evening boiling the crabs, and thoroughly enjoyed our meal. Next day we had a nice run to Milford Haven, and then up the Bristol Channel to Newport, arriving there at 10 a.m. on Sunday, May 30, much to the relief of everyone. We all had a good bath and a change, and then we were taken into the town and given a good meal in a café. When we came back on board and were being paid by the new owner for the trip round, our captain and navigator, who had been an officer in the Blue Funnel Line, was heard to remark that during the war he had made a passage of 28 days in an open boat with 50 passengers and very little of anything to add to their comfort, but he had had a far better time than he had just experienced in the *Protection*.

There were quite a few little incidents that had taken place on the trip to add to our discomfort—such things as her trick of rolling so violently as to throw the lamp glasses off the lamps. She also threw a mattress off a bunk on to the hot stove, which started a fire while no one was forward, a thing which could have had disastrous results if I had not managed to get there just in time. I was asked by the new owners to stay with them and help to work on the new job, which, actually, was her old job catching up with her again. She was going back into the stone trade; after all those years she was going back into one of the hardest trades for which a craft was ever built. I decided to stop with the old flat and see what happened.

While she was lying at Newport a new skipper came on board. A local man, he was born and reared on the River Severn where the *Protection* was going to trade, so was just the man needed for the job. We were going to use the anchor quite a lot, which meant we were going to need a third hand, and with having only the old-fashioned flat's windlass with which to work, the stronger the third hand was, the better. We were approached by one of the workmen on the quay. He was a fine big young fellow who must have weighed nearly as much as the skipper and I together. He had never worked afloat before, but with his mighty strength we decided he would be just the man to help with the anchor, which, as I said, was worked by "Armstrong's patent."

We set off from Newport on the Thursday following for Chepstow. We came out of the Usk into the Severn and were light ship, having discharged our ballast of granite chippings at Newport. When we entered the Severn there was a fresh breeze blowing and quite a nice sea getting up, and, of course, the old *Protection* resumed her habit of jumping around again. The propeller wouldn't stay in the water and the engine started racing again. After an hour of this I noticed big George, the third hand, was missing, so I went to see where he was. There he was forward, lying full length on the cabin sheets, sick as a dog and looking in terrible shape. Talk about the mighty fallen; it wasn't in it!

I might add that before we decided to take him on he had passed the remark that he was living with his mother-in-law and they didn't get on very well together and he thought it would be a good thing if he could get away from home for a while. His idea was that if he were away from home for a while he would be kind of missed, and then when he went back he would be a little more appreciated. Anyway, as soon as George was able to step ashore he beat it, and hitch-hiked back home, setting off shortly after 11 p.m. He wouldn't stay on board a minute longer than he could help. He went off with the remark that he would rather face his old mother-in-law a dozen times than have a job like that. I should add that since the rig was taken off the *Protection* she was very irritable. When she was rigged she used to roll very steady; roll she did alright at times, but not as lively as she does now as a barge.

The next day a young man of 32, who had been 12 years in the Navy, came aboard, and this was his first job in civil life since he had been demobbed. He was a born sailor and just the man for the job we were going on. Now we were all set to make a start. This is the work we have to do. We sail up the River Wye—up the beautiful Wye Valley. It is nice to look at, but the tide is terrific. We run to a small jetty and load block stone which is carried down from the quarry on a long conveyor belt down to the flat, and is dumped into the hold. It comes down so fast that 100 tons can be loaded in half-an-hour. After loading we come down the Wye and let go the anchor at the river mouth. On the next tide the anchor is hove up and we proceed up the River Severn.

All along the River Severn is a sea wall, and this block stone is being used to repair and fortify it in different places, and this is the procedure as I have seen it. We sail up the Severn until we come to the place in the sea wall where the stone is required, the place being marked out by long stakes driven into the beach. Sometimes it is soft mud, sometimes it is all rock, the stakes having been made fast to lengths of iron which had been driven into the rock at low water. The idea is to time the run to get to the place just on the turn of the tide, run off so far, let go the anchor, drop the ship back alongside the stakes, and get a head-rope ashore as quickly as possible. Now she is being held off in the tide with the anchor down off the port bow and a long lead ashore off the starboard bow. For the next operation, a light anchor is bent on to a handy rope and sculled off the port quarter, and another handy rope is taken ashore off the starboard quarter, all the slack taken in all round and the flat held in the strong tide which is now running, until she grounds. The job needs to be well understood, for no time must be lost getting her into position. We all had to start from scratch. None of us had done this kind of thing before, but after a time we got used to it and were able to do it in the dark, two big headlights having been fitted, one on either bow.

When the ship has dried out, as many as 20 men come on board and man-handle the block stone out of the holds on to the deck, and then over the side, and place it to form a breakwater to strengthen the sea wall, which alone is preventing the surrounding countryside from being flooded. When the stone has been discharged, the next worry is to get the flat off the beach as soon as possible; in fact, as soon as she floats. It can be readily understood that this job cannot be done unless the weather is suitable. If there is any jump at all, it is not safe to go near the beach. There is always the danger of staving in her bottom. The tide which lifts you on to the beach may be a nice quiet one, but by the next tide there may have been a great change in the weather.

Well, the cargo is out and it is lying on the inshore side of her, and we are waiting for the tide to get off again and keeping our fingers crossed hoping that the weather holds good. All the moorings and the light anchor have been got aboard, all that is left out is the big anchor, way off the port bow, the idea being that as soon as she starts to float again the engine will be started up and we shall endeavour to heave her off the beach to the anchor. Sometimes we are caught napping with the weather, and instead of heaving off to the anchor, the anchor hasn't held and it has been hove home without the flat coming off the beach, and quite a hectic time is had by all. With a bit of good luck, however, and lots of good management we manage to get her off, and sail back to the mouth of the Wye, let go the anchor and wait for the next flood, heave up, go up the Wye, load stone and start the whole crazy business again.

As far as seamanship goes the whole operation is crazy, but it is a very important job all the same, it being impossible to get the stone to the required places overland. I would like to say something about the type of anchor gear we have to work with. We have the old-fashioned flat's windlass, which has no gypsy, no brake—just a barrel round which three turns of the anchor chain are taken. When the anchor is let go, it has to be let go in a hurry over the barrel of the windlass as required, about 30 fathoms of chain (we are using three-quarter-inch chain and the anchor is supposed to weigh 8 cwt.). The chain is passed over the barrel to the far side of the windlass, then laid back and to across the fo'c'sle deck, the stopper, or devil's claw, being left in the hawsepipe to prevent the chain from running out. Now a piece of handy two-inch line is taken and made fast with a bowline to a link in the chain, short up against the stopper, and wound on the barrel, normally used for the barrel line. This is hove tight until the weight is taken off the stopper. When the "let go" order is given, the stopper is taken out, the line is out and the whole lot goes out in a hurry, the bight of the chain having been weather-bitted, after side of the windlass, to prevent all the chain running out of the box overboard.

On big spring tides the stone is taken up through the Severn bridge and the tide certainly "rips" through there alright. It is not safe to take the bridge until about a quarter-of-an-hour before high water. The tide has to be seen to be believed. No words of mine could describe it. We were the only craft to go that far up the Severn while I was there, and each time we went up above the bridge all the way along the banks of the Severn everyone turned out to see us go by. Well, we travel on and on until we come to where the stone is wanted, but sometimes we don't dry out. We stay afloat in a bit of a channel alongside the river bank, but the same procedure of mooring goes on as before. Now this is where we get the well-known Severn bore. We are lying off to an anchor waiting for the tide to come back. We can hear it coming miles away before we see it; that is when I start the engine up and stand by and wait for the surge, and it is certainly some surge. We have been on big spring tides with 40 fathoms of chain out and the engine going full speed ahead against the bore, and the old flat has been going *astern* at quite a nice turn of speed. As the tide eases we gradually steam back to the anchor, heaving up as we go. One night we had that much chain out the anchor must have buried itself in the sand and taken a good hold, and when we eventually got it home we found out the stock had broken. It's a wonder to me the windlass didn't go over her bow, the run of tide was so strong it was pulling her head down and making her jump about a bit.

Well, this game had been going on until around midnight on Monday, October 4, 1948. We came off the berth, after getting rid of the stone, well up the River Severn at a place called Longney Crib, when it came on a thick fog, and the Severn bore put her high and dry on top of a breakwater made of stout wooden piles, and there she stuck. To have seen her in the position she was when all the water had gone from her it would have seemed incredible to think she could have been put there.

The old *Protection* is now in the hands of the salvage people. She looks a sorry sight with her head stuck high in the air, listing over about 15 deg. across those big wooden piles. I came home two days after and that is the last I saw of her. It would be very interesting to know what will happen to her, and very nice to hear she has been salved and is able to carry on with a very exciting job. The trouble is, she went ashore right on top of high water on the biggest tide of the year, 31.9ft. The next tide gave 10in. less in the table, and with all our efforts, even to the extent of rigging blocks and tackles astern and putting the hauling part on the windlass and working the engine full speed astern, she did not even budge.

# Appendix 9: *Coastwise in the* Agnes Craig (reproduced from *Sea Breezes*, October 1947)

## Coastwise in the "Agnes Craig"

**In "Sea Breezes," Vol. II, the author of this article wrote of his experiences during a trip in the "Brooklands", the last of the three-masted schooners once so numerous around the British coast. He details below his work as deck-hand on another Irish-owned coastal craft, the auxiliary "Agnes Craig"**

***by Richard J. Scott***

SITUATED on the Avoca River 52 miles from Dublin, the little port of Arklow is to-day the last home of the Irish sail coaster. Famous the world over for its intrepid seamen, this picturesque town can still boast ownership of no less than 10 fair-sized auxiliary schooners, all active traders manned mainly by Arklowmen. The majority of these vessels, though registered at Dublin, belong to the fleet of Messrs. Kearon and Tyrrell which includes such well known names as *Windermere, Harvest King, Agnes Craig, Happy Harry, M. E. Johnson,* and *James Postlethwaite*—all former British sailers which came to Arklow in the last decade or two.

Having spent over a month in the tops'l schooner *Brooklands,* I was particularly anxious to make a few trips on one of these auxiliaries to see how life compared with that on the old Corkonian.

My opportunity came in July, and I joined the *Agnes Craig* at Waterford. A typical model of the old British coasting schooner, she dates back to 1884 when she was built of wood at Connahs Quay by the firm of Ferguson and Baird. Formerly a three-masted tops'l schooner she has had her rig cut down to that of a two-masted fore-and-after with a 90 h.p. Alpha diesel engine now supplying the primary motive power.

For'ard a comfortable fo'c'stle has certified accommodation for four seamen, whilst aft, a mess room and two cabins provide quarters for the skipper and mate. The engine room is situated between the after hold bulkhead and the messroom companionway. A neat little wheelhouse, flanked on the port side by a lavatory and on the starboard by paint lockers, has been erected near the stern. For'ard of the officers' quarters is the companion leading to the engine room with an exhaust funnel on the starboard side, then the after hatch and a galley of very small dimensions which forms the "workshop" of the cook. Moving still forward we come to the mainmast, hand pumps, main hatch and small donkey room housing a winch geared to a six h.p. Lister diesel engine.

Next follow the foremast, fo'c'stle scuttle, a windlass of the old-fashioned hand type, and lastly the bowsprit itself. On the port side, between the fore and main rigging, two davits with the the aid of tackles serve to swing the lifeboat on to chocks on the main hatch. The hull, tarred black with a white painted rail, presents a pleasing picture to the nautical eye right from its round counter stern sheering up gracefully to a smart clipper bow. A real old-time figurehead nestles proudly at the stem, giving the vessel a distinctive flavour amongst her fellow schooners. Indeed I might truthfully venture the opinion that old *Agnes Craig* is the only Irish sailer with a figurehead. Those of the *Gaelic* and *Isallt* are but pitiful caricatures of their former selves, sadly battered and broken as the passing of time has taken its toll. A respectable bowsprit sweeps up sharply between the knightheads and though rigged to take two jibs, seldom sees more than the inner headsail set nowadays. The ship's gross tonnage is 128 and her dimensions of 94.7 ft. x 23 ft. x 10.4 ft. are about the average for her type.

The crew usually consists of four hands and my arrival completed the complement which was as follows:—

Capt. James McDonald, master, Roderick Heron, mate, Andy Harte, cook and ordinary seaman, together with myself as A.B. taking the place of an Arklow man who was signing off. The skipper was a salt-seasoned old mariner hailing from Arklow, a man to whom I took an instant liking; the mate, a heftily-built, good-natured, Dubliner who is also a qualified engineer, whilst Andy, a typical Arklow lad, had seen service on the *Gaelic* and *Harvest King* before shipping on the *Craig*.

I went aboard on Monday, July 7, to find work nearing completion on the discharging of a cement cargo which the ship had brought from Drogheda. That evening we shifted across to the grain stores to load wheat for Dublin, and there we found another Arklow schooner, the *Invermore*, waiting to take a similar cargo when we cleared the berth for her. Further upstream lay the runaway German motorship *Adelaar*, which had caused a little excitement by a recent escapade when attempting to enter the Irish coasting trade in preference to returning to her home port under Allied control. Needless to say, that venture was not greeted very favourably by our own, rather hard-pressed schoonermen.

By five p.m. on Tuesday we were on our marks with 180 tons aboard, and an hour and a half later, having had tea, (supper on a coasting schooner), we cast off our moorings with a local pilot at the helm. Here I noticed the first change from procedure on the old *Brooklands*. No warping lines were laboriously hauled in or slacked out with sails trimmed to swing the ship's head; no men were laid aloft to let go the tops'l gaskets, or swung along the bowsprit footropes to loosen the jibs. Instead, the mate merely started up the engine; and with little more ado, we were on our way. There was a two hours flood tide against us and once well into the stream we hoisted the foresail. Mooring lines were then coiled neatly on the hatches, fenders stowed away, and the boat lashed securely down under the fore boom.

At about 8.15 we had Passage off the starboard beam and there the pilot disembarked. We were then entering the more open waters of the Suir estuary and by nine o'clock Credan Head lay astern. A fresh S.W. breeze outside boded no good, as I was to learn in quick time. Off Dunmore we plunged straight into the thick of it with heavy beam seas throwing us about at will, as they rolled in unrestricted from the Atlantic. Hook Head light flashed to port at 9.15 p.m. when we set up our navigation lamps on the stern, foremast, and on the port and starboard side amidships. The schooner by then was labouring heavily with a turbulent roll under darkening skies. First she would lie over on her starboard side shipping a green sea through the rigging and then, almost with an agonised groan, would fall over to port under the cruel onslaught of those robust combers. A glance at the trucks fascinated one; it seemed amazing that the masts could withstand the strain as they described wild arcs across the dull, overcast heavens.

Suddenly we were galvanised into action by the sound of a sharp report forward, followed by a frantic flapping noise. Yes, the foresail had carried away from the boom and was endeavouring to take the mast overboard with it. Led by the mate we managed to subdue the battling canvas and effect a temporary lashing at the clew and along the foot of the sail. Shortly afterwards the wind dropped considerably and the fore boom started to swing and tug at the whim of every roll, leaving us with no alternative but to get the canvas off. Under bare poles we ran for the Coninbeg lightship and as it was then 10.30 I gratefully accepted an invitation to turn in for a spell.

Midnight saw us passing the lightvessel which lay about a mile to the south'ard. With the seas more on our starboard quarter and a slight improvement in the breeze we slapped on the jib, stays'l (stay fores'l as it is known to schoonermen) fores'l, and mains'l. As though joyous in her relief the *Agnes Craig* plunged ahead at a steady six and a half knots, tossing clouds of spray over her bows. By 1.15 a.m. we had the Barrels Rock off the port beam and there the wind veered over to nor'west necessitating a change over on to the port tack, an operation which was extremely simple when one recalls that we had only four sails to deal with. The *Brooklands* had 10!

Rounding Carnsore Point at 3 a.m. under the guiding arms of the Tuskar light we steered for the Lucifer Buoy, nine and a half miles ahead. Our motion was much easier with more of a steady, pitching movement compared with that sickening roll off the Hook. Familiar coastline marks were made and passed at regular intervals—Lucifer Bay, 4.30 a.m., Blackwater, 5.30 and Glassgorman at 6.30 Our course took us on the inside of the dreaded Blackwater Bank, which in bygone days wrought heavy toll from unwary sailing ships venturing within its treacherous realm. Little wonder then, that there, more that at any other part of our trip, extreme care had to be observed by the helmsman. All through the night either the skipper or mate remained on deck keeping constant vigil whilst we passed through that tricky channel. Again there was a pronounced difference in the method employed by Capt. Creenan in the *Brooklands*. He usually stood out to sea, keeping the Bank to west-'ard, as he could not afford to be trapped either on a lee shore or to be driven on to the sands before a sudden off-shore blow.

**Capt. James McDonald, of the "Agnes Craig"**

In wintertime the schoonerman's lot is not to be envied, especially in waters like those when bitter cold, combined with fog or gale makes the negotiation of such channels a difficult task indeed. However, on that occasion our motor, in contrast to the general run of auxiliary sailing coasters, gave faithful service in response to the diligent care bestowed upon it by the mate.

At 6.30 a.m. Andy was roused out and by 7.15 a hearty breakfast was ready, consisting of tea, fried eggs, toast and butter. Having satisfied our ravenous appetites all hands adjourned on deck and set about their respective duties, the skipper at the wheel, Andy in the galley, the mate paying a call on his mechanical ward in the engine room, whilst I prepared my camera for a few snaps. I may add at this stage that in the *Agnes Craig* we did not follow a regular system of watches such as the traditional four hours on and four hours off which was customary in the *Brooklands*. Spells of duty were irregular, though that was of little consequence considering that as an auxiliary we were able to observe a more strict time schedule on short coastal passages than is possible for a pure sailer.

When he had his work completed I enlisted the aid of Andy for my photos. From the knightheads he passed out the camera to me at my perch on the end of the bowsprit, an excellent position for views of the ship. On one occasion the mate came out with me and, balancing himself on a bowsprit guy, held the camera with one hand. Gripping the outer jib stay I leaned over and pressed the shutter release with my free hand. The result proved to be one of the best prints I got and subsequently led to no small measure of controversy between "Jimmy the One," and myself as to who was the actual photographer. My grounds as a claimant lay in the fact that I did the adjusting of the apparatus as well as "pulling the trigger". However, were it not for my shipmate's excellent placing of the schooner in the viewfinder there would have been little or no picture!

**Taken from the end of the bowsprit, this view of the "Agnes Craig" called for both agility and ingenuity on the part of author and mate**

At this period we altered course to stand in towards Tara Hill, hugging the coast right up to Arklow Bay which we reached about 10 a.m. Work, as regards sail trimming, was practically negligible — certainly a change from the old tops'l schooner days. With the aid of a powerful diesel throbbing steadily one can sail nearer the wind close hauled than in the same vessel 25 years ago when the helmsman had to keep an ever-watchful eye on that quiver at the throat.

Past Arklow, we skirted round Mizen Head, a point where the schooner *M. E. Johnson* drove ashore five years ago. Her crew were rescued then by breeches buoy and fortunately the vessel herself was later refloated and taken to Arklow for repairs.

Abeam of the Poolbeg lighthouse we passed the steamer *Lady Anstru-*

*thers* of London, outward bound, and by 5 p.m. were alongside the South Quays, moored between the massive, steel hulls of two ocean - going steamers. Next morning we moved round into Alexandra Basin to discharge at the grain silo there. Work was finished by 5 p.m. that same evening when the news arrived that our next passage was to Wexford to load malt for Dublin.

Having replenished our provisions, we sailed light at noon on Friday. An ebb tide helped us to clear the Dublin river and once into the Bay we set all canvas with a good W.S.W. breeze keeping us on the starboard tack. In fact, the sails were drawing so well that the engine was kept just ticking over at half speed. By that time the first of the flood tide had turned against us but the skipper once again showed his unrivalled knowledge of local conditions by keeping in as close as possible to the coast where the flow was weakest. A steady speed of six and a half knots with only half motor power proved the wisdom of his action.

As a result of an off-shore breeze, the sea was rather smooth with a very slight swell, and under those ideal conditions we made a fast and pleasant passage, clearing Wicklow Head at 3.30. Arklow at 5 and Cahore Point at 7 p.m. From there we stood out in the channel between the Rusk and Blackwater Banks. Three hours later we were swinging into the placid waters of Wexford Bay and there we let go the port anchor with about 25 fathoms of chain.

Watches were then picked and I was allotted a spell lasting from 3 to 6 a.m. That subsequently proved to be the best period of all as the quiet beauty of the scenery, tinted by the dawn-hues of a new day, held me fascinated with its exquisiteness. Amidst those lovely surroundings, all the more enhanced by my environment of masts and rigging, I sighted another schooner away out to sea, bound South. As she came closer I recognised the long, grey hull, small topmasts, and graceful counter to be that of the auxiliary *De Wadden*. She had only her main and fores'l set, as there was little or no wind at the time to justify the use of the mizzen, jibs, or squares'l.

At 6 a.m. I was relieved by Andy and took the opportunity for turning in for an hour and a half before breakfast. The morning was spent washing down the decks and getting everything shipshape and Bristol fashion before making port. The mate considered it would be an insult to the harbour if we entered it in an untidy state, so he saw to it that the task was performed diligently. About noon the pilot came alongside and with the anchor hove we got under way. The channel winds about, making a narrow and difficult passage, and the marking buoys must be followed with meticulous care as the bar is constantly shifting and silting and can only be crossed within two hours or so of high water. Near the mouth of the harbour I saw the last broken ribs of a Danish schooner wrecked there 14 years ago. She was the four-masted *Svanen* (ex *Sigrid*) hailing from Svendborg, and on Nov. 16, 1933, caught in heavy seas off the Wexford Bar, was blown ashore to become a total loss.

We docked at 1 p.m. and having made all lines fast were free until Monday morning when loading operations were to commence. Thus came to an end the second of three passages which I have made on an auxiliary schooner this year, and here I would like to express my indebtedness to those who made it possible, Mr. Roy Kearon, the *Agnes Craig's* owner, Capt. J. McDonald; and my firm friend, Roddy Heron, the mate. If any readers who are interested in the fortunes of these sail coasters would care to write to me c/o the Editor, "Sea Breezes", to exchange information, gossip or photos, I would be delighted to entertain their correspondence.

# Appendix 10: Auction of Property of Robert Eyton, 16th November 1849

(Information from *Chester Chronicle* advert of 2nd November 1849)

To be sold by Auction at the White Horse Hotel, Holywell, order of the Administrator of the late Mr Robert Eyton.

Lot 1 4/16 share of S Mostyn Colliery.

Lot 2 3/16 share of S Mostyn Colliery 18 years unexpired.

Lot 3 3/16 shares in Mostyn foundry and shipbuilding yard.

Lot 4 Various shareholdings in lead mines.

Lot 5 16/64 of following sailing vessels-

*Flint Castle*

Flat *Betsey*

Flat *Lloyd*

Smack *Industry*

Plus 4/64 of *Flint* (built Chester 1810).

2/64 of *Marquess of Anglesea*.

2/64 of *Unity*, sloop.

Lot 6

| | | |
|---|---|---|
| 12/64 | *Taliesin*, steamer | |
| " | *Edwen*, schooner | |
| " | *Maid of Mostyn*, schooner | |
| " | *Lady Harriet* | " |
| " | *Sophia* | " |
| " | *Sir Edward* | " |
| " | *Black Diamond* | " |
| " | *Caroline* | " |
| " | *Dispatch* | " |
| " | *Gronant* flat | |
| " | *Sluice* flat | |

Lot 7.

4/16 of six leasehold cottages

# Appendix 11: Description of the construction of the *Royal Charter* given by William Patterson at the Board of Trade Enquiry into her loss at St George's Hall, Liverpool in 1859

I have been engaged for many years building both wood and iron ships. The *Royal Charter* was built in April 1855. The ship was contracted for by Messrs Charles Moore & Co. of Liverpool with Mr George Cram of Chester Messrs Gibbs Bright & Co. then purchased the ship of Messrs Moore and I became Inspector of her. When I became acquainted with her, nearly all the frames were up and part of the plating commenced.

After Gibbs Bright became purchasers I went down to superintend the building when Cram failed in 1854. We were very particular as the ship progressed to see that all the rivets were good.

The keel plates were 1" thick, the following plates were ½" and ¾ thickness up to round the turn of the bilge in the midship body and continued to within 30' of each end of the ship; the two ends being 1/8" less. The plate opposite each tier of beams was ¾", extending 250' of the ship's length. Her keel was about 12" x 4". The rivets I think were 1¼", but I am not quite sure. Round the turn of the bilge the rivets were one inch. All the plates and butts were double riveted.The frames were 18" from centre to centre and 5" x 3" and ¾ thickness. The lower tier of beams was 10" by 5/8" The upper edge had an angle iron riveted on3" x 3" x ½". The second tier of beams were 9" x 5/8" The angle iron riveted on the upper edge was 3"x ½". The upper tier of beams were 8" and 9–16" and the angle iron was the same in the lower beams. The upper tier of beams were tied together by fore and aft plates. The inside tier only were secured with diagonal plates. On each deck strong teak waterway pieces about 14–15" square were bolted to the shaft pieces and to the beams. There were six bulk heads about ½ inch, five of them being water tight. The bulk head at the after part of the engine had an archway through it leading to the screw tunnel, which was water tight. There was a watertight bulk head on the after side if the stuffing box, further secured by a water-tight deck over it. These bulk-heads were put in before the ship was launched and after she was designed for a screw steamship. The bulkheads were riveted to angle irons of the floor, round up the sides of the ship and it appeared to be good. The rivets appeared to be of very good iron

and anything I saw the least defective was put aside. The ship was lengthened before I took to her. She was not cut in two and lengthened in the midship body; but she was lengthened at the two ends and her original keel was not cut, so that it did not make her one bit weaker in consequence of being lengthened The riveting was countersunk and every care was taken. The workmen were paid more for their work upon her than I ever remember them to have been paid before. I have seen the ship in dock previous to each voyage (except the last) and I have never found a loose rivet and I can say the same of the *Great Britain* which I also built.

The engines were horizontal. I was present at the launch of the *Royal Charter*. Her heel went into the sand but I saw no sign of straining and I don't think she did strain She afterwards ran ashore and broke her keelson at Flint. She was put into dock at Liverpool and was thoroughly over-hauled. The repairs were done by Mr Vernon, a Liverpool gentleman who shall be here. As a shipbuilder, I think the damage was capable of being affectually repaired. I have no doubt that the violence of the seas and the weight of the ship caused the bottom to break and that the effect of the sea at the two ends would cause the parting so quickly. I believe any ship in the same position, wood or iron, would have broken. I believe the *Royal Charter* was a strong as, or stronger, than any ship of that day. In my opinion I think we might build a ship eight times the length of its beam, having regard to strength. The ship would be very little below Lloyd's classification as at present existing. The engines were 200 nominal horsepower. The upper deck was 4½" and the middle deck 3" American pine.

There was no contract when I took the building of the ship. I had no restrictions and was ordered to spare no expense to make her a good ship. Had she been stronger and consequently heavier she would have gone to pieces quite as soon. If she had been built like our floating batteries of 4" iron her very weight would have broken her to pieces on the rocks.'

The court adjourned at half past five pm.

The following day Mr Patterson was back in the witness box and again examined by Mr O'Dowd:

His foreman had been employed by me in the building of the *Great Britain* – consider him a competent judge in matters connected with iron and riveting. Of the iron which I found on the premises when I took to the *Royal Charter* there was some angle and beam

iron which would not stand the sudden bend that was required. There was also some floor iron which I objected to. The rivets werwe 1½" or 1¼" in dia in the keel; but the plating rivets were 1" dia. I think they were sufficiently large for a ship of the magnitude of the *Royal Charter*. I don't think there were more beams required in a ship of that bulk. I am in the habit of using what are called boiler plates.

# Appendix 12: Timeline of Chester River shipbuilding

| Date | Chester River Activity | National Events |
|---|---|---|
| 1798 | | Battle of the Nile, August |
| 1799 | | |
| 1800 | | |
| 1801 | | |
| 1802 | William Cortney commences shipbuilding in Chester | |
| 1803 | *Lord Forbes* built by Carson Forbes Cortney – largest vessel built to date | |
| 1804 | *Contest,* gun brig., first naval vessel by C.F.C. at Chester | |
| 1805 | | Battle of Trafalgar, October |
| 1806 | | |
| 1807 | | British government declares buying, transporting and selling of slaves illegal, but not ownership |
| 1808 | | |
| 1809 | | |
| 1810 | *Charles Mills* built by C.F.C. for E.I.C. at Chester | |
| 1811 | | |
| 1812 | | War between Britain and U.S.A. until 1815 |
| 1813 | | |
| 1814 | William Mulvey Snr builds first vessel at Chester, *Limerick Trader* | Sir John Gladstone sends first vessel from Liverpool to India (*Kingsmill*) after end of East India Co. monopoly |
| 1815 | | July 1815 end of war with France after 22 years of conflict. First steamboat on the Mersey |
| 1816 | Hanshall says shipbuilding trade is flat a Chester. Three vessels launched the same day. | First vessel towed out of Liverpool *Princess Charlotte* by *Harlequin*, October. Economic depression prevails in Britain. |
| 1817 | Fire at the Cortney yard, June | Economic depression in Britain |
| 1818 | | |
| 1819 | John Troughton dies 21 October | Peterloo Massacre, Manchester |
| 1820 | | |
| 1821 | Cortney gives up more land January. William Cortney dies February | First steam ferry running Birkenhead–Liverpool |
| 1822 | John WIlson Jnr launches P.S. *Lord Melville* and William Mulvey builds first paddle steamer *Sir Joseph Yorke* at Chester | |
| 1823 | | |
| 1824 | | |
| 1825 | | |
| 1826 | First steam tug on the river Dee. John Wilson marries Margaret Cortney | |

| | | |
|---|---|---|
| | and launches *St George* at Chester, largest vessel to date | |
| 1827 | Four vessels laid down at Chester for the merchants' cheese service to/from London. John Wilson leaves Chester to live in Devon | Newspapers report a tunnel under the Mersey is contemplated |
| 1828 | First vessel built by Thomas Eyton at Flint | |
| 1829 | | |
| 1830 | John Rigby opens Sandycroft site building *Kingfisher* | September opening of Manchester–Liverpool railway |
| 1831 | | |
| 1832 | Grosvenor Bridge in Chester opened by Princess Victoria | |
| 1833 | | Slavery Abolition Act passed, slaves gradually freed in the British Empire |
| 1834 | | |
| 1835 | | |
| 1836 | First recorded vessel built at Kingsferry (Queensferry) | |
| 1837 | | Princess Victoria becomes queen |
| 1838 | | System of slave apprenticeship abolished throughout the colonies |
| 1839 | William Mulvey Snr dies aged 67 | S.S. *Great Britain* laid down at Bristol |
| 1840 | Peggy Mulvey signs off her first 3-masted ship. Michael Parry employs F.M.B. to build the *Malcolm* at Flint | First transatlantic crossing by Cunard from Liverpool |
| 1841 | Thomas and William Mulvey sign off first 3-masted vessel themselves. Death of Sr Edward Mostyn | |
| 1842 | | Britain experiencing severe economic depression |
| 1843 | First screw steamer on the Dee, April visit by *Liverpool Screw* | Brunel and Patterson launch the S.S. *Great Britain* at Bristol. In 1845 she became the first iron screw steamer to cross the Atlantic |
| 1844 | | |
| 1845 | | Irish potato famine begins, lasting until 1849 and leading to huge emigration, mainly to North America |
| 1846 | | |
| 1847 | Last vessel completed by Rigby at Sandycroft | |
| 1848 | Last vessel completed at the Mulvey yard | Chester–Bangor railway opens |
| 1849 | Death of Robert Eyton | |
| 1850 | | |
| 1851 | | Gold discovered at Ballarat, Australia. Great Exhibition opened at the Crystal Palace in Hyde Park, London |
| 1852 | Death of Edward Eyton | 65,000 British people emigrated to Australia in one year. First steam collier, *John Bowes*, launched by Palmers on the Tyne |
| 1853 | First iron vessel *Amelia*, launched at Chester by George Cram. *Cobre* sails from Chester–Australia. Cram takes over Sandycroft yard in December | |
| 1854 | Six vessels built or converted at the Cram yard in Chester. *Winefred* launched at Sandycroft in December | Crimean War begins |
| 1855 | George Cram declared bankrupt. First wooden schooner, the *British Oak*, | |

| | | |
|---|---|---|
| | built by William Bishton at Chester. September *Royal Charter* is launched at Sandycroft | |
| 1856 | Roodeye Iron Shipbuilding Co. takes over the Cram yard | Crimean War ends. Bessemer process makes steel cheaper to mass produce |
| 1857 | George Cram's final involvement with Roodeye yard in the autumn | Launch of the *Great Eastern* on the Thames. Indian Mutiny begins |
| 1858 | First vessel built at Connah's Quay by Jones and Hooson in March | Formation of the liverpool Iron Register. Indian Mutiny ends |
| 1859 | William Parkes is first listed as a shipbuilder at Chester – schooner *Eclipse* | *Royal Charter* lost off Moelfre, Anglesey, 26 October. First oil discovered in the U.S.A. |
| 1860 | Firs full-rigged iron sailing vessel *Wayfarer* built at Chester | American Civil War begins |
| 1861 | *Gitana*, the largest iron sailing vessel built in Chester is launched | |
| 1862 | | President Lincoln proclaims the emancipation of slaves in the U.S.A. w.e.f. 1 Jan. 1863 |
| 1863 | | |
| 1864 | | |
| 1865 | Last vessel built at the Roodee Co. shipyard, the *West*. Last vessel built at Flint, the schooner *Alfred*, launched | American Civil War ends. Slavery abolished in the U.S.A. Nathaniel Cox sets himself up as a shipbroker in Liverpool |
| 1866 | | Wrexham, Mold & Connah's Quay Railway opens to frieght 1 January. 10 May declared Black Monday and a 5-year depression ensues |
| 1867 | | |
| 1868 | Last schooner built by Bishton at Crane Wharf, the *Imperial.* Bishton files for bankruptcy in Wolverhampton | |
| 1869 | | Opening of the Suez Canal reduces the voyage to India from Britain by six weeks |
| 1870 | Roodee Shipyard land sold to build new gas works. *Balogun* completed at Chester by Allsup of Preston – the last sea-going commercial vessel to be built at Chester | The Liverpool Iron Register and Lloyd's Register merge after twelve years independence. Major economic depression in Britain |
| 1871 | | |
| 1872 | | |
| 1873 | | |
| 1874 | | |
| 1875 | | |
| 1876 | | |
| 1877 | | |
| 1878 | | |
| 1879 | | |
| 1880 | Death of Daniel Ferguson Snr | |
| 1881 | | |
| 1882 | | Death of Giuseppe Garibaldi, Italian revolutionary, aged 74 |
| 1883 | | Krakatoa erupts |
| 1884 | | |
| 1885 | | |
| 1886 | | |
| 1887 | | Golden Jubilee of Queen Victoria |

| | | |
|---|---|---|
| 1888 | | |
| 1889 | | |
| 1890 | | |
| 1891 | | |
| 1892 | | |
| 1893 | | |
| 1894 | | |
| 1895 | | |
| 1896 | | |
| 1897 | | |
| 1898 | | |
| 1899 | | Outbreak of Second Anglo-Boer War |
| 1900 | *Lizzie May* built by Ferguson & Baird at Connah's Quay. Abdela & Mitchell open up at Brimscombe, Glouscester | |
| 1901 | | Death of Queen Victoria |
| 1902 | Death of James Baird Snr, aged 87 | End of fighting in Second Anglo-Boer War |
| 1903 | | |
| 1904 | | |
| 1905 | | |
| 1906 | Last wooden sailing vessel, the *Malvina*, built at Connah's Quay | |
| 1907 | | |
| 1908 | Abdela & Mitchell open at Queensferry | |
| 1909 | | |
| 1910 | | |
| 1911 | Last vessel built by A. Ferguson at Connah's Quay – the *Nora Bate* | |
| 1912 | | |
| 1913 | First vessel launched by Crichtons at Saltney | |
| 1914 | | Outbreak of the Frist World War |
| 1915 | | |
| 1916 | | |
| 1917 | | |
| 1918 | Summer Ferguson Yard at Connah's Quay acquired by Crichtons | Armistice signed ending the First World War |
| 1919 | | |
| 1920 | | |
| 1921 | | |
| 1922 | | |
| 1923 | | |
| 1924 | | |
| 1925 | | |

| | | |
|---|---|---|
| 1926 | | General Strike |
| 1927 | | |
| 1928 | | |
| 1929 | | Great Depression begins |
| 1930 | Last A & M vessels completed at Queensferry | |
| 1931 | | |
| 1932 | Crichtons cease building vessels at Connah's Quay. Sudden death of James Crichton | |
| 1933 | | |
| 1934 | | |
| 1935 | *D.B. Crane* (Yard N° 548) final vessel built by Crichtons at Saltney. | |
| 1936 | Shipbuilders' Security Ltd scheme to reduce overcapacity | |

# Bibliography


Anderson, John, *Coastwise Sail* (London, 1948).

Andrews, Graeme, *The Ferries of Sydney* (Sydney, 1975).

Bateson, Charles, *The Convict Ships 1788–1868* (1969).

Baughan, Peter E., *A Regional History of the Railways of Great Britain, Vol. 11, North & Mid Wales* (Newton Abbot, 1980).

Bennet, Douglas, *Schooner Sunset — the last British Sailing Coasters* (London, 2001).

BBC *Your Paintings* website

Brodie, Ian, *Steamers of the Forth, Vol. 1* (Newton Abbot, 1976).

Chester Ship Registers at Flintshire Records Office and National Archives Kew.

Colledge, J. J., *Ships of the Royal Navy, Vol. I, Major Ships* (Newton Abbot, 1969).

*Ships of the Royal Navy, Vol. II, Navy built Tugs, trawlers etc.* (Newton Abbot, 1970).

Coppack, Tom, *A Lifetime with Ships* (Prescot, 1973).

Dixon, John & Geoff Pickard, *J. Crichton & Co., Shipbuilders, Saltney and Connah's Quay* (Cleckheaton, 2002).

Duckworth, C. L. D. & G. E. Langmuir, *West Coast Steamers*, 3rd ed. (Prescot, 1966).

Eames, Aled, *Ships & Seamen of Anglesey* (1973).

*Ventures in Sail* (Caernarfon, 1987).

Emery (ed), Gordon, *Chester Canal* (Chester, 2005).

Fenton, Roy, *Mersey Rovers* (Gravesend, 1997).

Greenhill, Basil, *Schooners* (London, 1980).

Hawkes, G. I., 'Shipping on the Dee: the Rise and Decline of the Creeks of the Port of Chester in the Nineteenth Century' in *Maritime Wales*, Vol. 11 (Caernarfon, 1987).

Hocking, Charles, *Dictionary of Disasters at Sea during the Age of Steam, 1824–1962, Vols. I & II* (1969, London).

Holden, Chris & Leslie, *Life & Death on the 'Royal Charter'* (Chester, n.d.).

Household, Humphrey, *The Thames & Severn Canal* (Newton Abbot, 1969).

Jones, Clement, 'Pioneer Shipowners', *Journal of Commerce, Vol. 2* (Liverpool, 1938).

*Illustrated Catalogue of Marine Paintings of the Board of Trustees of the National Museums & Galleries of Merseyside* (1999).

Ingram (ed.), C. W. N., *New Zealand Shipwrecks*, 4th ed. (Wellington & London, 1972).

Kerr, David, *The Bowring Story* (London, 1962).

Kilgour, Owen F. G., *Caernarfonshire Sail* (Llanrwst, 2008).

*Lloyd's Registers 1800–2015* (London).

Lyon, David, *The Sailing Navy List, 1688–1860* (1993).

Lyon, David & R. Winfield, *The Sail & Steam Navy List* (2004).

MacGregor, D. R., *Merchant Sailing Ships, 1815–50, Supremacy of Sail,* (London, 1984).

*Merchant Sailing Ships, 1850–1875, Heyday of Sail* (London, 1984).

McNeil, D. B., *Irish Sea Passenger Steamship Services, Vol. 2, South of Ireland* (Newton Abbot, 1971).

McRonald, Malcolm, *The Irish Boats, Vols 1–3* (Brimscombe, 2006).

Mahon, John, *Kate Tyrell Lady Mariner (Dublin,* 1995).

Maritime Trust *The Story of the Kathleen & May* (1972).

Benn, W. Martin, *Closing Down Sail* (2011).

Maund, T. B., *Mersey Ferries, Part 1* (Glossop, 1991).

*Mercantile Navy List, 1858–19.*

Morgan, D. W., *Brief Glory — The Story of a Quest* (Liverpool, 1948).

Munroe, Colin, *Sailing Ships* (Lodon, 1973).

Pemberton, Barry, *Australian Coastal Shipping* (Melbourne, 1979).

Roberts, T. W., *Ellesmere Port, 1795–1960* (Gisborne, 1995).

Robins, Nick, *The Coming of the Comet — the Rise and Fall of the Paddle Steamer* (Barnsley, 2012.

*Sea Breezes Magazine,* 1932–2016.

Shaw, Captain Hugh, *Schooner Captain* (edited by Norah Ayland, (Truro, 1972).

Shropshire Union Railway & Canal Company Minutes, 1870–1.

Stammers, Michael, *Mersey Flats & Flatmen* (Lavenham & Liverpool, 1993).

*Sailing Barges of the British Isles* (Stroud, 2008).

Stammers, Michael, 'Emigrant Clippers to Australia — the Black Ball Line, its operation, people and ships 1852–1871', *Waterways Journal,* Vol. 8 & 12.

Stephen (ed), Patrick, *British Vessels lost at Sea 1914–18* (1977).

Winchester (ed), Clarence, *Shipping Wonders of the World, Vol. I & II* (London, 1938).

# Index

**Vessels**

**People and Companies**

**Places**